Date Due

# CELTIC TIDES

## By the same author

Bachman-Turner Overdrive: Rock Is My Life, This Is My Song (1976)

Century Of Sound: 100 Years Of Recorded Sound (co-author) (1977)

Heart Of Gold: 30 Years Of Canadian Pop Music (1985)

The Supertramp Book (1986)

1985 MuchMusic Rock Handbook

1986 MuchMusic Rock Handbook

1987 MuchMusic Rock Handbook

Oh What A Feeling: A Vital History Of Canadian Music (1996)

# CELTIC TIDES

## Traditional Music in a New Age

Martin Melhuish

QUARRY
MUSIC
BOOKS

The book *Celtic Tides* is a companion to
the documentary film *Celtic Tides*, produced
by Hallway Productions, Inc., with a
companion music album and video
from Putumayo World Music.

The publisher gratefully acknowledges
the support of The Canada Council
for the Arts and the Department of
Canadian Heritage for the arts of
writing and publishing in Canada.

The quotation of lyrics from songs
composed by the artists profiled in
this book is intended to illustrate
the cultural information and criticism
presented by the author and thus
constitutes fair use under existing
copyright conventions.

ISBN 1-55082-205-5

Cover design by Nicola Heindl,
copyright Putumayo World Music.
Text design by Susan Hannah.

Printed and bound in Canada by AGMV
Marquis, Cap-St-Ignace, Quebec.

Published by Quarry Press Inc.,
P.O. Box 1061, Kingston, Ontario,
Canada K7L 4Y5 www.quarrypress.com

# Contents

⊕ Preface  7

⊕ *One:* Nashville *Craic:*
The Celtic Connection  25

⊕ *Two: Keltoi:*
Celtic History and Mythology  39

⊕ *Three:* Celtic Soul:
Ireland and The Chieftains  51

⊕ *Four:* Scots Wha Ha'e:
Scotland and Dougie MacLean  89

⊕ *Five: Ceilidh* Trail:
Cape Breton and The Rankins  121

⊕ *Six:* Beyond the Ninth Wave:
World Music and Loreena McKennitt  161

⊕ Celtic Music Discography  179
⊕ Celtic Music Festivals  221
⊕ Celtic Sites, Pubs, Museums & More  229
⊕ Bibliography  233
⊕ Acknowledgements  236

For my parents,
Edith and Philip Melhuish;

✦

And for the families Hall:
Greg, Barb, Abbey and Stephanie;
Mark, Michelle, Jason, Adam and Nicole;
Doug and Joyce.

✦

Thanks for *Ciad Mile Failte!*

✦

*In memory of*
*Arthur and Vaughn Donald*

# Preface

This book is the companion to the television documentary *Celtic Tides* produced by Hallway Entertainment of Nashville and Toronto in association with the Canadian Broadcasting Corporation (CBC). Filmed in Ireland, Scotland, and Cape Breton, the show is hosted by Cookie, ~~ather~~, and Raylene Rankin of the acclaimed Canadian group The ~~nkins~~, and features Altan, Mary Black, John Allan Cameron, Capercaillie, ~~e~~ Chieftains, Clannad, Seamus Egan, Mary Jane Lamond, Ashley ~~cIsaac~~, Dougie MacLean, Natalie MacMaster, and Old Blind Dogs.

The idea for a documentary that would shed some light on the ever-~~reasing~~ popularity of Celtic music in the 1990s originated with Hallway ~~sident~~ and producer Greg Hall and Chip Sutherland, manager of The ~~nkins~~, with whom Hallway had previously worked on the group's con-~~t~~ documentary television special, *Backstage Pass*. Shot at the Orpheum ~~eatre~~ in Vancouver and at various locations around North America by ~~lly~~ ~~founder~~ and director Mark Hall, the show subsequently aired ~~in~~ the Un~~ited~~ States and on CBC in Canada.

~~y~~ had the working relationship unfolded between Hallway ~~and~~ ~~that~~ both parties, recognizing a show-biz rarity when it ~~saw~~ ~~had~~ often talked of other times and other projects. In the ~~ly~~ ~~of~~ 1997, The Rankins were preparing to go into the studio to ~~record~~ ~~what~~ would become their UPROOTED CD for EMI Music Canada. ~~ne was~~ in short supply, but the Rankin sisters — Cookie, Heather, and ~~ylene~~ — loved the concept and out came the Day Timers to coordinate ~~eir~~ individual on-camera hosting activities, which would include a shoot ~~with~~ Heather Rankin in and around Dublin, a return to the group's home ~~wn~~ of Mabou, Cape Breton with Cookie and Raylene Rankin, and a per-~~formance~~ by all three with The Chieftains in a Halifax, Nova Scotia studio.

As head writer/producer at Hallway as well as honorary Hall brother, I ~~found~~ myself in Nashville one sweltering, mid-summer afternoon during this ~~period~~ for a brainstorming session with Mark and Greg Hall. Timing on the ~~Celtic~~ music project was tight, and as Mark sweat the details, production ~~associate~~ Kristen Topping put the finishing touches on a research document ~~which~~ would form the skeletal outline for the project Greg Hall would dub ~~"Celtic~~ Tides."

The book of the same title had its origin with a phone call to
Hilderley, publisher and editor at Quarry Press in Kingston, Ontario,
of the fastest growing book publishers in the field of music-related subj
in the world. I had worked previously with Hilderley and his partner Su
Hannah on the book *Oh What A Feeling: A Vital History of Canadian Mu*
The phone conversation that day was short: at the mention of the titl
the television special, Hilderley raised the idea of a tie-in book a
launched into a breathless rant on ways and means. You hold the result
our subsequent communications in your hands.

As scriptwriter on the television show with director Mark Hall a
with no pre-conceived notions as to a format for the companion book, I
off on a two-month research excursion in October of 1997 that took me
Cape Breton and the Celtic Colours International Festival there, then
Ireland, Scotland, Wales, and Cornwall, where I was born. Mark Hall he
ed out on a similar, yet truncated journey due to looming deadlines, wit
crew that included director of photography Gordon Judges, location sou
man Phil Jones, and production associate Kristen Topping. Our pa
crossed briefly at a pre-arranged evening pint and dinner that began at
Russell Pub on the outskirts of Dublin and continued, by chance, the
lowing day after their return from an early morning shoot on the Irish c
with Heather Rankin in the city's teeming Temple Bar area
the Dublin Marathon.

On the flight home, a conversation with the per
prompted the question: "What's this 'Celtic music thing' a

"You had to be there" — or more to the point —
there," was my immediate thought for a reply. This musi
enced live at the impromptu sessions that take place in the k
parlors and dance halls in Mabou or Glencoe Station in Cape Breton.
one of the many pubs in Dublin or Doolin, Belfast or Galway Bay, even
a concert stage in Glasgow or Inverness, at any of the many Celtic mu
festivals around the world where musicians from diverse backgrou
traditions find common ground for collaboration.

Celtic music is as improvisational as jazz, and in the hands of a gro
like The Chieftains, as glorious as a symphony orchestra. It has the pov
to rock and roll, though most of the traditional instruments are acoust
Many of the lyrics and melodies have a history that's centuries old, a h
itage that's been handed down over the generations by word of mouth. L
see if *Candle In The Wind* has that kind of staying power!

So, what's this 'Celtic music thing' all about?

Read on MacDuff, and see!

# Capercaillie

# Alisdair Fraser

# Natalie MacMaster

# The Barra MacNeils

# Nashville Craic: The Celtic Connection

with

Paddy Maloney (The Chieftains) ❊ The Saw Doctors ❊ James Horner ❊ Loreena McKennitt ❊ Karen Matheson (Capercaillie) ❊ Enya ❊ Maire Brennan (Clannad) ❊ Michael Flatley ❊ Maireid Sullivan ❊ Mary Jane Lamond ❊ Buzzby MacMillan (Old Blind Dogs) ❊ Davy Cattanach (Old Blind Dogs) ❊ Ciaran Carson ❊ The Lash ❊ Paul McCartney ❊ Natalie MacMaster

*Music City will be facing a craic epidemic today.*

*Not to worry. Craic (pronounced 'crack') is an elusive Irish term that means good times, good vibes or high spirits, especially when such vibes are conjured by traditional Irish folk music.*

*With today being St. Patrick's Day, look for the craic to be, as the Irish say, mighty. Several area Irish folk bands will unleash giddy-paced reels and jigs, played on the likes of fiddle, accordion, bouzouki, tin whistle and bodhran (Irish hand drum).*

— Nashville Tennessean

⊕ St. Patrick's Day, as the turn of the millennium approaches, and the world is greener than Kermit the Frog's buttocks. On this day, far from the madding crowd decked out in their "Kiss me, I'm Irish!" T-shirts and the pagan hordes guzzling endless pints of green beer, I'm holed up in a hotel room on the out-skirts of Nashville gathering my thoughts and watching the greening of America through the key hole of CNN, the fabled news network.

25

I'm reminded of a comment on the subject of the wearing of the green from Booster, a musician and guide on Dublin's Music Pub Crawl. "Americans want the chocolate box image of Ireland. They want us wearing little green outfits and being all cute and spritely. They really love all the tradition." It's a tradition that prompts traditional musicians of the Emerald Isle, like Paddy Moloney of The Chieftains, to get their 'Irish' up. "One thing we're all very particular about is getting away from this false impression of what Ireland's all about," Moloney once confided to *Rolling Stone*, just prior to a U.S. tour. Moloney wanted "to get away from shamrocks and heather and Mother Machree and all that sort of shit."

Although Nashville seems to be a relatively green-free zone, there is a Celtic connection to the reason for my presence here in the Mecca of country music. Music City U.S.A. is very much at the center of the story of Celtic music's migration to the New World. Over at the Country Music Hall of Fame and Museum, this relationship has been acknowledged in the history of country music contained in its official souvenir book.

"Country music is music of America," the book states. "Born of the folk songs brought to the New World by early settlers, country music springs from an Anglo-Celtic tradition of songs and singing and fiddling that is centuries old but has been continually revitalized by American change and diversity. Ultimately, its roots can be traced back to the ballads and tunes of long-ago Scotland, England and Ireland which came to the New World with its first settlers. These were authentic folk songs and fiddle tunes passed from one generation to the next without a word or a note ever written down, a tradition of songs and singing and fiddling common to every community." This oral tradition and the passing of songs and melodies from singer to singer and musician to musician by way of impromptu sessions or jams is a recurring theme in the history of Celtic music.

In recent years, the relationship between Nashville and the Old World, and in particular, Dublin, has warmed considerably. For example, Celtic Harmony, a week-long songwriter retreat organized by America's The Music Bridge and Irish rights society IMRO, recently saw twenty-five American and Canadian songwriters head for Galway and Dublin to collaborate with their Irish counterparts. Country superstar Garth Brooks sold out three shows at Dublin's Croke Park on a recent excursion. As promoter Jim Aiken noted, one in every twenty residents of Ireland wanted to see Brooks in concert. The Irish traditional group The Chieftains recorded their album ANOTHER COUNTRY in Nashville in the early '90s, and the joy of discovering the easy fit of both music styles is apparent. I have just finished reading John Glatt's fine biography of The Chieftains. He notes that it was

Nashville-based songwriter Marijohn Wilkin who co-wrote the song *The Long Black Veil*, the title track for the group's 1994 collaborative effort with some of the biggest names in rock music. Wilkin co-penned the song with Danny Dill in 1959, but she admitted that she'd never understood the song's mystery until she heard Mick Jagger sing it with The Chieftains.

"I didn't want anyone to be with me when I listened to it," Wilkin told *R&R* magazine. "I'm a strange person. When I heard it beside Sting doing an ancient Celtic melody, I just sat here and cried because every ounce of my heritage came through in that melody. Listening to The Chieftains' album, I thought, 'And they wonder where country music comes from.'"

Interestingly enough, north of the border in Canada, Celtic music has found a rather comfortable fit under the "New Country" banner, a category reviled by country and western purists but embraced enthusiastically by much of the record buying public. Artists like The Rankins, Rita MacNeil, Ashley MacIsaac, Natalie MacMaster, The Barra MacNeils, Great Big Sea, Spirit Of the West, The Irish Descendants, Rawlins Cross, and Leahy, among others, have had great success at home and abroad.

⚭

Back on CNN, they've cornered The Saw Doctors, an Irish rock group with a traditional soft center, who are preparing to do a sound check at New York's Irving Plaza. Though the luck of the Irish is not the obvious focus of CNN's presence on this day, the band, whose debut album bears the memorable title, IF THIS IS ROCK AND ROLL, I WANT MY OLD JOB BACK, knows a little something about the subject. In April of 1993, the group's resident Welshman and keyboard player, Tony Lambert, took a two pound flutter on the Irish lottery, making sure he included the number 17, inspired by the group's first single *N17*. As it happened, that was the last number drawn in the winning sequence, and Lambert, the only winner that night, pocketed more than £800,000. He subsequently left the group before the release of the single *To Win Just Once* in the summer of 1994.

Now, trapped like rats at the end of a gangplank and in a no-win situation once again, a couple of members of The Saw Doctors face the probing news camera and bravely attempt to sum up the current Celtic craze in a five-second, green sound bite. "I find it really hard to explain...," offers a group member, haltingly. "People come along and just sing along at gigs, so they must be listening to the songs and saying, 'Ah, I like that noise.'" Low marks for profundity; full marks for pith.

Over the years, "that noise" from an ancient past, the traditional music of the world's Celtic regions, has been woven, like the multi-colored threads of a fine tartan, into the very fabric of contemporary music and culture around the world. Songs and melodies of Celtic antiquity from Ireland, Scotland, Wales, The Isle of Man, Cornwall (in the southwest of England), Brittany (in the northwest of France), Galicia and Asturias (along the North Atlantic coast of Spain), and the east coast of Canada, specifically Cape Breton Island, have become an integral part of the soundtrack for the 20th century's fade-to-black and the dawning of the Third Millennium.

History will record that *Titanic*, the movie world's commercial block-buster of the century, spawned a similarly successful soundtrack album thanks in good measure to the melancholy grandeur of James Horner's Celtic-tinged score. "It's possible this is the first time [this music] has been painted on such a big canvas and such a big billboard," reckons Horner, who was also responsible for the evocative Celtic soundscape of Mel Gibson's epic film *Braveheart*. Speaking to *Entertainment Weekly* as the TITANIC CD moved into the Top Ten on the list of Best-Selling Soundtracks of all time in the U.S. on the strength of its eight million-plus sales, Horner cites the irresistibility of the music as a major element in its popularity. "If you have a penny whistle, play a pretty tune, it ends up being terribly melan-choly," the composer states. "There's something heart-breaking about it. That's the Celtic thing."

The "Celtic thing" has also caught the imagination of a number of mainstream pop, rock, and country artists. Sting regularly features the tal-ented Northumbrian piper Kathryn Tickell on his albums and tours, and you'll hear uilleann piper Davy Spillane on rocker Bryan Adams' UNPLUGGED album. Shania Twain, one of country music's biggest-selling acts of all time, gets "jiggy with it" on her video for the hit single *Don't Be Stupid* as she makes a splash step-dancing to a traditional fiddle chorus in a *Singing In The Rain*-style production number. Twain's much-anticipated North American tour during the summer of 1998 featured the Canadian Celtic group Leahy as her opening act. Even Winnie the Pooh has a Celtic/Folk CD out on Disney, FRIENDS FOREVER, featuring the Irish tradi-tional band, Solas.

Advertisers, who try to stay one-step ahead of public taste, have also come around to this traditional way of thinking. Uilleann pipes echo through ads for mega-corporations like Mobil Oil, while General Electric's aerospace division looks to the future to the strains of a tradi-tional Welsh folk song. When Tim Horton's, the Canadian coffee and doughnut chain, set out to find the ideal personality and music match for their TV commercials, they looked no further than winsome and talented Cape Breton fiddler, Natalie MacMaster.

The local record store has seen the light as well. Early on, Celtic music was bundled in with the mish-mash of music you'd find under the banner of "New Age" or within the bounds of that international musical potpourri known as "World Beat" or "World Music." Today, you'll find that Celtic music, while still embraced by these categories, has its own, rapidly expanding section.

The displaced New Age tag is more likely to denote old age than anything else. As a music category, New Age has always had the particularly disagreeable connotation of being music for an aging population who've either had it prescribed by their doctor or recommended by *Good Housekeeping* — musical wallpaper that lends itself to frequent washing. Chart-topping Canadian Celtic / World Music star Loreena McKennitt has no doubt sold thousands of records to New Age fans, but the term itself gives her some discomfort. She has said in the past that, by the mere nature of its structure, much of the New Age music extant is not very focused and lacks passion. "It's function is to provide a very comfortable, easy listening environment," she explained at the time of the release of her million-selling CD, THE VISIT. "I know that my music has provided a comfortable environment for a lot of my listeners but it also has provided a much more thought-provoking, passionate kind of environment."

But there's nothing like a sudden surge in record sales to render categories impotent or at least flaccidly inadequate. It's marketing musical chairs. Artists given the alternative tag were once consigned to a small section at the back of the store and most remained smug in their renegade ways. Now with the alternative category dominating the aisles of most record stores, "alternative" has become the new mainstream. Similarly, with the public's growing interest in all things Celtic and their subsequent sophistication with the music, catch-all categories have crumbled under the weight of a rapidly rising tide of popular Celtic music.

"There's been a real resurgence of the music over the past decade and perhaps that's a reaction to other styles of music," suggests Karen Matheson, singer with the Scottish traditional group Capercaillie. "Perhaps people are now looking at some of the popular music in the charts and finding that, for them, it doesn't have any substance. Perhaps they're waking up and saying, 'Hang on a moment, we want something with a bit more history and something with a story to tell.' I think that's a big part of the resurgence of Celtic music. There's an earthiness to traditional celtic music but, more important, it comes from the heart. It's music of the soul. "

29

An indication of the record-buying public's affinity for Celtic-flavored pop came in 1983 as Dexy's Midnight Runners, a group from Birmingham, England, described as "Celtic soulsters" by the *Billboard Book of Number One Hits*, topped the charts on both sides of the Atlantic with their rollicking *craic* of a single, *Come On Eileen*. It was the band's second number one single in the U.K. and their first in the U.S., where it knocked Michael Jackson's blockbuster hit, *Billie Jean*, from the top spot. During the same period, Blowzabella hit the Top 10 in Britain with the much-covered *Between The Wars*, swirling with hurdy-gurdy and pipes disguised as instruments of pop domination.

Eithne Ni Bhraonian (Brennan) of County Donegal, Ireland — Enya, as she is known to her legion of fans — was responsible for giving Celtic music a hefty push into the contemporary spotlight in 1989 as *Orinoco Flow* (*Sail Away*), from her WATERMARK CD, became her career-launching hit. Enya, who spent a few years in the early 1980s as a member of the group Clannad with her sister Maire Brennan, provided the hauntingly beautiful soundtrack for the critically-acclaimed BBC-TV series, *The Celts*, as a solo artist in 1986. Three years later, she was on top of the international record charts and Celtic music was suddenly in the news. Though purists were predictably in a flap over the embraced recording technology, the record buying public found the music's cathedral sound and mystic mood compelling. At the time of the release of her mainly retrospective CD, PAINT THE SKY, in the latter months of 1997, she had sold close to 35 million records worldwide.

"In my music, I hear a lot of the influences from Irish culture," Enya told an interviewer during the course of her VH1 music special. "Even if it's an up-tempo melody, there's a melancholy feel and I think that's something that's very inherent to being Irish. A lot of people in Ireland have that, whether it's in literature or music. I think I've taken that from the culture."

Then MOUTH MUSIC, a collaboration between Scottish TV producer Martin Swan and American born ethnomusicologist/singer Talitha MacKenzie, became one of the surprise dance and world music hits of the early '90s. Combining a rhythmic, a cappella form of traditional singing unique to Scotland known as Mouth Music (or *puirt-a-beul* in Gaelic) with the funk and flash of afro-pop music, the album garnered critical acclaim and chart-topping sales on both sides of the Atlantic.

Clannad, the Donegal group featuring Maire Brennan, would inadvertently provide the next mainstream jolt of popularity for Celtic music in 1993 when a portion of the track *Harry's Game* from the group's 1982 CD, ANAM, was used to underscore a television ad for the Volkswagen

Passat. Public reaction to the snippet of music was immediate, ultimately prompting the ad agency to take the unprecedented step of recalling the spot and adding the group's name and song title. Reportedly Passat sales jumped by 25 percent and ANAM became one of the top-selling World Music albums of the year.

"For me, and for Clannad, the area that we came from has a huge bearing and is a huge influence on what we've created — the Clannad sound or that mystical earthiness; I'd probably call it more earthiness than anything else," Maire Brennan of the group explained during a recent television special produced by Philip King of Dublin-based Hummingbird Productions when asked about the origins of the group's trademark sound. "When we wrote *Harry's Game*, it was after doing a long road of listening to traditional songs, especially from our own area, taking them and spending time and energy on arranging them with our instrumentation and our voices and everything. When we wrote *Harry's Game*, we had to stand back when people said to us, 'Where did you get the sound?' The only way I could actually explain that to them was to talk about where we came from where there are mountains and valleys. It's the landscape around us that created that kind of aura around the sound. Enya, my sister, has it as well and she comes from the same place. It has a huge bearing on the sound."

The impact of The Chieftains, Ireland's premier traditional music band, on the current Celtic music boom cannot be understated. Not only have The Chieftains shaped the sound of contemporary Celtic music, they have also directly influenced dance and film. In the early 1980s, Chicago-born, seven-time world champion step-dancer Michael Flatley toured the world with The Chieftains, and one evening, at Carnegie Hall in New York, he was given the opportunity to do a solo spot. "That was it," Flatley told interviewer David Frost. "That was the time. I did about five dances that night and I remembered the audience getting up and I remember doing a triple spin that night and using my arms — I could feel the audience reaction. Even if you couldn't see 'em, I could feel 'em, and I just knew, 'This is what I was born to do. I have got to find a way to dress this properly and take it to the world stage.'"

It took more than a decade from that defining moment for Flatley to realize his dream, but in 1994, a show originally conceived with Irish composer/record producer Bill Whelan as a seven-minute interval filler for the Eurovision Song Contest in Dublin, soon developed into the Irish dance extravaganza the world came to know as *Riverdance*. Jean Butler, one of the original leads, also worked with The Chieftains. Flatley would later depart over creative differences and put his own show, *Lord of the Dance*, on the road with a new score composed by Ronan Hardiman.

The spectacular success of *Riverdance* and *Lord of the Dance* can certainly take a great deal of credit for the Celtomania of the last half of the '90s. In 1995, *Billboard*, the music industry bible, had no less than 18 Celtic music CDs reach its Top 15 World Music chart compared to the handful that made the grade over the previous five years. Leading the way were The Chieftains, Clannad, Mouth Music, Mary Black, Nightnoise, Anuna, the original vocal group from *Riverdance*, and Loreena McKennitt, who was represented by two CDs. It was only a small taste of things to come for McKennitt who, in 1998, saw her single *The Mummers Dance*, a tune inspired by a folk tradition from a number of ancient sources, become a dance hit around the world.

As the public warmed to the music that they were hearing under the "Celtic" banner, they were not always sure of the repertoire or even the names of the artists. The record industry met the demand with an unprecedented number of releases featuring collections of artists and songs. In 1995, fully half of the Celtic CDs on the World Music chart were compilation albums led by the top-seller, CELTIC LEGACY: A GLOBAL CELTIC JOURNEY, on the Narada label.

And aren't movie soundtracks the most compelling samplers, asks Charly Prevost, a former president of Island Records in the U.S., a former management exec, who's had Supertramp and Chris De Burgh as clients and is now the Vice-President of Retail at the Los Angeles-based music trade magazine *The Album Network*. "They [soundtracks] really help to make an artist very visible; that's become evident in the last few years. When you look at the Top 20 of the charts these days, 25 or 30 percent of the records are soundtracks. They're a sample of an age or a style and that can lead a lot of people to the music. There have also been a lot of new labels open specializing in Celtic music, and these are the folks who have been leading the way to selling the music in book stores and coffee houses and other non-traditional outlets," adds Prevost. One such independent label is Putumayo World Music, which has released such compilations as WOMEN OF THE WORLD CELTIC, WOMEN OF THE WORLD CELTIC II, A CELTIC COLLECTION, THE DOUGIE MACLEAN COLLECTION, and CELTIC TIDES, the CD companion to this book, with strong presence in the Starbuck's and Timothy's coffee shops affiliated with Borders and Barnes and Noble bookstores in the United States as well as Chapters and Indigo Books in Canada.

"The style of music does lend itself to film because it conjures up images," contends Capercaillie's Karen Matheson of Capercaillie, who themselves have worked in the movies, most notably on the film *Rob Roy*, starring Jessica Lange and Liam Neeson, for which they contributed to the soundtrack. "We got involved through a woman from our village who had been asked to put the dancers together for a section of the film where Jessica Lange and Liam Neeson do this wee Scottish dance," explains Matheson. "She asked us if we'd come and play some tunes for them to dance to. We did that and the director asked me if I could sing some songs. It turns out that he had actually heard of us through Billy Connolly. Anyway this whole thing snowballed and we found ourselves writing music for the film — not only that, but actually performing in it as well, which was brilliant and good fun."

Paddy Moloney and The Chieftain's have provided the sonic ambience for feature film and television movie projects like *The Playboy of the Western World, Barry Lydon, Rob Roy, Circle of Friends, Treasure Island, Tristan and Isolde, The Grey Fox,* and *Far and Away.* Other Celtic-flavored soundtracks featuring a variety of artists from the genre have included *Michael Collins, Last of the Mohicans, The Secret of Roan Irish, Circle of Friends,* and *The Brothers McMullen,* on which the four-time all-Ireland champion instrumentalist Seamus Egan co-wrote the featured song, *I Will Remember You,* with Canadian singer/songwriter Sarah McLachlan.

"I see these [compilations and soundtracks] as samplers of the culture designed for people of Celtic heritage who are just beginning to notice the great value their cultural heritage can bring to their lives." That's the take on the current Celtic boom by Mairéid Sullivan, a singer/songwriter, poet, and self-proclaimed "student of history" who was born in County Cork Ireland and currently lives in California. Timothy D. Taylor, the author of *Global Pop: World Music, World Markets,* an admirably researched opus that "explores some of the new musics in the increasingly inter-connected global village," agrees. His explanation of the surge of interest in things Celtic, though stated in 'lingo academius', is that it has something to do with the increasing consciousness of ethnicity in contemporary American life and the concomitant commodification of ethnicity in music, even white ethnicities. In other words, "European Americans are loath to be left out." In an age where e-mail, cyberspace, and virtual reality have come to represent connection without contact, the idea of family music sessions around the kitchen table with neighbors and friends is an old one but not without its nostalgic appeal.

Mary Jane Lamond, a singer in the Gaelic tradition from Cape Breton Island in Canada, reckons that the current popularity of Celtic music is in part due to the fact that it is simply good music with a universal appeal that comes from people's desire to hold on to some of the more positive community values of times gone by. "Following World War II, there was this huge move to become 'white' and middle-class, no matter what color or background you were," suggests Lamond. "There was this whole movement for everybody to be the same and to have the electric range and all the modern conveniences. In some ways, I think that Celtic music plays to the backlash towards all of that. We've become more and more global and more alike as people. Across North America, we all watch the same television programs, and we now have the Internet, which has made the world smaller still. I just don't think a lot of people are able to handle all of it and many are finding the need to be part of a smaller community. People living in big cities need to find common interests with other people or at least have an understanding that the world can work on a smaller scale. Celtic music's appeal comes from the fact that it is rooted in an older tradition and in those small, close-knit communities that have kept this music going."

Buzzby MacMillan and Davy Cattanach are members of the Scottish traditional group Old Blind Dogs, who have spent many a long hour traversing the highways and byways of America on tour. It has given them ample opportunity to observe the natives in their natural habitat. "The crowds are brilliant in America," raves Cattanach in his strong Scottish brogue. "They really lap it up. That's partly due to the fact that a lot of people in North America have got Scottish roots. I can imagine if I was hauled off to America, I'd be hanging on to my roots and going, 'Yeah, I remember this song or that.' They've got a respect for their own roots and you know, it's quite funny, because they know more about our roots than we do — and certainly me because I never pay much attention to these kinds of things."

Adds band-mate MacMillan, "with a lot of the people who come to hear Celtic music in America, it's not like they're hearing it for the first time. The people who are hearing it for the first time, I find, are the most in awe and the most surprised because it's new to them. I find their reactions the most interesting. People who are Celtic music buffs, they've heard it all before and are always going to compare you with this or that or the next thing. They're always going to have opinions. The first time listeners are always the most fun to get feedback from."

In the mid-1980s, Irish author, poet, and musician Ciaran Carson was already seeing the Celtic tide rise in America. "In recent visits to the U.S.A. I have caught some glimpses of a mirror image of Ireland in the '20s; now it is young American musicians, often without any discernible Irish ancestry, who are turning to Ireland as a source of their music," he states in his book *Irish Traditional Music*. "Ireland is their America, representing not economic status, but cultural status, an escape from the American dream into a vision of poetic simplicity and Celtic spirals."

Carson's comments are echoed in the mission statements of a growing number of groups and artists in America who have gone the traditional route but with some pretty interesting side-trips along the way. For example, The Lash is a seven-piece group from the United States who call their brand of music Celtic Mayhem. "Take the attitude of The Clash, the look of The Commitments, the sound of The Pogues, and mix it together with seven musicians whose musical backgrounds range from jazz to punk to folk," they explain in their biographical notes, "and you have The Lash: a band that's taken a not-so-traditional approach to traditional music." The group also offers its unique perspective on the rising tide of interest in Celtic music in America. "Almost at its conception, Celtic music was a bridge that led people of different cultures to common ground," notes the group. "As Americans, we see the Celtic influence every day in our popular and theatrical music, in our styles of dance, even in the jewelry and tattoo art that is currently fashionable. The Lash is a further extension of this influence; seven people who have come from seven different paths not only to introduce the passion of Celtic music to a new audience, but to celebrate with those who already know the joy of high stepping to an Irish reel. It's folk music for rockers, rock music for folkies. It's traditional, it's contemporary, it's revisionist — give it any label you wish. We call it Celtic Mayhem, and it's spreading like wildfire."

Mairéid Sullivan reckons that it isn't just America where things are shaking Celt-wise. The voice of Celtic culture has reached the diaspora and Celts as far flung as Latin America and Australia are awakening to their ethnic heritage. "Musicians in all these places have been performing traditional Celtic music for years," states Sullivan, who has herself lived in Australia. "Most of the Australian folk songs were written to Irish or Scottish melodies. I know hundreds of musicians, personally, who play jazz, blues, and classical music and who also know and play the traditional Celtic repertoire. I have had discussions with many of these friends about the value of playing Bach and Celtic music as part of their skill development."

Sullivan, whose recording career has included a number of solo CDs of original and traditional songs as well as a live concert recording with Derek Bell, the "wandering harper" from The Chieftains, titled A CELTIC EVENING, has traveled the world as a performer and played her share of Celtic music festivals. "The U.S., Canada, Australia, as well as England, Scotland, Ireland, France, Spain, and Brittany host these festivals which have become important gathering places for thousands of music lovers, offering a heightened sense of community for organizers, local and visiting artists and their audiences. The spread of these festivals and the growing mainstream appeal of popular Celtic influenced music, and a growing fascination for unaccompanied singing, is finally reaching the larger population it belongs to and it brings with it riches beyond imagination. The music is a conduit to the ancient Celtic myths and philosophies which are coming to life again to feed starved imaginations."

It's a romantic notion and no less a pop icon than Paul McCartney has fallen under the spell cast down through the ages by the same folklore and mythology. In 1993, when McCartney was approached by EMI Classics with the idea of writing an orchestral work on the occasion of EMI's centenary year and in recognition of his own close-links with the record label over the years, his thoughts turned to his own Celtic heritage. An accomplished painter, McCartney's first inspiration came from two canvases he had completed, one dealing with the dawn of time and the other reflecting his wonder at the megalithic grave site at Newgrange (Brugh Na Boinne) in County Meath, Ireland, the surrounding standing stones and, in particular, the spiral design from the entrance stone at the doorway to the chamber. The paintings gave way to an extended narrative poem which synthesizes his own explorations into Celtic and other ancient legends. In turn, the poem became the story line for *Standing Stone*, his second large-scale classical work following the enthusiastically-received, *Liverpool Oratorio*.

Andrew Stewart, who notes McCartney's long-standing fascination with the ancient music and the religious and transcendental importance of music to the ancient world, spoke to McCartney for the project's liner notes. "When I started the work four years ago, the whole Celtic thing had yet to come into vogue," relates McCartney. "I also wanted to explore my Celtic roots. I paint and like surrealist images and so many of these Celtic myths fired my imagination. I decided that rather than slavishly copy one of these ancient stories, I'd invent my own. After all, my roots are Celtic and that's exactly what they would have done."

As wide as the boundaries of Celtic music may stretch geographically and musically, at its core, the traditional element remains. From the youngest to the oldest, no matter the part of the Celtic world from which they come, no discussion of the genre could be complete without a reference to the living tradition inherent in the music and the importance of maintaining its integrity.

The Saw Doctors, who stumbled in trying to explain the reason for the current Celtic music boom in ten words or less for the CNN cameras, were unambiguous in stating their objectives as a band in one of their tour programs. "Born into a repressed, Catholic, conservative, small-town, agrarian, angst-ridden and showband-infested society, we're trying to preserve the positive elements of our backgrounds and marry them to the sounds which have culturally invaded our milieu through TV, radio, 45s, fast food restaurants, 24-hour petrol stations and electric blankets."

Paddy Moloney of The Chieftains is renowned for defending the traditional core of the group's music to the last man no matter the breadth or scope of their musical experimentation or collaborations. "It's essential that we play the music as traditional as it always was," states Moloney. "And that's something, believe it or not, we still do."

Newcomers like Cape Breton fiddler Natalie MacMaster feel that sometimes subtlety is not what is needed when introducing the music to new audiences. "People who didn't grow up with the culture need to be hit in the face with the music," asserts MacMaster. "Now I couldn't do that if I went to Cape Breton because everybody knows the music, but you take the music outside of the traditionalists and you go into a crowd of people who aren't familiar with it, you have to go, 'Here it is; now go nuts!'"

# Chapter Two

# Keltoi: Celtic History and Mythology

*with*

D.H. Lawrence ※ Daphne DuMaurier ※ Paddy Moloney (The Chieftains) ※ Frank Delaney ※ Marie-Louise Sjoestedt ※ Dougie MacLean ※ Mairead Ni Mhaonaigh (Altan) ※ Mairéid Sullivan ※ Jean Markdale

❧

"I didn't feel Celtic as such until I visited other Celtic countries," I once heard a Cornish woman remark on a BBC 2 radio program profiling the duchy of Cornwall, in the extreme southwest of England. "All of us live on pretty rocky places and we always have the sea close by us . . . those things we have in common, plus our ancient roots, make us as thick as anything against anybody else."

I understood what she meant. Born in that same ancient, Celtic corner of England, I particularly came to know the ever-changing moods of the sea that foamed and crashed petulantly against its rugged coastline. As a child, I delighted in its sun-sparkled serenity, wondered at its reflective melancholy, and feared its sudden paroxysms of rage. It was a giver of life — and a taker of life — and its brooding presence was never far from your thoughts, awake or asleep.

And, of course, the mythology was everywhere. From a bedroom window, I could see St. Michael's Mount, the home of the giant slain by Jack, rising out of Mount's Bay. Beyond, lay the Lost Land of Lyonesse of Celtic Arthurian legend, where the lovers Tristan and Iseult drank the potion that would bind them forever to each other and where Arthur himself would ride to the hunt through a forest long ago buried by a restless sea.

Novelist D.H. Lawrence lived in the area during the First World War. "It is not England," he once wrote. "It is bare and elemental. Tristan's land.

I lie looking down at a cove where the waves come white under a low, black headland which slopes up in bare, green-brown, bare and sad under a level sky. It is old, Celtic, pre-Christian." As Lawrence added, "it is a cove like Tristan sailed into, from Lyonesse — just the same. It belongs to 2000 years back — that pre-Arthurian Celtic flicker of being which has disappeared so entirely. All is desolate and forsaken, not linked up. But I like it."

In her book, *Vanishing Cornwall*, long-time resident Daphne DuMaurier, the author of *Rebecca, Jamaica Inn,* and *Frenchman's Creek,* all set in the area, considered her own, and the area's, Celtic heritage: "There is in Cornish character, smoldering beneath the surface, ever ready to ignite, a fiery independence, a stubborn pride. How much of this is due to centuries of isolation after the Roman conquest of Britain, when Mediterranean trade no longer found its way to south-western estuaries but went direct from Roman France to the eastern channel ports, and how much to the legacy of those dark-haired invaders with their blue beads and their circlets of gold, heirs of a civilization existing long before Rome was even named, is something the Cornish can argue themselves. As an outsider, with Breton forebears, I like to think the two races, facing an Atlantic seaboard blown by identical gales, washed by the same driving mists, share a common ancestry, along with the Irish further west."

Irishman Paddy Moloney of The Chieftains had reason for similar thoughts in 1961 as he traveled to Brittany to attend the Celtic Congress. It was here that he first met Celtic folklorist Polig Montjarret and the young harper, Alan Stivell. "The word Celtic never meant anything to me before 1961," Moloney confided to biographer John Glatt. "That's when I fell in love with Breton music and I began to realize about the Celtic culture and all the similarities. The Breton music punched me completely with its incredibly melodic form that fit perfectly with traditional Irish music. I've never lost hold of it since."

Not much is lost in the trans-Atlantic migration either. Ashley MacIsaac, the "mad" fiddler of Creignish, Cape Breton, says he often feels some of that old Celtic blood running hot in his veins. "Sometimes, when I'm completely crazy and baying at the moon, I feel very much like I should have a much longer beard — as it gets sometimes — and enjoy stomping my foot as hard as I can when I play. It's that whole feel of the pagans around the fire."

Offers Frank Delaney, writer and presenter of the acclaimed BBC 2 series, *The Celts,* and author of the best-selling companion book, "the word 'Celtic' excites immediately, automatically, a host of images: memories of gold and music, of bards, princes and Druids, of fighting, talking and horsemanship — or pictures of thatched cottages, round towers, harps, high crosses, rocky coasts and shawls. A cliché is a phrase worn smooth by rubbing."

It is unlikely that one would go flitting back to pre-history to get to the roots of rock 'n' roll, but that is precisely the destination to which one must travel if there is to be any understanding of the survival of Celtic music through the ages and its current widespread appeal.

The stereotypical image of The Celts would seem to rule out any connection with couth and culture. History has long painted the picture of the Celts as a race of tall, fearless warriors with big hair and walrus mustaches who would charge naked and howling into battle, beating rhythmically on their shields. This spectacle obviously had a remarkable effect on the enemy. Even the mighty Romans fled in panic at the very sight of this crazed Celtic horde, who would subsequently march unchallenged into Rome where the terrified citizens had fled at news of their approach.

But there was another side of the Celtic character, one that would earn them the title "The Fathers of Europe." According to ancient chroniclers, The Celts originally emerged from eastern Europe and the area of the lower Danube (Austria) more than 2500 years ago. Herodotus and other Greek writers make reference to a people they call "Keltoi," which translates as "barbarian," but in the sense of "outsider" or "foreigner." By the third century BC, Celtic tribes had crossed the Alps and settled in Italy where they launched successful, but short-lived, conquests of the Romans and the Greeks, sacking the city of Rome and the great temples of Delphi in the process. For a brief, shining moment in Celtic history, they were the dominant race in the western world from the Bosporus (Turkey) to the Atlantic, from the Baltic to the Mediterranean. The Romans referred to the continental Celts as Galli or Gauls and those that had settled in Britain were known as Britanni.

But there was to be no Celtic empire, just a widespread, cluster of warlike tribes loosely bound by similar languages and a culture dominated by the influential and widely-consulted Druids, who were priests as well as philosophers, orators, scholars, natural scientists, judges, and bards or poets. Recruited primarily from the ranks of the nobility, the Druids established a formidable secret society. They alone communed with the deities of the natural world who were believed to exist as part of the land, the sea, and the sky and with the flora and fauna. They were the repository of all contemporary knowledge and they forbade all written language, in part, to maintain secrecy but also to uphold the sacred nature of an ancient oral tradition.

They believed in reincarnation and the immortality of the soul, a factor that the enemy certainly believed made the Celts fearless in battle. The Druids were not usually soldiers themselves — why would they be given their fearsome reputation of being able to bring a man or woman to their knees with a well-aimed jibe or satirical remark? They were spiritual leaders, who stood on the sidelines and urged the warriors to fight to the death. Their influence on the Celtic forces was not lost on the Romans. When they invaded Britain, one of their first strategies of conquest was to seek out and destroy the power center of the Druids and the spiritual center of the Celtic world, at the time located on the island of Anglesey. In 60 AD, Roman forces crossed the Menai Strait, massacred the Druids they found there, and burned their sacred groves.

It is said that it took 20 years to become a Druid, a period during which all existing knowledge was codified in verse and committed to memory. In this regard, all Druids were bards, though not all bards were Druids. Nonetheless, bards, poets, storytellers and musicians, were given a place of high honor in Celtic society. Sought after for their wisdom and perceived powers of providence, they delivered the orations, sang the praises of their rulers, lamented over fallen heroes and battles lost. They also held within their power of eloquence the instrument of shame and ruination for any warrior, chief, or king who crossed them.

The Celts invented trash-talk, not Dennis Rodman. Reminiscent of the stories of chivalrous battle that played such a part in the Celtic legend of King Arthur and his Knights of the Roundtable, the Celts favored settling their conflicts, one on one, rather than sending their armies into battle. Each side would pick their champion and to the victor's tribe or nation would go the spoils. As Greek historian Diodorus Siculus once noted: "And when someone accepts their [the Celts] challenge to battle, they proudly recite the deeds of valor of their ancestors and proclaim their own valorous quality, at the same time abusing and making little of their opponent and generally attempting to rob him beforehand of his fighting spirit."

In her book *Gods and Heroes of the Celts*, Marie-Louise Sjoestedt states, "Some peoples, such as the Romans, think of their myths historically, while the Irish think of their history mythologically." The same characteristic applies to most Celtic music, permeating it with the mystic quality that is still commented on today. The bards were the keepers of this Celtic mythology, in which nature is a prevailing theme. The ancient Celts saw a direct link between the fertility of the land and the wisdom and spiritual health of their kings. That harmony with the land is still prevalent in the symbolism and imagery of today's Celtic music. "They were very much in awe of nature and its mysteries and I think they viewed music the same way," suggests Scottish traditional folk singer, Dougie MacLean. "Music played a big part in their everyday life; it was more than entertainment. It was almost an extension of life itself rather than something that happens when you're not working."

"You have to think of where our people came from," states Mairead Ni Mhaonaigh, Donegal-style fiddle player and vocalist with the Irish traditional group Altan. "We were simple people without much except the land that we had and we were inspired by our environment. The land had gods and goddesses and they had magical qualities. The wells had magical qualities and certain mountains had that same magic. Nature ruled our lives then, so it makes a lot of sense that our music and poetry would be derived from the natural world. Water, wind, fire and the earth ruled us. They still do . . . well maybe, whisky too."

Though a patrilinear society, women stood on equal ground with men in virtually every area of Celtic life. Boudicca or Boadicea, queen of the Iceni tribe, became a British icon following her audacious, yet failed uprising against the Romans in 61 AD. From the perspective of the late 20th century, we discover that the main bearers of the oral tradition of storytelling and the singing of songs through later history were the women. This oral tradition became one of the major characteristics of Celtic music. Songs, music, and dance were preserved in the memory, handed down from one generation to the next or passed from one performer to another. In the 14th century, a Scottish bard by the name of John Barbour once wrote that he saw no need to chronicle the details of a particular battle because the local women were already singing about it. He was so sure that the battle would be documented for posterity by their songs that he didn't even bother to mention which conflict he was writing about.

Notes singer/songwriter Mairéid Sullivan, "the resurgence of Celtic music and culture reminds me of the comments of Jungian psychologist, Robert A. Johnson, in his book *We: Understanding the Psychology of Romantic Love*, where he points out that whenever there is a resurgence of women's freedom, there is an accompanying resurgence in Celtic culture. Celtic culture was, historically, a unique 'freedom domain' for women."

In his book *Women of the Celts*, poet, philosopher, historian, and story-teller, Jean Markale, the author of more than forty books on pre-Christian societies, alludes to the durability of the folklore and culture thus handed down through the generations: "There is nothing more tenacious than tradition, nothing more firmly rooted than the ancient beliefs and systems of thought when they are concealed within new forms . . . the myths never die, they are constantly being revived in new and varied shapes and sometimes surprise us in unexpected places."

"In the last analysis," writes Frank Delaney, "the Celts must be defined as an ancient European people who spread across the world and who created a civilization, with cultural and even genetic considerations. They had a grand mythology and they created exciting and profound art: these facts made them a most suitable case for heritage." Part of that heritage was political, as the following chronology shows.

# A Celtic Chronology

❋ c 3200 BC   Construction of the megalithic passage grave at Newgrange, County Meath, Ireland, the entrance stone to which will, in part, inspire Paul McCartney to write the orchestral piece *Standing Stone* more than 5000 years later.

❋ c 1100 BC   The Halstatt Period, named for an archaeological site in Austria associated with the Celts, begins.

❋ c 750 BC   The ancient Greeks come into contact with traders from Halstatt whom they call "Keltoi".

❋ c 600 BC   La Tène Period, named after an archaeological site in Switzerland associated with the Celts, begins. The first wave of Celts invade Ireland.

❋ 400 BC   The Celts cross the Alps into northern Italy.

❋ 387 BC   Celtic tribes (The Gauls) defeat the Romans in battle and move on to Rome, which they sack.

✸ 279 BC  Celtic tribes (Galatae) sack Delphi and cross into Asia Minor.

✸ 225 BC  Romans soundly defeat the Celts at the Battle of Telamon in Greece.

✸ 124 BC  Romans conquer the Celts in Gallia, an area on the Mediterranean coast of France.

✸ 59 BC  Julius Caesar begins his campaign in Celtic Gaul (France) and then moves against Celtiberia (Spain). With his victory in Galicia, all of Spain fell to Roman rule.

✸ 55 - 54 BC  Julius Caesar launches expeditions into Britain.

✸ 52 BC  Romans put down a Celtic rebellion led by Vercingetorix and become the rulers of France.

✸ 48 BC  Roman Emperor Claudius, so brilliantly portrayed in modern times by British actor Derek Jacobi in the critically acclaimed TV series *I Claudius*, overruns the Celts in Britain. The Celts are driven into the hills of Wales and Scotland.

✸ 61 AD  A rebellion, led by Queen Boudicca (Boedicea) of the Iceni, a Celtic tribe from the area in Britain now known as East Anglia, is put down by the Romans. This icon of British history is reputedly buried under the platform at Kings Cross railway station, where I frequently stand while awaiting my train up to see the football in Wolverhampton.

✸ 61 AD  Romans cross to Anglesey, the sacred island of the Druids, and massacre its inhabitants and burn the sacred groves.

✸ c 120 AD  Roman Emperor Hadrian begins construction of a wall across the North of England from Solway Firth to the mouth of the Tyne River to contain the Pict and Scot Celts to the north.

✸ 312 AD  The Roman conversion to Christianity begins with Emperor Constantine. The Celtic conversion to Christianity also begins during this period, marked by the gradual transfer of divine power from the deities of the natural world to a growing number of missionaries who were preaching the Christian gospel throughout the Celtic world and had attained sainthood.

❀ 410 AD   The Romans depart and the pagan Germanic tribes, the Angles, Saxons and Jutes, move into Britain. Over 1500 years later, the tide would turn as waves of soccer hooligans cross back over into Europe to plunder and pillage.

❀ 432 AD   St. Patrick, son of a middle-class Roman family in Britain, returns to Ireland, where he had once been held captive, and converts Irish Celts to Christianity.

❀ 493 AD   According to legend, the British Celts, under King Arthur, win the Battle of Badon during their campaign to drive the Saxons out of Britain.

❀ 498 AD   Irish Gaels, called "Scotti" by the Romans, establish the kingdom of Dal Riada in Argyll on the west coast of Alba. Alba later becomes known as Scotland, named after the same tribe.

❀ c 500 AD   Celtic Brythonic tribes migrate from Britain to the province of Amorica, known today as Brittany.

❀ 563 AD   St. Columba crosses from Ireland to Iona in Scotland where he begins his Christian missionary work among the Picts.

❀ 795 AD   The Vikings, who will establish the cities of Cork, Dublin, Limerick, Waterford, and Wexford, invade Ireland. (It wasn't such a stretch after all to feature Norwegian singing star Sissel on the Celtic-flavored soundtrack for the blockbuster movie *Titanic*.)

❀ 843 AD   Kenneth MacAlpin (Kenneth I) unites the Picts and Scots in Alba and becomes the first ruler of Scotland.

❀ 1040 AD   "Is this a dagger which I see before me, the handle toward my hand?" Macbeth, later immortalized by William Shakespeare, kills Duncan, who had previously killed his grandfather, Malcolm II, and becomes king of Scotland.

❀ 1207 AD   The first coins struck in Ireland incorporate the Irish Harp (cithara) in the design.

❋ 1297 AD   The British are defeated at Stirling Bridge by a Scottish army of foot-soldiers, led in part by Scottish patriot William Wallace, whom Mel Gibson would portray in the 1990s blockbuster movie *Braveheart*. Wallace was captured seven years later and taken to London for execution.

❋ 1314 AD   Scottish king Robert the Bruce defeats the English at the Battle of Bannockburn.

❋ 1348 AD   One third of Ireland's population is wiped out by the 'Black Death'.

❋ 1494 AD   First written reference to Scotch Whisky — *aqua vitae* ("water of life") in the Latin or *uisge beatha* ("whisky") in the Gaelic.

❋ 1532 AD   Henry VIII splits with the Catholic church — the real beginning of 'The Troubles'.

❋ 1536 AD   The Act of Union between England and Wales attempts to expunge the Welsh language from common usage.

❋ 1537 AD   The Irish Supremacy Act asserts the English king's power over Irish churches.

❋ 1603 AD   Sweeping cultural changes in Ireland occur as England outlaws the speaking of Gaelic and abolishes the Brehon Law.

❋ 1629 AD   The establishment of Scottish colonies in Nova Scotia (Canada) begins, though it is short-lived due to a revival of French power in the region a few years later.

❋ 1690 AD   England's Protestant conquest of Ireland is complete as William of Orange defeats James II at the Battle of the Boyne, a victory the Orangemen still celebrate.

❋ 1704 AD   Irish Catholics are restricted by English law from holding public office or owning land.

❋ 1707 AD   The Scottish parliament is dissolved as the Act of Union between Scotland and England is ratified.

✳ 1720 AD   The Declaratory Acts puts legislative power over Ireland in the hands of the Westminster Parliament in London.

✳ 1738 AD   Revered Irish harper and celtic bard Turlough O'Carolan dies.

✳ 1745 AD   Remembered as "The 45," Bonnie Prince Charlie and his Jacobite forces push across the English border to Derby, 130 miles from London.

✳ 1746 AD   The Jacobites are defeated at the Battle of Culloden by English and Lowland Scottish troops. The aftermath of the defeat saw the eradication of the Highland culture and the clan system. Land was seized from the Jacobite chiefs and the wearing of Highland dress was banned. Even bagpipes were outlawed as they were considered an instrument of war.

✳ 1759 AD   St. James Gate Brewery in Dublin is bought by Arthur Guinness.

✳ 1789 AD   Brittany's autonomy is lost with the outbreak of the French Revolution.

✳ 1796 AD   Robert Burns, the national poet of Scotland, dies.

✳ 1800 AD   The Act of Union between Britain and Ireland is passed.

✳ 1807 AD   The Highland Clearances begin in Scotland, resulting in waves of immigration to the New World, primarily to places on the east coast of Canada like Cape Breton, Nova Scotia, Prince Edward Island, and New Brunswick.

✳ 1845 AD   The Great Hunger — or the Irish Potato Famine as it came to be known — forces a mass migration of Irish to the North America, Australia, and the United Kingdom.

✳ 1916 AD   Proclamation of the Republic in Ireland as a country independent of the United Kingdom.

✸ 1919 AD   Sinn Fein convenes Dail Eireann, a revolutionary parliament.

✸ 1920 AD   The Government of Ireland Act splits the country.

✸ 1922 AD   Outbreak of Irish Civil War and the establishment of Irish Free State. Irish patriot Michael Collins dies and James Joyce's *Ulysses* is published.

✸ 1937 AD   The Irish ratify a constitution that, among other things, returns Irish to the position of being the primary national language.

✸ 1949 AD   Under the Republic of Ireland Act, six of the nine counties of Ulster become Northern Ireland, under British rule.

✸ 1997 AD   Scotland and Wales vote "yes" for their own parliament.

✸ 1998 AD   Referendum in Southern and Northern Ireland overwhelmingly ratifies the proposed peace accord.

✸ 1999 AD   129-member Scottish parliament elected.

⊕ If indeed the Celts think of their history mythologically, they also think of their politics poetically. In most Celtic regions, it is not possible to talk about the development of culture and music without understanding the political and social upheavals these communities have created and endured. Many of the songs handed down through the ages echo equally fierce cultural pride and doleful laments, like the Irish standard *Wearing Of The Green*.

*Wearing Of The Green*

*Oh Paddy dear and did you hear the news that's going round?*
*The shamrock is forbid by law to grow on Irish ground.*
*No more St Patrick's Day we'll keep, his colours can't be seen*
*For there's a cruel law against the wearing of the green.*

*Oh I met with Mappertandy and he took me by the hand*
*And he said, 'How's poor old Ireland, and how does she stand?'*
*She's the most distressful country that ever yet was seen*
*They're hangin' men and women for wearing the green.*

*And if the colour we must wear is England's cruel red*
*Let it remind us of the blood that Ireland has shed.*
*Then take the shamrock from your hat and cast it on the sod*
*And never fear, 'twill take root there, tho' underfoot 'tis trod.*

*When laws can stop the blades of grass from growing as they grow*
*And when the leaves in summertime, their colour dare not show*
*Then I will change the colour that I wear in my caubeen*
*But 'till that day, please God, I'll stay a-wearing the green.*

As I continue my quest for this Celtic 'thing', I take a cue from the lyrics to *Off To Dublin (In The Green)* by the Abbey Tavern Singers and join a crowd of Friday night revelers in Leeds, England, for the short flight with Ryanair across the Irish Sea to the fabled Emerald Isle where Celtic history and mythology, politics and poetry, are very much alive.

# Chapter Three

# Celtic Soul: Ireland & The Chieftains

with

Anne Bianchi & Adrienne Gusoff ● Mareid Sullivan ● Maire Brennan (Clannad) ● Mary Black ● Mairead Ni Mhaonaigh (Altan) ● Seamus Egan ● Peter Woods ● Bob Dylan ● Tommy Makem (The Clancy Brothers) ● John Allan Cameron ● Ashley MacIsaac

*The great Gaels of Ireland,
the lord hath made them mad,
for all their wars are merry
and all their songs are sad.*

— G.K. Chesterton

It's a dreary fall morning in Dublin and through the haze of an uneasy half-sleep, I'm sure I can hear the wailing of the Banshee, the female spirit of Gaelic legend, whose presence is said to be the portent of imminent death. My head's buzzing like a "b"-hive from the bouzoukis, bodhrans, and beer of the previous evening's *craic* at the residents' bar of The Harcourt, but, to tell you the truth, I'm feeling pretty good. If the grim reaper is on his way, I'm hoping it's with a cup of hot coffee from Bewley's and the morning paper.

Sliding into wakefulness, with this unholy caterwaul now directly outside my hotel room door, I realize it's the house maid doing a frightful

51

injustice to one of the catchier pop songs of the day. She knows the chorus in a couple of different keys and she's playing no favorite with either one. The movie version would have had *How Are Things In Glocca Morra?* I've got *Barbie Girl* by Aqua in the key of B flat and F sharp.

But why should this pop sensibility come as a surprise? After all, this is Dublin on the doorstep of the 21st century, a bustling, cosmopolitan city, that cherishes its cultural heritage but dances with destiny. There is perhaps no city in the world, outside of Nashville, where music and its traditions are as ubiquitous. Music pours forth from every corner of the city, whether its from the traditional music sessions, known as *seisiuns* or *ceilidhs*, held at the inordinate number of pubs to be found here, or from the buskers along Grafton Street, who can trace their tradition back to the 19th century when artists of legend like Zozimus, a blind poet and ballad singer, and, in more recent times, the Benzini Brothers, later to find fame on the international pop charts as Hothouse Flowers, took it to the streets in the name of art and coin-toss commerce.

And you don't have to wander far to run into other sites of musical import. On Grafton Street, there's Bewley's 24-Hour Oriental Cafe, the coffee house where Bob Geldof and his late-'70s group The Boomtown Rats convened regularly and where their hit single *Rat Trap* was conceived, undoubtedly in the James Joyce Room on the first floor. Just up the street is Captain America's, the burger joint where, as a Trinity College student, chart-topping singer/songwriter Chris de Burgh once sang for his supper.

Over on Merrion Row, a short walk from St. Stephen's Green and the trendy Horseshoe Bar of the Shelbourne Hotel with its impressive solid-oak bar, stands O'Donoghue's, the center of traditional music in Dublin in the early 1960s and the meeting place for most of the top traditional musicians and singers in the city during that period. This is where those internationally-renowned rabble rousers, The Dubliners, came together as The Ronnie Drew Group in the early '60s and where they learned the controversial song *Seven Drunken Nights* from another of the regulars, *sean nos* singer Joe Heaney. The song earned them their first chart hit in 1967 and an appearance on the influential *Top of the Pops* TV show in the U.K. The late Seamus Ennis, the revered uilleann piper, played his share of sessions here, as did fiddler Sean Keane of The Chieftains, who worked at O'Donoghue's early in his career with his brother James in the Castle Ceili Band.

O'Donoghue's is just one of the many pubs in Dublin — and throughout the rest of Ireland — where traditional music and songs thrive in impromptu sessions of instrumental music and unaccompanied solo singing of the old ballads. "The pubs of Dublin are not simply places to have a drink," note Anne Bianchi and Adrienne Gusoff in their highly-recommended travel book, *Music Lover's Guide to Great Britain and Ireland*. "They are theaters for storytelling, backdrops for romance, homes away from home, keepers of the spirit of the city and — of course — repositories of Dublin's own blend of music and performance. In the best of places, you'll find throngs of people joyfully involved in pursuit of 'the crack' which means — not what you think — but literally 'having a good time.' In specific terms they're drinking, shooting the breeze and listening to the music of the ancients."

Mairéid Sullivan, whose debut album THE DANCER was produced by Donal Lunny, who has been called "the uncrowned king of the Irish music scene," has had her share of "the crack" over the years and recommends it for whatever ails you: "The *craic* is an Irish expression for good, fun conversation amongst equals — 'the gift of the gab' or 'the blarney' — good story-telling and conversation with plenty of music and laughter. This is the main focus of Irish social life today and it has its roots in their most ancient Celtic ancestry."

"The crack," you will find, has many moods and faces.

A Sunday afternoon session at Dublin's Mother Redcaps Tavern is a mellow but ultimately entertaining, even moving, affair. One by one the musicians drift in, with instrument cases in hand, working-class men drawn together for the mutual pleasure of playing the ancient music. There appears to be no organization, no set schedule for this impromptu gathering, though, suddenly, one corner of the bar is occupied by a few of these players who, having carefully set their pints of Guinness down on the table before them, quietly begin to tune up their fiddles and guitars and to breath life back into the old tin whistle that has been idle since the previous session.

Slowly, the few become many, and the clicking sound of instrument cases being opened and the dissonant drone of instruments being tuned joins the ceaseless chatter of the tavern's patrons and the clinking of beer glasses. The music takes form from this, haltingly but with increasing purpose. There's a snatch of a recognizable melody and then sporadic tuning. A number of tunes are begun and then abandoned until an unspoken consensus is reached and a melody, unchained, bursts forth into the smoke-filled room.

They get on with it from there as the old tunes are randomly selected and given an airing, much to the delight of the tavern regulars as well as the tourists who have dropped in for a taste of the "reel" thing in Irish music. The highlight of the session, and one of many as it turns out, comes unexpectedly. With no obvious prompting or invitation, a member of the audience, undoubtedly a regular, breaks into song following a short musical intro by the assembled musicians. A hush falls over the crowd. At first, it's hard to identify the source of this remarkable voice. He is sitting, unmoving, at his table amongst the other tavern patrons as he sings his song of Irish patriotism and heroes of days gone by. The singer is a mountain of a man, whose appearance suggests that he's a member of the local farming community. His voice points to a past career on the concert stage.

As it turns out, there are many here up to a good ballad well-rendered. Fact is, as you travel around Ireland, you are left with the impression that every man, woman, and child has a set-piece drawn from a repertoire of songs and ballads, often indigenous to the various regions, but certainly handed down over the generations. Even the beloved Irish novelist James Joyce won a bronze medal singing at a Dublin music festival, though, reputedly he was less than impressed and threw the award into a river.

Back at Mother Redcaps, one of the musicians is airing out a beautiful old ballad that hints at sex but settles for seduction and a quick shoe buckling. (Give me a penny for every time a petticoat is lifted in one of these ancient songs and a man is struck pie-eyed by a glimpse of white stocking at the ankle of his lady-friend, and I'd be a rich man.)

*Easy And Slow*

*'Twas down by Christchurch that I first met with Annie*
*A neat little girl and not a bit shy.*
*She told me her father who came from Dungannon*
*Would take her back home in the sweet by and by.*

*Chorus:*
*And what's it to any man whether or no*
*Whether I'm easy or whether I'm true*
*As I lifted her petticoat easy and slow*
*And I tied up my sleeve for to buckle her shoe.*

*All along Thomas Street down to the Liffey,*
*The sunshine was gone and the evening grew dark,*
*Along by Kingsbridge and beggor in a jiffy,*
*Me arms were around her beyond in the park.*

*From city or country, a girl is a jewel,*
*And well made for gripping the most of them are*
*But any young man is really a fool,*
*If he tries at the first time to go a bit far.*

*Now if you should go to the town of Dungannon,*
*You can search till your eyes are weary or blind.*
*Be you lyin' or walkin' or sittin' or runnin'*
*A girl like Annie you never will find.*

These ballads, sung in English, represent one side of the singing tradition in Ireland. The other side involves the more ancient custom of singing in Gaelic, singing *sean nos* or "in the old style."

If your first thought is that songs sung in a language that had long been given up for dead would have limited appeal beyond the Irish counties in which it is still spoken, you haven't been watching the pop charts. The pioneering Celtic rock group Horslips of the early 1970s included a number of songs in Irish on their albums, but in the 1980s, two of the Brennans of Donegal, Enya and sister Maire of the group Clannad, took the Gaelic language to the top of the charts and into millions of homes around the world with the great success of their recordings.

"When we started to sing Gaelic, we were encouraged not to," Maire Brennan has said. "We had a nice sound but people felt to sing in Gaelic was sort of wasting time because they felt the language was going to disappear in ten years time. I actually think that it's got a bit stronger, and maybe we are one little part of that, helping it along, so that young people are not ashamed to speak it. When I first came to Dublin, people were ashamed."

As far as *sean nos* singing goes, Brennan says she has never regarded herself as a traditional singer. "My mother's people came from Donegal and that's where my Gaelic comes from. On my father's side, it was very much the music halls and the show bands and that. So there was always a fusion within the family and what we grew up with and really we've let that develop rather than trying to compete with *sean nos* singers or traditional singers. We've let what was there within our own house, within what was available to us, just develop into our sound. I would have to say that singing in Gaelic has probably 90 percent to do with the sound that we've created. We would never have got that sound if we were singing in English and that's very, very important to us all the time. Sometimes my singing in Gaelic is very different to what it is singing in English. I just sing it differently. I feel different.

"There is a spiritual element in singing Gaelic songs from where they came from originally. The *sean nos* is really just a form of how people used to sing it long ago. It was just a style, but a very strong style at that.

"There was a woman in Dore that used to give songs. She would give you any song that she knew and one of the amazing things about it was that she would always tell you the story and the source of the song first. Then she would give you the words and the last thing that she would give you was the melody. Then she would say, 'Now go off and sing it your own way!' I think that taught me an awful lot. She wasn't saying, 'This is a precious song. This is the way to sing it and this is the only way to sing it.' For somebody that grew up with *sean nos* to approach me — and she knew I was young and would approach it differently — to give me that freedom was very important to me and it probably affected me greatly, to not be afraid to sing Gaelic songs and know that I wasn't singing them traditionally in the way that one is meant to, that I could do it in my own style."

With the perspective of history, it comes as no surprise that it is two women — Enya and Maire Brennan — who have given the Irish language its biggest international boost to date. "Traditionally, the women were the ones who carried the songs and passed them down from generation to generation," relates Mary Black, a singer who has herself found international stardom by never letting tradition — though it's still at the core of much of her recorded work — become a creative strait-jacket. "That's not to say that the men didn't sing as well. The men seemed to be more inclined to carry the traditional tunes; the fiddle playing and all that."

Mary Black was born and married in Dublin. Her father, who played fiddle and mandolin, came from a very traditional background in a very remote place called Rathlin Island, on the Antrim Coast, at the northern tip of Ireland. "Traditional music would have been the main kind of music that he would have been involved in," says Black. "He played fiddle and mandolin and all of his brothers and sister also played, which is the way of a lot of Irish families. My mother, who came from Dublin, loved to sing. They both did it purely for the pleasure and enjoyment that they got from it. They were never in it professionally. There were five children and my three brothers and my sister Frances luckily inherited this same passion for music. We all sing, which I think is our forte, but my brothers play and we grew up playing and singing as a family.

"I feel, there's a great strength in Irish women and they don't have any problems in standing up there and pushing themselves to the front. That has something to do with the fact that there are so many successful and good female artists in Ireland."

That was certainly true in 1992 when Dara, a small Dublin-based record label, released an album titled A WOMAN'S HEART, which sold well-over 200,000 copies in Ireland, reportedly making it the country's biggest selling album of all time with enough copies eventually sold for each household in Ireland to own at least a copy. The record showcased the work of six of the country's top female performers, including Mary Black, her sister Frances Black, Eleanor McEvoy, Dolores Keane, Maura O'Connell, and Sharon Shannon. A companion book was also published, to which writer Eddie Rowley added profiles on Maire Brennan of Clannad and Mary Coughlan "in order to give a comprehensive picture of how women have made the breakthrough to stardom on the music scene, sometimes against seemingly impossible odds." Coughlan was included on A WOMAN'S HEART 2, released in 1995, along with Mary Black, Frances Black, Delores Keane, Sinead Lohan, Maura O'Connell, Sinead O'Connor, Maighread Ni Dhomnaill, and Sharon Shannon.

Acclaimed vocalist/fiddler Mairead Ni Mhaonaigh of the Irish traditional group Altan can speak with a great deal of understanding of not only the Donegal-style of fiddling but also traditional Gaelic songs and singing *sean nos*. She was raised in the *Gaelteacht* (Irish speaking area) of Gweedore in Donegal, a stone's throw away from where Enya and Maire Brennan grew up.

"Most of the Gaelic songs are love songs," Ni Mhaonaigh explains, "but there isn't a story line to them. They're little instances, little pictures and images. Every verse is an image, say, of a loved one, usually a woman. The songs are usually from a man's perspective but a lot of the ladies would sing these songs as well. They're images of love, of the loved one, of their beauty. They go on for hours, adjective upon adjective about someone's beauty. They remind me sometimes of Japanese poetry, just little snippets of images and you make up your own story.

"Sometimes the singer would start the song by telling the story of the song and then sing it. If you just saw the song in written form, it wouldn't give you a story line as such. In a lot of the songs, if the meter was similar to the meter in another song, they would swap the very good verses from one song to another. I think it is a very modern way of thinking about something and it leaves things wide open as well for the interpreter."

Maire Brennan agrees with Ni Mhaonaigh's characterization of the Gaelic song. "If you look at a lot of the Gaelic songs particularly, the way they were written was very cryptic; they weren't straightforward. They were absolutely, beautifully painted in the way they used to write the words, and I think that that's something that we've brought into our music."

Brennan says that her first memories of these songs come from her time at school with her grandparents. "They were very much into setting aside at least a couple of hours during the week during my school time for learning Gaelic songs and old songs that my grandmother would teach us. I also remember very vividly a sort of — I don't know if you would call him a tramp as such — but he would visit the school just once a year, and my grandparents would always bring him in and he'd tell us stories and sing all these old songs. I'm sure they're songs that have been lost now, which is a shame."

Gaelic was also Ni Mhaonaigh's mother tongue, and she reckons she was just lucky to be brought up with such an ancient language and its accompanying philosophies. "It wasn't a big deal to be brought up with Gaelic," she states, "but then I realized in leaving home that it was really special, that it had a magical quality and another dynamic. For instance, when I speak English, I think in a different way. When I speak in Gaelic, it's totally another way of thinking completely. If the language died, I think a way of thinking would die along with it. It's a very poetic way of thinking, and the closest examples in the English language that would come near to it would be James Joyce's *Ulysses* and Yeats' poetry."

Yeats' *Down by the Salley Gardens* is not only an example of the style of poetry of which Ni Mhaonaigh speaks but also of the indomitability and the far-reaching influence of the Irish song tradition.

### Down By The Salley Gardens

*Down by the salley gardens my love and I did meet;*
*She passed the salley gardens with little snow-white feet.*
*She bid me take love easy, as the leaves grow on the tree;*
*But I, being young and foolish, with her would not agree.*

*In a field down by the river my love and I did stand,*
*And on my leaning shoulder she laid her snow-white hand.*
*She bid me take life easy, as the grass grows on the weirs;*
*But I was young and foolish, and now am full of tears.*

— W.B. Yeats

*Down By The Salley Gardens* is a ballad of some renown in Ireland with lyrics that were adapted by Yeats from a song he had heard in County Sligo during his youth. The remarkable aspect of this is that research has connected the song to an 18th or 19th century ballad titled *Rosey Connelly*, the song Yeats no doubt heard, which is also known in America as *Down In The Willow Garden*. In Ireland, a willow tree is also known as a salley tree. The Everly Brothers, quoted in Nuala O'Connor's companion book to the BBC-TV series *Bringing It All Back Home: The Influence of Irish Music*, indicated that they had long been aware of the song in America. In the early 1990s, the legendary duo recorded *Down In The Willow Garden* in Nashville for the TV project and accompanying record.

A Sunday visit to Mother Redcaps Tavern provided a glimpse of the more subdued *craic* experience, but if you're in search of a *seisiun* of a more robust nature, a Saturday night at the residents' bar of the Harcourt Hotel in Dublin certainly fits the bill. A rollicking good time, some rousing tunes in the ancient tradition, and a very late night await you.

The Harcourt is the former residence of British, yet Irish-born, author George Bernard Shaw, but these days it has become one of the primary gathering places for traditional musicians in Ireland's capital city. The group Stockton's Wing is in the house most Saturday nights when they're not on the road, and you can expect a lot of drop-in guests to share the stage, especially at the traditional music concerts held on Monday nights and during the informal sessions on Tuesdays.

Irish music journalist/author Sarah McQuaid says that members of big-name bands like Altan, Clannad, and the recently disbanded Four Men & A Dog regularly turn out to support their fellow artists, and when local heroes Steve Cooney and Seamus Begley played a gig at the Harcourt not so long ago, contemporary singer/songwriter Luka Bloom, the brother of Irish folk legend Christy Moore, showed up unannounced and joined them onstage for a few songs.

The instrumental music you hear at these pub sessions is for the most part dance music — the jigs, reels, hornpipes, polkas, and *scottiches* once played at country house or crossroads dances, parish halls, and in the tighter confines of the kitchen or family parlor. Talk to any traditional music artist from Ireland and they'll tell stories of being raised with this rich musical heritage that has been as much a part of their lives as eating, drinking, or sleeping for as long as they can remember.

Paddy Moloney's grandfather was from a place in the center of the country he refers to as "the big lands of Ireland," up in the Slieve Bloom Mountains. "He was a flute player and had a little farmer's cottage up there," recalls Moloney. "There was no television and practically no radio; in fact, there was no electricity in some cases. The source of entertainment was house parties — house hooleys, we called them. The people were called ramblers. They would just ramble in and sit down and maybe they would have a fiddle or flute and there would be a few tunes and a few dances. Stories would be told and songs would be sung. I remember all this from my early days. We used to have a melodeon up on the dresser in the kitchen and you'd take it down and the dancing would start. I started to play a tin whistle my mother had bought me when I was four years old. I just taught myself because there was always music happening. That was my beginnings with the music and from there I started with the pipes when I was eight or nine years old."

Donegal, the home of Altan's Mairead Ni Mhaonaigh, is very much fiddling country. "Even though my father played fiddle, it took a while for me to start playing because I was into rock'n' roll and artists like David Bowie, but, when I was about ten years old, I started getting interested again," recalls Ni Mhaonaigh. "As soon as my father heard that someone in the family was interested in the music, he went out to find an instrument for me to play. An old neighbor of ours gave him a fiddle. 'I hear your daughter's interested in playing?' My father said, "Yeah, you have an old fiddle up there, would you give it to her?' It was full of cobwebs and everything and he gave it to me free of charge. My father wanted to buy it off him, but he said as long as it is being played, I'll be happy. So, I still have the fiddle and my father tuned it up for me and since then I haven't looked back."

Ni Mhaonaigh may not have looked back, but there were certain to have been moments of second-thoughts. "In the older society, as women came into child-bearing age, they weren't supposed to be playing fiddles or pipes," she points out. "They would be looked down upon and if you were a fiddle player, you'd be looked on as a rebel. I had a first-hand experience with this in the last 15 years.

"I went to an old fiddle player that I used to get a lot of music from and he said to me, 'You play the fiddle?' and I said, 'Yes.'

" 'And, you're a woman?' I said, 'Yes.' I knew what he was getting at and I said nothing. I just wanted him to realize himself that it could happen.

"It was just an older society, but it's changing very rapidly. It's not considered as rebellious these days. Long ago in Donegal, it was mostly men who played fiddles and instruments, but then I think this century, the women's movement helped and it was just easier to get instruments as well. A lot of these musicians came from very poor areas and they wouldn't have had the money to buy instruments, so they were very scarce."

Accomplished multi-instrumentalist Seamus Egan was born in Philadelphia, but moved to Ireland with his family in his infancy. "My father's from Mayo and my mother was born and raised in Philadelphia but her parents were from Donegal," explains Egan. "The whole family moved over to Mayo when I was about three years old. That's where I first started to play music. My grandmother played the melodeon, the one row accordion, so my father had some tapes of her laying about. We heard that and the other music that was always played around the house, so it was always in our ears. Our parents made sure we were exposed to it. My sisters and myself sort of gravitated towards it and have been at it ever since.

"At the time we lived in Ireland, we didn't have a television. One night, my mother and father had heard that there was going to be this special on with Matt Molloy and James Galway. They took us down to our neighbor's house, which had a television, and put a tape recorder up to the television and taped the program. I just remember being fascinated by the sound of the flute at that stage. Up until then I'd tried to play it but not with much success and much frustration. But after I saw that program, I got it into my head to try it."

One of Egan's earliest mentors was Martin Donaghue, an amazing man, who, though he was paralyzed and confined to a wheelchair, would come up to Foxford where he lived and give music classes at the local town hall. "He played the button accordion himself," recalls Egan, "but he didn't play any of the other instruments and he would just talk us through it. He'd talk about how this and that should be played and the things you need to do. We'd come back the next week and play it for him, and he'd say that's right, that's wrong, try it this way or that way. It was a great experience."

Egan reckons that if you had to name one thing that's identifiable with Irish music, it's the melody. "If the melody isn't strong, it won't last. There's a reason these tunes have lasted so long. They have a quality, whether you can write it out on paper or it's just something that you feel, there's something inherent in these melodies. That's the reason why they've endured and why people want to play them and listen to them.

"The other thing about Irish music is, you do have a fair bit of variation. If you look at Irish music on the written page, for the most part it's the skeleton of the tune. It's the rule book, more or less, of how this particular piece is to be played, but it's wide open for interpretation. That would include how you choose to phrase it. It's a guide more than a hard and fast rule, but you're still even given the leeway to operate within a certain musical structure or eight-bar form. Any variations that occur,

occur within these eight-bar segments. That may sound limiting, but it actually isn't. There's an almost infinite way of changing what's in between those eight bars, but at the end of the day, you're still maintaining that structure and you're still maintaining the integrity of the initial melody. Anything you're doing is to embellish that as opposed to taking it apart and rebuilding it.

"With these tunes or songs, at the end of the day, all you're left with is the emotion that's conveyed either through the interpretation of the word or of a note. You could have a great series of notes or a great series of words and if they're not delivered in a way that has some sort of meaning to you personally, as the person giving it out, then it's probably a safe bet that it is not going to connect with someone else with any impact, so it's important as much as possible to keep the feel."

In his book *The Heartbeat of Irish Music*, a heart-warming tale of growing up with the traditional music at the heart and soul of Ireland, author/musician Peter Woods writes: "There was music before me and after me — on both sides of my family they could play. There was music in nearly every house where we came from, up in the humps and hollows, wet, bad land, all bog and lake . . . it was within you and you could take it with you wherever you went in life." Not only did the Irish carry this music with them, they clung to it as if it were a life preserver tossed to them upon the cruel sea that was their country's history. Through political upheaval, murderous famine, and mass emigration, the instrumental music and songs, many still sung in the original Gaelic or *sean nos* style, have not only survived but now thrive in the hands of a new generation of singers and musicians. They call it the living tradition, and the story of its perseverance is made all the more remarkable by the fact that, early on, nothing of the music was ever written down.

From early Celtic Ireland, where it is said that no Roman could ever boast of conquest, to Saint Patrick's mission of salvation to Ireland; from the arrival and settlement of the Vikings on Irish shores, to the reign of Brian Boru, the legendary king of Tara; from the Norman invasion by "Strongbow" in the 12th century, to the subsequent generations of Anglo-Irish conflict — music has always played an integral part in Irish history.

Evidence of a drum much like the shallow, goat-skin covered bodhran (pronounced boran) still in use in Irish traditional music today, dates back to the Bronze Age, while as far back as the 9th century, the image of the harp was beginning to show up on the sculptured stone crosses that dotted the landscape of Ireland and Scotland. The harp, which is Ireland's national symbol, enjoyed its greatest popularity between the 10th and 17th centuries; in fact, in 1207 AD, the first coins struck in Ireland incorporated the Irish harp design. The harpers were the pop stars of the day, elevated to positions of privilege within the courts of the ruling chieftains and princes who were their patrons.

This tradition was devastated in the early 17th century as the Catholic/Protestant and Anglo/Irish conflicts, which had their beginnings in 1532 with Henry VIII's split with the Catholic church, ended in Irish defeat and the confiscation of their land by Protestant settlers from England and Scotland. The chieftains fled the country in the face of the subsequent harsh Penal Laws introduced by the British, and without their patronage, the once esteemed harper became an itinerant musician forced to wander from house to house, depending on the goodwill and patronage of the people with whom he came in contact.

The last of Ireland's vagabond harpers and composers was Turlough O'Carolan, born in 1670 near Nobber in County Meath. After being blinded by smallpox at the age of 18, O'Carolan was urged to take up the harp by the wife of his father's employer, Mrs MacDermott Roe. She subsequently apprenticed him to a harper and, after three years of training, gave him money, a guide, and a horse as he set out to travel the length and breadth of Ireland as an itinerant harper. Having taken up the instrument so late in life given the harp's relative difficulty to master, O'Carolan was never considered a great performer. He did, however, show a great aptitude for composing, which he did prolifically.

O'Carolan died in 1738, and it was possible that his music and that of other traveling harpers would have been lost had it not been for archivists like Edward Bunting, a renowned piano teacher and organist in Ireland during the late 18th and early 19th century who notated the performances of traditional Irish players. Much of his work in this regard was published in the three-volume collection *The Ancient Music of Ireland*. The Chieftains' CD CELTIC HARP: A TRIBUTE TO EDWARD BUNTING won a Grammy Award in 1993 as Best Traditional Album.

The traveling community of musicians was not limited to harpers. Over the years, Uilleann pipers like Johnny and Felix Doran, John and Paddy Keenan, and The Furey Brothers, as well as fiddlers like the Dohertys of Donegal, have taken the music to every small village and town in Ireland, in effect keeping the traditional music alive and vital.

The Potato Famine, which struck Ireland to such devastating effect between 1845 and 1849, caused the death of more than one million people and prompted hundreds of thousands more to immigrate to places as far afield as Australia and North America. Though no one will ever know how much of the music and how many of the songs were lost during this period, we do know that the survivors carried with them to the New World many of the old tunes and ballads.

Once again, Ireland's musical heritage found it had another guardian angel watching over it, this time in the unlikely person of a remarkable, young adventurer by the name of Daniel Francis O'Neill. O'Neill, who was born in County Cork in 1848 during the Potato Famine, was surrounded by music in the rural society in which he grew up. He learned to play the wooden flute at an early age, but by the age of 16, he ran away to sea and spent the next six years traveling the world. By the year 1870, he had settled in America, initially working as a teacher and a shepherd before moving to Chicago and joining the police force.

It was during this period that Francis O'Neill met James O'Neill, a young fiddler, who could read and write music, but at that point was working as a common laborer. Francis, who would later rise to the position of General Superintendent of the Chicago Police, subsequently used his influence to get James a job on the force, and over the next few years, they teamed up to begin collecting Irish folk melodies and dance music from many of the immigrants who had carried the music with them from various regions of Ireland. The result of their work was two books, *O'Neill's Music of Ireland* and *The Dance Music of Ireland*, both known by most traditional musicians as simply "The Book" and widely regarded as the standard reference work for players of Irish traditional music.

By the 1920s and '30s, Irish music had a ready audience with the thousands of immigrants who were then living in America. This was not lost on a recording industry that at the time was in its adolescence. During this period, 78 RPM recordings by expatriate Irish fiddlers, like James "The Professor" Morrison, Hugh Gillespie, Packie Dolan, and flute player John McKenna, all had a tremendous impact on future generations of musicians, though none was more influential than expatriate Sligo-style fiddle player Michael Coleman, whose spectacular ornamentation and inspired technique could make the less demonstrative styles of fiddling found in some areas of Ireland sound drab and unexciting in comparison. This undoubtedly influenced the playing styles of many a young fiddling hopeful who naturally turned to the more flashy delivery of Coleman for inspiration.

There are many distinctive fiddle styles throughout Ireland, as Altan's Mairead Ni Mhaonaigh explains. "I've heard it said that the more south you go in Ireland, the more fluid the sounding of the bow was. The more northern people were associated with Scottish people because the bowing was more staccato and it had more attack. That makes geographical sense because a lot of Donegal people used to go to Scotland for work and they used to mix a lot with Scottish people, so Scotland is part of our land as well.

"In Donegal, where I come from, there used to be a lot of twin fiddling. Most of the music long ago, I guess, would have been solo music, but when it came to fiddle music, fiddles blend very well, and no matter if it's a good and a bad fiddle player playing together, they seemed to blend very well.

"In Donegal, there also used to be a lot of octave playing. A fiddle player would play in a low octave and then the other player would take it an octave higher, which would give it a sense of harmony and a wider and bigger sound. We do that a lot in the band. The other fiddle player would take the octave while I would play the straight melody. He would play an octave lower and then embellish on that octave as well. Sometimes, along with that, they used to drone. If you were playing an E minor and A major, they'd drone the A note to give it that piping sound. Again, that would expand it and give it a bigger sound. That was done frequently in Donegal music."

With a combined population of less than five million, Ireland and Northern Ireland have contributed more than their fair share of world class talent to the pop charts internationally.

"In the past 10-12 years, it has opened up enormously and it's not necessary to go into England anymore to make your mark," reckons Paddy Moloney of The Chieftains, who traveled far and wide to make their international mark. "Now, we go direct throughout the world. At long last, it's recognized that this is the great thing about the Irish, the music and the arts. You think of our poets, authors, playwrights, and filmmakers and then the music itself in all forms like U2, The Cranberries, Sinead O'Connor, and young people like that, and that's not the end of it. You just have to visit and you find out that the whole place is coming down with music." Moloney could have added artists like Thin Lizzy, Van Morrison, Enya, The Pogues, Chris de Burgh, Clannad, Luka Bloom, Hothouse Flowers, The Waterboys, The Corrs, Boomtown Rats, and the late Donegal-born bluesman, Rory Gallagher. Few of these artists remained untouched by the traditional music around them and most retained ties with it throughout their careers. "Celtic Soul," they call it — and it recognizes no musical boundaries.

In 1973, the Irish ballad *Whiskey In The Jar*, a staple of The Clancy Brothers & Tommy Makem, became the first hit for Dublin-based rockers Thin Lizzy, fronted by the late Phil Lynott. A ballad may have seemed a strange choice for the repertoire of a rock group, but a song which dealt with armed robbery and a woman's treachery and had a rollicking drinking chorus to boot, well, that was something they could get into late at night in the studio when the whiskey and other potables had been flowing freely.

*Whiskey In The Jar*

*As I was going over the Kilmagenny Mountain,*
*I met with Captain Farrell and his money he was counting.*
*I first produced my pistol, and then I drew my sabre,*
*Saying, 'Stand and deliver, for I am a bold deceiver.'*

*With me ring dum a doodle um a dah,*
*Whack fol the daddy o, whack fol the daddy o,*
*There's whiskey in the jar.*

*He counted out his money and it made a pretty penny,*
*I put it in my pocket and I gave it to my Jenny.*
*She sighed and she swore that she never would betray me,*
*But the devil take the women, for they never can be easy.*

*I went into my chamber, all for to take a slumber,*
*I dreamt of gold and jewels and for sure it was no wonder.*
*But Jenny drew my charges and she filled them up with water*
*And she sent for Captain Farrell to be ready for the slaughter.*

*And 'twas early in the morning before I rose to travel,*
*Up comes a band of footmen and likewise Captain Farrell.*
*I then produced my pistol, for she stole my sabre,*
*But I couldn't shoot the water, so a prisoner I was taken.*

*And if anyone can aid me, it's my brother in the army*
*If I could learn his station in Cork or in Killarney.*
*And if he'd come and join me, we'd go roving in Kilkenny,*
*I'll engage he'll treat me fairer than my darling, sporting Jenny.*

The 1985 collaboration between Irish traditional group Clannad and U2's Bono resulted in the hit single, *In A Lifetime*, and in 1987, The Dubliners and The Pogues got together to record a rousing version of the classic ballad, *The Irish Rover*. It resulted in the second appearance in two decades by The Dubliner's on the U.K.'s *Top of the Pops* TV show.

## The Irish Rover

*On the fourth of July, eighteen hundred and six,*
*We set sail from the sweet cove of Cork*
*We were sailing away with a cargo of bricks*
*For the grand city hall in New York.*
*'Twas an elegant craft, she was rigged fore and aft,*
*And how the wild wind drove her*
*She could stand a great blast in her twenty-seven masts*
*And we called her the Irish Rover.*

*We had one million bags of the best Sligo rags,*
*We had two million barrels of stones,*
*We had three million sides of old blind horses hides,*
*We had four million barrels of bones.*
*We had five million hogs, six million dogs,*
*Seven million barrels of porter,*
*We had eight million bales of old nanny goats tails,*
*In the hold of the Irish Rover.*

*There was Barney McGee from the banks of the Lee,*
*There was Hogan from County Tyrone,*
*There was Johnny McGuirk who was scared stiff of work,*
*And a chap from West Meath called Malone.*
*There was slugger O'Toole who was drunk as a rule,*
*And fighting Bill Tracy from Dover.*
*There was Dolan from Clare, just as strong as a bear,*
*All aboard on the Irish Rover.*

*We had sailed seven years when the measles broke out,*
*And our ship lost its way in the fog,*
*Then the whole of the crew was reduced down to two,*
*Just myself and the captain's old dog.*

The ship struck a rock; Lord what a shock,
The boat, it was flipped right over,
Turned nine times around and the old dog was drowned,
I'm the last of the Irish Rover.

These were certainly not the first Irish ballads to cross into the world of contemporary music. For that you'd have to go back to the early 1960s as the folk boom was in full nova in the United States. The Clancy Brothers & Tommy Makem arrived in New York at the time with a repertoire of songs that had never been heard by the local folkies, who were immediately and completely taken with these traditional ballads.

Bob Dylan was one of the group's biggest fans, a fact he confirmed during an interview with Bono of U2 prior to his show at Slane Castle in Dublin in July 1984. In the interview, which appeared in the Irish music paper, *Hot Press*, Dylan talked about hanging out with the group in the early '60s and seeing them pack some pretty large venues to the rafters. The group even performed on the *Ed Sullivan Show* during this period. "One of the things I recall from that time is how great they all were," Dylan told Bono. "There is no question, but that they were great. But Liam Clancy was always my favorite singer, as a ballad singer. I just never heard anyone as good, and that includes Barbra Streisand and Pearl Bailey."

Tommy Makem from Armagh, the fourth member of the original group featuring Liam, Paddy, and Tom Clancy of Tipperary, is an acclaimed singer, songwriter, actor, banjo player, and storyteller in his own right. He recalls their connection with Dylan during their time in New York. "Dylan would come in and listen to what we were doing," Makem told Craig Harris, author of *The New Folk Music*. "Then he would make up songs with the same tunes. We'd meet him at Sixth Avenue at three o'clock in the morning and he'd stop us to sing a song that he had written. He wrote *With God On Our Side* to the tune of *The Patriot Game*. The funny thing was that it had originally been an American pop tune, *Hear The Nightingale Sing*, which had been recorded by Patti Page and Jo Stafford. It had gone over to the other side and been adapted by Dominic Behan. It was a lovely tune."

The Clancy Brothers, with a new line-up that included brothers Pat, Bobby, and Liam Clancy as well as their nephew Robbie O'Connell, played the star-studded Bob Dylan tribute at Madison Square Gardens in 1995. *Rolling Stone* talked about "the timeless traditional Irish grace of the Clancy's" and their "breathtaking" performance of *When The Ship Comes In*.

John Allan Cameron, a troubadour of note himself from Canada's Cape Breton Island, remembers all too well The Clancy Brothers With

Tommy Makem's impact on the folk scene of the '60s. "Tommy Makem once told me — and I'll always love Tommy Makem and the Clancy Brothers — that when they came over from Ireland to New York in the '50s, they brought the guts of Irish music," imparts Cameron. "They were raunchy and would sing songs like *Isn't It Grand Boys To Be Bloody Well Dead*. I mean, that is so far removed from a song like *Did Your Mother Come From Ireland?* or the stuff that Dennis Day used to do on the *Jack Benny Show*. The Clancy Brothers brought the rawness and the real energy of the roots of Irish music to the American and Canadian public. I was influenced by that and songs like *Brennan On The Moor*."

Brennan On The Moor

'Tis of a brave young highway man this story I will tell
His name was Willie Brennan and in Ireland he did dwell.
'Twas on the Kilworth mountains he commenced his wild career
And many a wealthy noble man before him shook with fear.

Chorus:
And it's Brennan on the moor, Brennan on the moor,
Bold, brave and undaunted was Brennan on the moor.

One day upon the highway as Willie he went down
He met the Mayor of Cashel, a mile outside the town.
The Mayor, he knew his features, and, young man, said he
Your name is Willie Brennan, you must come along with me.

Now Brennan's wife had gone to town, provisions for to buy
And when she saw her Willie, she began to weep and cry.
She said, hand to me that ten-penny, as soon as Willie spoke
She handed him a blunderbuss from underneath her cloak.

Then with the loaded blunderbuss, the truth I will unfold
He made the Mayor to tremble and robbed him of his gold.
One hundred pounds was offered for his apprehension there
So he with horse and saddle to the mountains did repair.

*Now Brennan being an outlaw upon the mountains high*
*With cavalry and infantry to take him they did try.*
*He laughed at them with scorn until at last 'twas said*
*By a false-hearted woman, he was cruelly betrayed.*

In the late '60s and early '70s the North American pop charts could even boast a few hits by Irish artists like The Irish Rovers, who hit the Top 10 of the influential Billboard singles chart in America with a little ditty called *The Unicorn* written by Shel Silverstein. In his book, *Children of the Unicorn: The Story of the Irish Rovers*, group member Will Millar recalls those early days and the immigration to Canada of this group of five young men of mixed Catholic and Protestant backgrounds from Belfast and North Antrim. "There were grey days once and Canada had no singing pubs. You couldn't open your cheeper, or they would whisk your salty beer away: you would find yourself in the glare of Yonge Street, with a song on your lips; the dismal hum and clink in the smoky room now closed behind you.

"But civilization prodded its way across the land and in 1968 the Irish Rovers got on the hit parade of the world. We played the fancy Crystal Light, Royal York's Imperial Room — once the hallowed confines of Al Martino and Tony Bennett sounds — now rattling away starting slowly but surely, echoing the drunken strains of 'Me father he was Orange and me mother she was Green.' Folkies from Scotland and Ireland started groups by the dozen. The Abbey Tavern Group, from Dublin, did a commercial for Carling's Brewery and everyone in Canada roared, 'We're off to Dublin in the Green, in the Green.' The Irish Rovers came in long before all that culture took a hold of Irish music. Any group of Irish singers, if they are even half presentable, would never be out of work in North America."

Of course, when the folks at home in Ireland saw the tremendous success that The Clancy Brothers With Tommy Makem and others were having in North America, it made many look at the music that had been an integral part of their lives for generations in a new light. This had the effect of actually creating a resurgence of interest in these traditional ballads in Ireland.

Besides the folk boom, the early 1960s also produced the late Sean O'Riada's ensemble Ceoltoiri Cualann, later to evolve into The Chieftains. "Sean O'Riada came to public notice during the 1960s in Ireland as a pioneer in the conscious revival of ancient Celtic musical traditions," observes singer/songwriter Mairéid Sullivan. "He was the first to take the traditional melodies and give them harmonic structure. The Chieftains were his experimental group. Many other musicians began to explore the melding of traditional forms with classical and popular styles. But today more than any other of the many musicians working with the traditional music, O'Riada's student, Micheal O'Suilleabhain, carries on the intelligent and sensitive focus on the music tradition's capacity for improvisation and alignment with 20th-century music. Micheal's partner, Noirin Ni Riain, has become a leader in the restoration of the *sean-nos* (old style) singing tradition, bringing new life in a variety of traditional and contemporary settings." The Irish World Music Centre was established by O'Suilleabhain in 1994, who became the first holder of the new Chair of Music at the University of Limerick.

The rejuvenated music scene of the early '60s in Dublin produced groups like The Dubliners, who in 1967 took the controversial, and oft-banned ballad *Seven Drunken Nights* to the upper echelon of the British charts. The Dubliners differed from The Clancy Brothers in a number of ways. They had a reputation as hell-raisers and they also made wider use of traditional instruments, like the fiddle, tenor banjo, and tin whistle, within the group. By the late '60s, this would become the norm for many of the popular groups of the day, including The Johnstons and Sweeney's Men, the first group to introduce the bouzouki — played by Johnny Moynihan — to Irish traditional music.

Singer Mary Black had her beginnings in this same Dublin music scene. "There was a folk revival going on in Dublin as well as in England and Ireland," she recalls, "and my two older brothers were playing and going to folk clubs. As I got older, I was always the one who was encouraged to go out front and sing.

"There were a lot of good folk clubs around and, therefore, there were a lot of opportunities to hear Irish folk and traditional music, Scottish-influenced music, and English folk music. There was lots to listen to and learn from. Of course, there was the traditional influence coming from my father and my mother loved to sing the songs of her day and we were listening to the radio and groups like The Beatles. There was a lot of music that influenced me in those early days.

"When I was eight or nine, my brother Shay got an old reel to reel tape recorder. He was about 13 or 14 at the time and his voice was cracking and breaking so he couldn't sing. He used to get me up to the bedroom to sing into this big microphone. Those songs helped me to learn my trade as well as to branch out into the folk clubs of Dublin.

"There's a strong folk influence in what I do, there's no doubt about that. I would like to think that's obvious or somewhere there to be heard. But over the years the sound has developed and changed, as I would like it to because I have a great broad interest in music myself. If you're listening that closely to all kinds of music, you're bound to be influenced by what you're hearing. I've always been experimental and wanted to try new ideas. My first solo album had a Lovin' Spoonful song on it and one from Karla Bonoff, so over 50 percent was folk and traditional and the other half was kind of trying things out, even that early in my career. I've always done it for the pure love of it and never dreamed that it would actually go as far as it has gone."

In the early 1970s, musicians who had grown up with the traditional music were now filtering the influences of the contemporary music of the day, which at this point was running the gamut of styles from hard rock to folk, from psychedelia to the blues. The traditional music was starting to take on a harder edge, and not unexpectedly, its popularity was on the rise locally. The '70s in Ireland was destined to become the decade of the Celtic supergroup and the super session which featured a new generation of accomplished musicians whose names would recur over a number of ground-breaking recording projects and whose influence on Ireland's traditional music scene is still being felt today.

Celtic rock was born with Horslips, who arrived on the scene in 1972 with their debut album, HAPPY TO MEET, SORRY TO PART. (Just over a decade later, one of the group's guitarists, Declan Sinnott, who has also worked with Moving Hearts, would produce singer Mary Black's critically-acclaimed, self-titled debut album.) That same year, Planxty was formed during the sessions for folk singer Christy Moore's PROSPEROUS album. (A 'planxty' is a song written in tribute to a musician's patron.) The group, which could match any rock 'n' roll band for sheer power and excitement on traditional instruments alone, featured contributions from a wide-range of outstanding singers and musicians during their decade-long career, including Christy Moore; uilleann piper Liam O'Flynn; Donal Lunny; ex-Sweeney's Men members Andy Irvine and Johnny Moynihan; Paul Brady; and flute player Matt Molloy, who's now with The Chieftains. Pianist Bill Whelan, the composer of the score for *Riverdance*, was also an early member of the group.

Planxty, which broke up in 1983 as Christy Moore and Donal Lunny took their leave to devote more time to Moving Hearts, an Irish traditional group with jazz, blues, and folk/rock leanings, created a fusion of folk and traditional music which had instant appeal with audiences not only in Ireland, but throughout Britain and continental Europe as well. Planxty's Paul Brady, a former member of the Johnstons, would emerge as a major pop singing star in his own right as well as an in-demand songwriter whose material has been covered by artists as diverse as Tina Turner, Bonnie Raitt, Mary Black, Carlos Santana, Cher, and Bryan White.

The Bothy Band, which formed in the mid-1970s and only had a four-album, three-year career, nonetheless made a lasting impact with a driving rhythm section that transformed their repertoire of Irish traditional music. The group, named after the bothy huts in which migrant laborers were forced to live, featured over its history uilleann piper Paddy Keenan, singer/keyboardist Triona Ni Dhomhnaill, singer/guitarist Micheal O'Dhomnaill, fiddlers Paddy Glackin, Kevin Burke, and Tommy Peoples, flute player Matt Molloy, accordion player Tony MacMahon, and the ubiquitous Donal Lunny on guitar. Following the break-up of the group, Triona and her brother Micheal moved to the U.S. and formed the groups Nightnoise and Relativity with Scottish accordion player and keyboardist Phil Cunningham.

De Dannan is another of the ground-breaking groups from this era which at their peak featured future solo stars Mary Black, Delores Keane, and Maura O'Connell on vocals. And though they formed in North London in the early 1980s, it would be difficult to ignore The Pogues — originally Pogue Mahone or "kiss my ass" in Gaelic — and their iconoclastic frontman, Shane MacGowan, in any discussion of Irish music. MacGowan, who can make an old ballad crackle with dramatic tension when he wants to, also knows what to do with a rollicking old standard like *The Irish Rover*, which he and the group recorded with The Dubliners back in 1987.

"There's not just one particular type of Irish music," says Seamus Egan, who, along with Irish accordion and fiddle player Sharon Shannon, is one of the most spectacular solo instrumentalists I've ever seen play live. "There's so many ways of playing it and people are playing it in so many ways. No matter how it is being played, at the end of the day, it still has the same emotional impact the musician gets from it and that comes through to the person who is listening. If you were to look for one fundamental thing, I would say that's probably it."

"Since becoming a republic in 1948, Ireland has seen tremendous progress in the reclamation of the Irish Celtic culture through its language, literature and music," observes Mairéid Sullivan. "A celebration of freedom is evident in the diversity of musical styles embraced as popular culture. For example, the annual jazz festival in Cork is considered to be an important part of the European circuit for jazz lovers. Billboard's Top 10 includes Irish musicians from rock, world and new age music genres."

"We should never be worried about the identity of Irish music because it has survived so much worldwide," declares Clannad's Maire Brennan. "If you look at the population of our land, it's still around four million, and where do they all go? There's families of nines and tens or twelves or whatever, and they're spread all over the world, who have kept the tradition going. And the great pipers and the other musicians that went to America, they didn't lose it. Also, people that have touched on Irish music or have ever heard of it just feel a huge sense of spiritual kind of feeling. They really do feel something deep down from it, because that's where it comes from and that's why I don't think it will be lost.

"The energy will always go back into the music because of, for example, Comhaltas Ceolteori Eireann that has created classes of young people playing uilleann pipes, harps, fiddles, tin whistles, flutes in this country. Now the young people go out and develop it in all sorts of directions but their source is good and it's always there."

As Paddy Moloney of The Chieftains notes with characteristic Celtic pride, "its the arts that have held us together in Ireland and people have at last realized that. We have a wonderful language, which is just holding on. We are just commemorating the 150th anniversary of the Irish Potato Famine. That was the Irish holocaust where we lost two million people through starvation and almost the same number through emigration. The language suffered greatly and the music emigrated. A lot of the musicians went to Australia, the north of England and particularly Canada. They came up the St. Lawrence River on what we call the coffin ships to the Island of Grosse Ile for quarantine and from there they took off throughout America where they made their mark. It was a dreadful shock and a terrible thing to happen but being the sort of people that we are, we didn't just lie down, we still have our time for songs and dance and music."

If the political events drove the Irish to immigrate to the New World between the 17th and early 20th century, thereby spreading the *sean nos* abroad, Paddy Moloney and The Chieftains have taken up the cause of reviving the traditional ways of singing and playing through their extensive work internationally as "musicianers" to the world.

"Musicianer" is a title of great respect in Ireland. It is not only an acknowledgment of instrumental virtuosity, but also of a player's wider gift of musical understanding. "You da' man!" is a close North American translation.

Past and present, Ireland has had its fair share of "musicianers" — artists like accordion players Seamus Begley, Dermot Byrne, Joe Cooley, Jackie Daly, Tony McMahon, Mairtin O'Connor, Colette O'Leary and Sharon Shannon; bodhran players Tommy Hayes, Johnny MacDonagh, Gino Lupari and Peader and Mel Mercier; composers Sean O'Riada, Shaun Davey, Donal Lunny, Peader O'Riada, and Micheal O'Suilleabhain; concertina players Terry Bingham, Noel Hill, and Niall Valelly; fiddlers Maire Breatnach, Kevin Burke, Nollaig Casey, Frankie Gavin, Paddy Glackin, Kevin Glackin, Seamus Glackin, Martin Hayes, Eileen Ivers, Mairead Ni Mhaonaigh, and Tommy Peoples; flute players Kevin Crawford, Brian Finnegan, Frankie Kennedy, Emer Mayock, Michael McGoldrick, and Desi Wilson; guitarist Steve Cooney; harpers Patrick Ball, Paul Dooley, Laoise Kelly, and Maire Ni Chathaisaigh; whistle players Mary Bergin, Packie Byrne, Micho Russell, and Sean Ryan; uilleann pipers Ronan Browne, Willie Clancy, Seamus Ennis, Finbar Furey, Robbie Hannon, Tommy Keane, Paddy Keenan, Maire Ni Ghrada, Liam O'Flynn, Sean Potts, and Davy Spillane; and multi-instrumentalists Seamus Egan and Alec Finn.

Shortly before his tragic and untimely death at the age of 40 in 1971, musician/composer Sean O'Riada called Paddy Moloney of The Chieftains the best musicianer in Ireland. This was high praise indeed from the man most responsible for the revival of Irish traditional music back in the 1950s. O'Riada, born John Reidy, played the traditional fiddle as a youngster, and, having shown great promise as a musician, he ultimately studied music at University College, Cork where, later in life, he would join the music faculty. Upon graduation he became the assistant musical director for Radio Eireann, Ireland's national broadcasting company, before spending a year in Paris where, as a musician, he immersed himself in the jazz and Be-Bop music which was all the rage in the City of Lights during that period. When he returned home to Ireland, he took up the position as musical director at the Abbey Theatre. It was at The Abbey, in the mid-1950s, that O'Riada's love affair with Irish traditional music was re-ignited.

O'Riada was a classically-trained musician in the European style, which certainly fit the job description for his work at the theater. But O'Riada was a creative man of restless and adventurous spirit who had begun to rediscover the ancient music of his own country. His initial notoriety in Ireland came in the late 1950s with the film *Mise Eire* (*I Am Ireland*), the story of the country's struggle towards nationhood, for which he handled the score. He arranged traditional Irish song airs for full orchestra to stunning effect and struck a chord close to the heart of the Irish people. Overnight, he became a household name.

During this same period, when one particular Abbey production, *The Golden Folk*, cried out for the inclusion of some traditional music, he decided to augment the orchestra with a number of the traditional players who were to be found in great numbers in Dublin's pubs at the time. Through a mutual friend, accordion player Eamon de Buitlear, O'Riada was introduced to uilleann piper and whistle player Paddy Moloney. Together, they recruited a group of traditional musicians for the production.

So enthusiastic was the audience reaction to the traditional players, O'Riada decided to put together a contemporary folk orchestra which would not only feature Irish traditional music, but also showcase the talents of the musicians on instruments like the uilleann pipes, accordion, fiddle, harp, bodhran, and even the harpsichord, which O'Riada himself played. The result was the ensemble Ceoltoiri Chualann, which featured, among others, Moloney, Sean Potts, and Abbey Orchestra regular, violinist Martin Fay.

Moloney and O'Riada subsequently became close friends and would regularly meet at the Trinity Bar in Dublin's Pearse Street to discuss the music from their differing perspectives. Moloney was a self-taught musician, who in common with the best players in the jazz world, played extemporaneously, inspired by the spirit of the moment. O'Riada was an academic, who, as fascinated as he was by Moloney's improvisational abilities, undoubtedly felt more at home with the music notated.

Ceoltoiri Chualann became hugely popular in Ireland and O'Riada's dream of bringing Irish traditional music to a contemporary mainstream audience had been realized. When he disbanded the ensemble in the mid-1960s, in part due to the health problems he was experiencing from his heavy drinking, he could not have known the impact that his initiatives would have on future generations of Irish traditional musicians and the so-called supergroups of the 1970s "Celtic revolution" in Ireland like Planxty, The Bothy Band, De Dannan, among others.

Moloney and O'Riada collaborated for the last time in the summer of 1971, shortly before his death, on sessions for the record that became known as O'RIADA'S FAREWELL. "Guided by O'Riada's vision, traditional music changed radically, and became accessible to a modern Irish audience, and through this traditional music, the cultural life of Ireland was invigorated," writes Nuala O'Connor, author of *Bringing It All Back Home: The Influence of Irish Music*, the companion book to the TV documentary and record set of the same name. "The consequences of O'Riada's work were far-reaching: contemporary, classical, folk and rock musicians of recent years, who have chosen to work with Irish idioms, cite him as a creative source in their work; generations of Irish people are indebted to him for restoring to them their nation's music."

When, in 1962, Paddy Moloney was offered the chance to put a group together to record for Claddagh Records, the label created by his close friend Garech Brown, an heir to the Guinness Brewery fortune, he knew without hesitation where he wanted the sessions to go. The group, which also featured Martin Fay, Sean Potts, Michael Tubridy, and elderly bodhran player Davy Fallon, was originally to be called The Quare Fellows after a Brendan Behan play. Kind providence surely smiled upon them when poet John Montague, a director of the record company, suggested the name The Chieftains from one of his books, *The Death of a Chieftain.*

Despite working in the shadow of Sean O'Riada for many years, Moloney had always had his own vision of how a traditional folk orchestra should sound. As the years rolled on, Moloney and the group began to see Ireland's traditional music in the context of the wider Celtic community internationally, delighting in the similarities and exploring its variations. If O'Riada had put the traditional music of Ireland's past into the spotlight at home, Moloney and The Chieftains subsequently carried it to the rest of the world.

"I did the usual school of music trip and took piano lessons and things like that but traditional Irish music was what I really wanted to do," recalls Moloney. "During my teens, I had barber shop quartets and played a ukulele and the washboard and went through all that but I eventually went back to playing Irish music."

The Chieftains current line-up includes Moloney as uilleann piper and whistle player, flute player Matt Molloy, harper/keyboardist Derek Bell, fiddlers Sean Keane and Martin Fay, and vocalist/bodhran player Kevin Conneff. Over more than three decades of history, there have been relatively few changes in the line-up, though Moloney and Fay are the only two remaining members of the original group. Sean Keane made his debut at the Edinburgh Festival in 1968, while Derek Bell, whom Moloney had met in Belfast in 1966 during a performance of *Carolan's Concerto* on a special St. Patrick's Day broadcast, officially joined The Chieftains in 1974 prior to a North American tour. Kevin Conneff replaced Peader Mercier in 1976. In 1979, with the departure of Michael Tubridy, Sligo-style flute player Matt Molloy joined up. Molloy, an old friend of Moloney's from the days they used to play together at The Old Sheiling Hotel in Raheny, was also a former member of the ground-breaking Irish traditional bands Planxty and The Bothy Band.

"Each individual in the group is a soloist in his own right," explains Moloney prior to giving a brief thumbnail sketch of each of the current members of the group. "Matt Molloy has several solo albums. He comes from the west of Ireland. He has his own pub in Westport, which is very handy. Sean Keane has the connection with Longford and County Clare. His parents are from there but he's a Dubliner. He's a tremendous fiddle player. Martin Fay comes from a classical background. He used to play in the Abbey Orchestra. Derek Bell is a concert pianist. He plays all four families of instruments, so he was a prize to find. I was always looking for a harper who would blend into our situation. He arrived in 1972. Kevin Conneff will tell you himself that he came into music at a late stage. He's a wonderful ballad singer. He went on to the bodhran in his teens and he's now our percussionist."

If Celtic music's current international momentum is a train under a full head of steam, then surely the track upon which it has run for the last four decades was laid, in good part, by Moloney and the other members of The Chieftains. Through their world tours and recordings, The Chieftains also became the conduit to broader international acceptance for a wide range of artists from other Celtic regions who perhaps would never have received a hearing without Moloney and the band's intervention. Albums like CELTIC WEDDING and SANTIAGO, the latter featuring the young Galician piper, Carlos Nunez, introduced the music of Brittany and Galicia, respectively, to a wider international audience.

Noted Cape Breton fiddler Ashley MacIsaac is one of many of a new generation of Celtic music artists who have toured extensively with The Chieftains. "Everytime I've gone on the road with The Chieftains, it has been completely amazing because you have a ready, built-in audience of traditional music lovers," says MacIsaac. "I feel right at home with them because they are a bunch of traditionalists and like hanging out with Cape Bretoners, even though they're Irish. Although most of the people are usually there because of the Irish music, they typically connect with me easier than if I were to go into a rock club, although if I go into a rock club, I play a lot harder than I do with The Chieftains."

Irish dancers Michael Flatley and Jean Butler of *Riverdance* and *Lord of the Dance* fame worked with The Chieftains for a number of years long before the runaway success of the two blockbuster productions that generated a new interest in all things Celtic in recent years. Their arrangements and subsequent performances and recordings of music by the revered Irish harper Turlough O'Carolan, in particular on their Grammy Award-winning album THE CELTIC HARP: A TRIBUTE TO EDWARD BUNTING, not only carried on Bunting's work in keeping the music alive, but also opened it up to an audience the size of which even a traveling musician like O'Carolan would have found mind-boggling.

Another of the group's Grammy-winning CDs, THE LONG BLACK VEIL, with its impressive list of guest performers, including Mick Jagger, The Rolling Stones, Sting, Van Morrison, Sinead O'Connor, Marianne Faithfull, Mark Knopfler, Tom Jones, and Ry Cooder, among others, is a testament to the esteem in which they have always been held by their peers in contemporary music circles.

The Chieftains recorded their album ANOTHER COUNTRY in Nashville in the early '90s, demonstrating the historical connection between the ancient Celtic music of Ireland with "America's music." The timing was perfect, as a new wave of interest in country music was on the rise across North America. They played the *sanctum sanctorum* of country music, the Grand Ole Opry, thanks to country singer/musician Ricky Scaggs, whose own family originated in Donegal, Ireland. With the help of TV executive Brian O'Neill, who had produced a one hour show with the group during this period featuring Scaggs, Chet Atkins, and the Nitty Gritty Dirt Band, they entered the studio with a long list of special guest performers, including Willie Nelson, Waylon Jennings, Kris Kristofferson, Don Williams, Chet Atkins, Emmylou Harris, the Nitty Gritty Dirt Band, Bela Fleck, Jerry Douglas, Sam Bush, and Ricky Scaggs. The easy fit of the music and the musicians was a revelation.

Moloney's work on film and TV soundtracks, including his Oscar-winning score for the film *Barry Lyndon* (1975) and the three-part PBS-TV series *Long Journey Home* (1998), has also had the incalculable effect of popularizing the music genre beyond its traditional borders. The soundtrack to the *Long Journey Home* was released on Unisphere Records, the new joint venture label formed by Moloney and BMG Classics, which will focus on Celtic music and artists. FIRE IN THE KITCHEN, a compilation of Canadian Celtic musicians, is a recent release from Unisphere (now known as Wicklow Entertainment).

"There's something about it that just gets you in the gut," British actress Susannah York is reported to have said after listening to a particular Chieftains album. It's a comment similar to that made by others about Celtic music as a whole and one that would come as no surprise to Moloney. "Once you get people to sit down and listen, you win them over eventually," he claims. "It was one of the missions of The Chieftains when we set out to spread the gospel of the real thing, the music itself. The roots of an awful lot or rock 'n' roll and other songs have come from this folk music which for all intents and purposes started as a mother singing to her child. "

Tommy Mackem
(The Clancy Brothers)

Will Millar
(The Irish Rovers)

Christy Moore

Seamus Egan

# De Dannan

# Steeleye Span

Sharon Shannan

Wolfstone

ERECTED
BY THE DESIRE OF SYDNEY LADY MORGAN
TO THE MEMORY OF
CAROLAN
THE LAST OF THE IRISH BARDS
———
OBIIT
A·D·MDCCXXXVIII · AETATIS·SVAE·AN·LXVIII

TO
CHARLES STEWART PARNELL

"NO MAN HAS A RIGHT TO FIX THE
BOUNDARY TO THE MARCH OF A NATION
NO MAN HAS A RIGHT
TO SAY TO HIS COUNTRY
THUS FAR SHALT THOU
GO AND NO FURTHER
WE HAVE NEVER
ATTEMPTED TO FIX
THE NE PLUS ULTRA
TO THE PROGRESS OF
IRELANDS NATIONHOOD
AND WE NEVER SHALL"

# Chapter Four

# Scots, Wha Ha'e: Scotland and Dougie MacLean

*with*

Colin Irwin ❋ Ailie Munro ❋ Steve McGrail ❋ Buzzby MacMillan (Old Blind Dogs) ❋ Jonny Hardie (Old Blind Dogs) ❋ Davy Cattanach (Old Blind Dogs) ❋ Karen Matheson (Capercaillie) ❋ Robin Williamson ❋ Helen Hopekirk ❋ Aonghas MacNeacail ❋ John Ramsay ❋ Rob Gibson ❋ John MacLeod ❋ Alasdair Fraser ❋ Robin Morton

ॐ

*Disgruntled Scots arriving from Edinburgh by plane for the Brazil-Scotland match showed their displeasure when Paris airport officials displayed the British flag instead of their own Cross of St. Andrews. To the tune of Flower Of Scotland, groups of Scots took turns raising their kilts to moon the Union Jack.*

— The Globe & Mail

❋ *"Donald Where's Your Troosers?!"*

The very mention of the '60s hit by the late Andy Stewart, the Glasgow-born music hall entertainer and recording artist, brings "Gaels" of laughter. One of my travel companions is in hysterics.

"Now, there's another of the great Scottish clichés!" she laughs, her eyes rolling skyward.

There are four of us sharing a table in the crowded, smoke-filled sleeper lounge car on the overnight train from London's Euston Station to Inverness in the heart of the Scottish Highlands, and our idle conversation is now lurching like the train itself between the subjects of Scottish nationalism and the country's music heritage, and, at this relatively late hour for dining, the contents of the menu that has been handed to us by the steward.

There's a tempting main course of traditional haggis, neeps and tatties, and a steamed treacle pudding and custard for afters, but, for the sake of digestive harmony and a restful night's sleep, I decide to stick with a wee nightcap of the stuff that Kilmarnock grocer Johnnie Walker began blending and bottling in 1820. This becomes an increasingly popular choice for all concerned as the night wears on and our discourse on the shape of Scotland's future becomes more strident.

Scotch Drink

O Whisky! soul o' plays an' pranks!
Accept a Bardie's gratefu' thanks!
When wanting thee, what tuneless cranks
Are my poor verses!
Thou comes — they rattle i' their ranks
At ither's arses!
— Robert Burns

The earlier judgement passed on Andy Stewart, who also topped the charts with songs like A Scottish Soldier and Campbelltown Loch I Wish You Were Whisky, had earned a nod of general agreement from the other Scots at the table, though, across the aisle, a man of an older generation who has overheard our conversation is not so quick to dismiss the singer who had hosted the popular live TV show known as The White Heather Club. After all, in his day, this was an island of Scottishness in a sea of British-dominated television, and though it reinforced many of the old Scottish stereotypes, it made stars of Stewart and other show regulars like accordionist Jimmy Shand, whose name has become synonymous with Scottish dance music over the past half century. (The Jimmy Shand Story, written by Ian Cameron it takes 22 pages to list his recordings and compositions.)

Nonetheless, there are a number of observers of the Scottish music scene who regard The White Heather Club and the subsequent international popularity of a number of the artists of the period as a blot on the landscape of Scottish music. "The show ran for many years, and — let's not be mean — probably gave an awful lot of people an awful lot of pleasure," writes Colin Irwin beneath the headline, "The Curse Of the White Heather Club: Scottish Music Has Survived Andy Stewart," which introduces his chapter on Scotland in the authoritative *Rough Guide to World Music*. "It also damned Scottish music with an image of banal glibness from which it looked like never recovering. . . . Scots musicians were donated a legacy that was to dog them for the next two decades. To make any credible headway beyond the shackles of an image decimated by kilt and highland flings, they were forced to deny the very thing that provided their one claim to be unique in the first place — their Scottishness."

Ailie Munro, author of *The Democratic Muse: Folk Music Revival in Scotland*, agrees, noting that a significant factor in the musical background to the revival of Scottish folk music was a reaction against Scottish 'popular' music as promulgated by artists like Stewart, Shand, comedian Will Fyffe, Harry Lauder, Robert Wilson, Kenneth MacKellar, Moira Anderson, Peter Morrison, Calum Kennedy, the Alexander Brothers, and various pipe bands. This is music aimed at the tourist market, she suggests, and is found in most record stores under "Scottish."

"Some of it is good stuff — Will Fyffe's songs have lasted well, and piano accompaniments are coming back into fashion," states Munro. "But one cannot ignore the mawkish, kitsch element in it: what has been described as 'cultural sub-nationalism' [by Tom Nairn] , and as 'the persistent curse of Scottish music at the international cultural level' [by Kenneth Elliot]."

It's a pretty dire assessment of dear old Andy and his kilted contemporaries, but I suppose it's no less unkind a cut than the pox that Paddy Maloney of The Chieftains and others have wished upon those who would trade in the blarney and "leprecorn" element of Irish culture.

ᘓ∕ᕲ

To the average Scot on the street — or on the train — the focus is not so much on Scottish stereotypes, most of which they now laugh off, as it is with recent events which relate to the country's status as it enters the 21st century. These are surely historic times for Scotland, which had been a sovereign state for hundreds of years when, in 1603, England and Scotland were united under King James the VI of Scotland, who had also became James I of England. James subsequently moved his Court to London and in the process impoverished a country that was also in a constant state of political upheaval. Scotland was eventually brought to her knees in 1707, partly out of fiscal necessity. The Treaty of Union was signed with England as Scotland closed its Parliament — referred to as "the end of an auld sang" — and ceased to be an independent country.

Almost three centuries later, the Scots voted a resounding "Yes" to the establishment of their own Parliament which was to hold its first assembly in the early months of the new millennium following the voting to elect a 129-member devolved Scottish Parliament. The general feeling is that this truly is the silver lining to Scotland's clouded history and optimism for the future is high.

In the latter stages of the 13th century, Scotland's greatest patriot, William Wallace, the hero of Mel Gibson's epic film, *Braveheart*, dreamed of a free Caledonia, as he called Scotland in those days. Centuries later, popular traditional folk singer/songwriter Dougie MacLean, a former member of ground-breaking Scottish traditional folk groups the Tannahill Weavers and Silly Wizard, would write a song of praise for the Highlands he called *Caledonia*, inspired by an acute bout of homesickness while traveling in Europe, and featured on his 1983 CD CRAIGHIE DHU. It now rivals *Flower Of Scotland*, the song written by the late Roy Williamson of the '60s Scottish folk group The Corries, as Scotland's unofficial national anthem.

"This wee song has become part of the whole movement of creating a little bit more self-determination for Scotland," MacLean explains. "I feel very proud that it has become something bigger than just a song you sing and has almost become a national symbol.

"It's funny because it was a song I wrote on a beach in France when I was in my late teens. I was just very homesick at the time. I had been traveling with these three guys from Ireland and we had been playing in the streets across Europe. When I finished writing the song, I played it to them at the youth hostel where we were staying, and the next morning the three of them left on a ferry back to Ireland and I got on a ferry back to Scotland. We couldn't handle it. All of us were homesick and hearing the song was sort of the last straw."

*Caledonia*

> I don't know if you can see the changes
>     that have come over me
> In these last few days I've been afraid
>     I might drift away
> I've been telling old stories, singing songs
>     that make me think about where I came from
> And that's the reason I seem so far away today.

*Chorus:*
*Let me tell you that I love you*
*and I think about you all the time*
*Caledonia, you're calling me*
*and now I'm going home*
*For if I should become a stranger*
*you know that would make me more than sad*
*Caledonia's been everything I've ever had . . .*

Shortly after the referendum for a Scottish Parliament, *Scottish Life* magazine suggested a link between the people's changing outlook and the apparent boom in traditional music sessions in pubs, private homes, mountain bothies, and village halls all over Scotland. "Some of the events are organized, many just happen, and they seem to be increasing," wrote journalist/photographer Steve McGrail. "From Shetland to the Borders, they're a sign of the vibrancy of Scottish traditional music. And in their ways, perhaps, they reflect the growing self-confidence of Scots, expressed most dramatically in the recent vote for a Parliament for their small nation.

"Such vibrancy hasn't always been there, though. Despite having a history stretching back eons (harpers, for example, play a tune first heard at the Battle of Harlaw in 1411), Scotland's traditional music has had its ups and downs. It's been very much a story of change."

Dougie MacLean came from a Highland family and knows the value that was placed on music as he was growing up. "My father's father came from the Isle of Mull, so there was always a lot of music around. These people had a mysterious side to them and a kind of belief in mystery of which music is one of these things. They were very much in awe of nature and the mysteries of nature. Music was a part of that, so it was more than entertainment. It was almost like an extension of life itself."

"My mom plays the melodeon and my father played a bit of fiddle. Whenever there was something happening in the house, my mother would drag out the melodeon and we'd play. They were very basic players, but I remember my mother teaching me a tune on the melodeon when I was about five or six years old, and it just sort of developed from there.

"I suppose if I was to be honest, apart from our own traditional music, I was also influenced by American acoustic guitar songwriters because there's a bigger tradition of that in America. We don't have that in Scotland, a guitar-playing songwriter. I grew up listening to people like

James Taylor and Joni Mitchell and artists like that."

The Aberdeen-based group Old Blind Dogs could never be accused of conservativism in their approach to the traditional music at the core of their repertoire, which never allows the rhythm to take a back seat. "I suppose Scottish music is characterized for me by things like the strathspey and the two-four and six-eight marches, the piping music, the punctuation of the music and the kick that it has got to it," states band member Buzzby MacMillan. "That's the definitive Scottish music for me . . . and *pibroch* [piper's musical repertoire], of course."

Fellow Old Blind Dog, Jonny Hardie, adds that along the way there was the realization that traditional music was more than music that the old folks liked. "It's actually funky," states Hardie. "It's got all kinds of elements to it that you can latch on to, and there's the pure skill of the musicianship. I realized that it wasn't just people who were doing it for fun. By this time, there were people doing it professionally and playing it really well; bands like De Dannan and Silly Wizard and people like that. They're really good players and I respect good musicianship of any kind.

"That was a big lead into it, as well as the local language. We have something quite unique in this part of the world, and in the Northeast in particular, where a lot of the traditional songs have survived and are written in the language that we speak when we're not putting on our best English when we're traveling aboard. It's our own language and that's great."

The members of the band play the usual array of Celtic instruments, including the mandolin, fiddle, cittern, whistles and border pipes, but you'll also find a well-stocked arsenal of non-traditional percussion instruments within striking distance of the band's percussionist/backing vocalist, Davy Cattanach. "We do things with the band that are contemporary but we also try and keep it as much in the tradition as we can, with the possible exception of myself," says Cattanach, smiling as he looks down at the African drum he's holding between his legs. "But my theory is that 500 years ago people weren't playing bodhrans, they were playing all kinds of stuff.

"When we first started recording with the Old Blind Dogs, there was quite a lot of material, but as we go through the albums, it gets more difficult to come up with songs that we can do in our style because we decided that we should try as much as possible to stick to songs from the Northeast because we are a traditional band. "

Buzzby MacMillan reckons that the blend of the contemporary and, in part, the traditional Doric folk music of the region in the Old Blind Dog's music is never achieved through conscious effort. "We don't think, 'Let's take all our influences and graft them on to our traditional roots.' The traditional music is there if you strip away all of the influences that we hang around it. If you just leave the fiddle or the pipes or the voice by themselves, you'd find it hasn't changed at all. The stuff that we graft on, that's done unconsciously. It's just that these are the influences that have surrounded us and when we get together to create music, that's just what happens. We don't say, 'Let's try and make this one reggae or let's make this one rockier or let's use a pop riff.' We don't go out of our way to fabricate anything, it's just the way it happens."

The innovative Scottish group Capercaillie, fronted by acclaimed vocalist Karen Matheson, may make frequent forays of experimentation into the latest music technology and other ethnic cultures, but they never stray too far from their traditional core. "There's an inevitable push there for any band to experiment," explains Matheson. "We came from this very Celtic tradition, but we were always anxious to push the boat out and, from the very early days, we had synthesizers and other things, which were considered quite alien to the traditional music field. But we always felt that it was very important to experiment and to bring in other styles of music. Within the band, there are other elements apart from Celtic music. There are elements of rock and jazz and other styles of music, and it's just like throwing it all into the melting pot and seeing what comes out.

"Definitely, on our last album, BEAUTIFUL WASTELAND, we've almost come full circle to where the music is practically all traditional. Nearly all of the songs, maybe bar one, are songs that I've known all my life, songs that I didn't actually have to learn — they were just there. That's an incredible feeling, to be able to draw on material that you knew as a child and be able to rehash it in a way that's accessible for people now and to re-invent it in a way. That's one of the most exciting parts of what we do. It's a cyclic thing and I think you always end up coming back to where you started. If you've grown up with this traditional element, even when you start writing in English, it still pours through; it bleeds through regardless. It's a spiritual thing that we grew up with and you can't really get away from it."

Matheson, whose voice *The Times* of London has described as "easily the equal of Sinead O'Connor or Enya," notes that the group often gets caught up in the issue of musical categorization. "You're always going to be pigeon-holed regardless of what you do, but it really doesn't bother us to be honest. We've been called all kinds of things. Actually, one thing we did quite like was the term 'Celtic soul,' so we clung to that."

Capercaillie and Old Blind Dogs, along with artists like Dervish, Clan Alba, Wolfstone, The House Band, Ceolbeg, Shooglenifty, Jennifer and

Hazel Wrigley, Deaf Shepherd, Rock, Salt & Nails, and the "hip-hop piper" Martyn Bennett represent a varied and relatively new wave of the Scottish Celtic music revolution that had its beginnings in the folk scene of the '60s in Glasgow and Edinburgh that produced The Corries, The Fishers (Archie, Ray and Cilla), The McCalmans, The Ian Campbell Folk Group (led by the father of contemporary pop music chart-toppers Aly and Robin Campbell of the reggae-flavoured group UB40 and featuring future Fairport Convention members Dave Swarbrick and Dave Pegg), and The Incredible String Band (co-founded by multi-instrumentalist/singer-songwriter/story-teller Robin Williamson).

Robin Williamson is highly regarded for his visionary approach to the fusion of traditional music with a variety of contemporary and exotic idioms. He reminisced about the early days of the folk scene in Edinburgh and his discovery of the music that would become his passion in the introduction to a published collection of the traditional music of Britain he selected and annotated in the mid '70s called *English, Welsh, Scottish & Irish Fiddle Tunes*.

"In Edinburgh, Scotland, 1956, I first heard the words folk music," Williamson recalled. "I suppose it was about then it occurred to me that the country dance music I was hearing on the radio, the drunken warblings of old street singers, and the rabid ravings of football devotees had some connection with the medieval ballads we were dryly taught in poetry class. I had heard the radio ballads that Ewan McColl was doing at the time. Startling collages of traditional tunes and the taped speech of fishermen, lorry drivers, boxers, and the like. An eye-opener. It merged with the smatterings of history I had absorbed and exposed me to the vast tale of betrayals, rebellions, and all the anguish of the Celtic soul, continually at war with reality."

Williamson would later find himself "at a place where an era was emerging, curiously enough, in the undercurrents of Edinburgh." The action was at a folk club called The Howff where young artists of the day, like Archie Fisher, Davy Graham, and others, would play. Williamson would subsequently team up with one of the regulars, Bert Jansch, who would later go on to form the folk/rock group Pentangle, and spend the winter of 1961 working at various folk clubs in London. By the spring, Williamson had returned to Edinburgh and had begun playing traditional music around the clubs with banjo player Clive Palmer.

"Frankly, in 1962, the pickings were slim, and I was getting thinner," Williamson continues. "One day, when winter was making itself felt, I was standing on a particularly windy corner when I pricked up my ear to the sound of bagpipes. A little further on were a couple of tinker pipers sitting on some steps, with their hats on the pavement, huffing and puffing and skirling away at some reel tunes. I could see that they were fatter than me and drunk to boot. It struck me then that I'd never need to starve if I could learn to play the jigs and reels."

Williamson bought a fiddle he saw hanging in a junk shop window the following day. A subsequent gig with Tom Paley of the New Lost City Ramblers and an inspiring encounter at a local party with banjo player Barney McKenna of The Dubliners stirred him to further musical ambition. He formed The Incredible String Band with Clive Palmer and Mike Heron in 1965, and before the group broke up in 1974, they had toured the world and recorded 17 albums.

Williamson perhaps speaks for a number of emerging Celtic music artists of the 1960s and '70s in describing his motivations for adding to the traditional repertoire by writing material of his own. "I first began writing songs to fill a lack I sensed in the music that was available to me, and to communicate first to my friends and then to an unknown group I sensed in the world," Williamson explains. "An audience evolved of people who heard and liked these songs. I hit on the idea of using different styles of music even within the same song to achieve the emotional results. I began to use a variety of exotic instruments to add sound-color and began to present certain ideas in a theatrical or ritualistic way. I drew from all cultures and periods of history. In looking back, it is easy to see that these ideas were instrumental in the rise of 'flower power'. Such people as Mick Jagger, Robert Plant, The Beatles, and Dylan have expressed interest in and regard for my work, and the course of rock through the last decade has absorbed and utilized some of these innovations."

The mid-1960s was a turning point for Scottish traditional music in a number of ways. As American rock 'n' roll was stealing the headlines at home and abroad and the musical troops were being mustered south of the border for the imminent British Invasion of the pop charts, the interest in Scotland's own musical heritage seemed to be at a low ebb. Yet in 1966 a festival (*feis*) of traditional music was organized in Blairgowrie which exceeded all expectations of its promoters. Charged with renewed optimism and sensing that there was, at the very least, a silent minority at large interested in the survival of music indigenous to Scotland, an intrepid few decided that it was time to organize.

Subsequently, the Traditional Music & Song Association of Scotland (TMSA) was formed with the stated intent of actively promoting Scottish traditional music at festivals, ceilidhs, concerts and competitions, and, in general, helping to create an environment in which it could flourish. It wasn't the answer to every problem dogging the trad scene in Scotland but it was a start, and within a few years, traditional music festivals, which would become a major factor in the revival of interest in the country's musical heritage, began cropping up across the length and breadth of the country. At last count, there were close to 70 traditional music and folk festivals in Scotland, the largest of which is the annual Celtic Connections festival in Glasgow each January.

The survival of Highland music, in particular, has also been greatly aided by the National Mod, now more than a century old, and the work of the University of Edinburgh's School of Scottish Studies — and Hamish Henderson specifically — in making field recordings of traditional music, both in Scotland and Canada's Cape Breton Island. The National Mod, which evolved from a festival of Gaelic song and literature organized in 1892 by the newly formed Gaelic society An Comunn Gaidhealach, subsequently became an annual, competitive event. The work of the University of Edinburgh's School of Scottish Studies can be found on the ear-opening "Scottish Tradition Series" of CDs and cassettes released by the Scottish record label, Greentrax.

Through the late 1960s and into the 1970s, Scotland saw the emergence of a number of other musically adventurous groups, including Boys of the Lough, the Tannahill Weavers, Battlefield Band, Runrig, Silly Wizard, Ossian, Alba, and Gaberlunzie, many of which featured musicians whose impact on the music scene is still felt today. The formation of Boys of the Lough in 1967 brought together musicians and singers dedicated to the Celtic music tradition from both Scotland and Ireland, led by master fiddler Aly Bain, who had previously toured the Scottish folk circuit with Billy Connolly, later to become an internationally known comedian and comedic actor. Bain, who is arguably the savior of the Shetland-style of fiddling, has in recent years toured extensively with accordionist/composer Phil Cunningham, a former member, with his fiddle playing brother John, of Silly Wizard. The 1997 Celtic Connections Festival in Glasgow kicked off with the world premiere of Cunningham's "The Highlands & Islands Suite" with Bain as a featured soloist. Acclaimed traditional Scottish ballad singer Andy M. Stewart was featured vocalist in Silly Wizard, while Dick Gaughan, like England's Billy Bragg, one of a dying breed of socially and politically active singer/songwriters, was once a member of Boys of the Lough.

❧ The oral tradition in Scotland is of a varied and ancient origin encompassing work and communal songs, battle songs and laments, praise songs (panegyric), religious and love songs, *puirt-a-beul* (mouth music), Muckle Sangs, Gaelic psalms, pibroch songs, and ballads. But as the late Scottish composer, pianist, and collector of tunes Helen Hopekirk, points out, the Scottish traditional folk song belongs to two racially different peoples, the Celtic Scot, with a direct connection to Celtic music, and the Lowland Scot, with the poetry and song of Robert Burns as the epitome. "Lowland Scottish music and Celtic music, although talked of collectively, are widely different in character," Hopekirk notes in the introduction to her published song collection, *Seventy Scottish Songs*. "The Lowlander is placid, pastoral, canny, pawkily humorous, somewhat matter of fact, good-hearted, reserved. The Celt is imaginative, 'dreaming dreams and seeing visions,' unpractical, superstitious, tender, of quick perception, living an inner life, a good lover, a good hater. The Lowlander would die for a dogma, the Celt would die for a dream."

In *A Celtic Resurgence: The New Celtic Poetry*, contributor Aonghas MacNeacail quotes the late Scottish Gaelic poet and author Sorley MacLean, who pays tribute to the anonymous (largely female) composers of the classical repertoire of traditional Gaelic song. Maclean, who is heard reciting his poem "Hallaig" in the background of a particularly haunting track of the same title on Scottish fiddler/piper Martyn Bennett's 1997 BOTHY CULTURE CD, speaks of "those Gaelic songs of the two and a half centuries between 1550 and 1800 — the songs in which ineffable melodies rise like exhalations from the rhythms and resonances of the words, the songs that alone make the thought that the Gaelic language is going to die so intolerable to anyone who knows Gaelic, and has in the least degree the sensibility that responds to the marriage, or rather the simultaneous creation of words and music." MacLean also expresses his conviction that "Scottish Gaelic song is the chief artistic glory of the Scots, and of all people of Celtic speech, and one of the greatest artistic glories of Europe."

The best-known Gaelic women poets and praise singers include Mary MacLeod in the 17th century, Maighread Ni Lachainn in the 17th and 18th centuries, and Sileas of Keppoch in the 18th century. Karen Matheson of the group Capercaillie knows first hand about the Scottish Gaelic tradition having grown up in Taynuilt, a small village on the west coast of Scotland where there's a real wealth of Gaelic songs and fiddle music. "My whole family was really absorbed in that whole culture," relates Matheson. "My grandmother came from the island of Barra, one of the Outer Hebrides, and she spoke Gaelic in the house and sang Gaelic songs to me. The first songs I ever learned were in Gaelic, so for me it was more natural for me to sing in Gaelic than it was to sing in English. We also had a primary school teacher locally who came from the mainland and brought us a different element of the Gaelic culture and was very influential in the early years in teaching all the school children in the area to sing and to recite Gaelic poetry. There was just a real wealth of tradition there when we grew up, but I think it's got even healthier in the past 15 years. There's a real resurgence and interest in the language and in that style of music."

*See Afar Yon Hill Ardmore*
*(The Praise of Islay)*

*See afar yon hill Ardmore,*
*Beating billows wash its shore;*
*But its beauties bloom no more*
*For me, now far from Islay.*

*O, my island! O, my isle!*
*O, my dear, my native soil!*
*Naught from thee my heart can wile,*
*That's wed with love to Islay.*

*Tho' its shore is rocky, drear,*
*Early doth the sun appear*
*On leafy brake and fallow deer,*
*And flocks and herds in Islay.*

*Eagles rise on soaring wing,*
*Herons watch the gushing spring,*
*Heathcocks with their whirring, bring*
*Their own delight to Islay.*

*Birken branches there are gay,*
*Hawthorns wave their silver'd spray;*
*Ev'ry bough the breezes sway,*
*Awakens joy in Islay.*

*Mavis sings on hazel bough,*
*Linnets haunt the glen below;*
*O, may long their wild notes flow*
*With melodies in Islay.*

(Ancient Gaelic Verse, translated by Thomas Pattison)

In the 18th century, John Ramsay of Ochtertyre wrote, "over all the Highlands, there are various songs, which are sung to airs suited to the nature of the subject, are in general very short and of a plaintive cast, analogous to their best poetry; and they are sung by the women, not only at their diversions, but also during almost every kind of work, where more than one person is employed, as milking cows, and watching the folds, grinding of grain with the quern, or hand-mill, hay-making and cutting down corn. The men too have *iorums*." The men were, for the most part, the bardic praise singers, who, as in Celtic days of old, toasted the virtuous deeds of the aristocratic warrior-hunters and generally upheld the political and social values of Gaelic society. But a woman's work was never done, and during the course of their communal labor, most of which was tiring and repetitive, they would sing.

"These work songs, or the *waulking* songs as they are known, are very similar to African work songs," explains Karen Matheson of Capercaillie, who in May of 1992, spent two weeks on the British hit singles chart with their EP *A Prince Among The Islands* from a TV documentary series of the same name, which included the 400-year-old waulking song *Coisich A Ruin/ Walk My Beloved*. The record peaked at Number 39, making it the first Scots Gaelic song to crack the Top 40 singles chart in the U.K. "The connection is not only through the rhythm, but also through the poetry as well, the yearning, the longing. There's something very spiritual about them; something very earthy and timeless." *Beann a' Cheathaich*, an up-tempo waulking song, was recorded by The Poozies on their 1995 DANCEOOZIES CD, as well as by Christine Primrose.

Waulking, which is done almost exclusively by women in Scotland but mostly by men at gatherings called "milling frolics" on Canada's Cape Breton Island, describes one particular "fulling" treatment for wool cloth that ameliorates the Velcro-like characteristics of the wool hair in order to make the finished fabric stronger, more air-tight, and waterproof. The fulling process, traditionally done by either hand or foot, involves weaving the wool into a long cloth, which is then wet down. The traditional fixing agent was male urine, but one can imagine that, more often than not, hot water sufficed.

The women, who were usually seated around a large table, would then grasp a section of the cloth in both hands. To the rhythmic singing of their waulking songs, they would bang it on the table in front of them, causing the fibers to mat together and bind the strands in place, before passing it on to the woman to the left of them, who would repeat the process. The clockwise direction of the movement was notable in that it was in keeping with ancient belief that all circular movements should be accomplished in the direction of the sun's movement across the sky. This process, from which the surnames Fuller and Walker are thought to have derived, died out in the 1950s in Scotland. The famous Harris Tweed is machine fulled these days, though crofters still hand weave the material in the home.

Another style of singing, called *puirt-a-beul* or mouth music, involved the a cappella and rhythmic performance of nonsensical lyrics written for dance tunes that accompanied the reel, strathspey, or jig. It is a music form unique to the Scottish Highlands and, in particular, The Hebrides, according to Karen Matheson. "The Irish culture doesn't have it, neither do the Welsh. They are very fast, very rapid songs which they used to make up and sing when the playing of the bagpipes was banned [mid-18th Century]. If you travel around the world and listen to the music of other cultures, you get this kind of rhythmic singing, and although it's unique to the Highlands, there's so much that connects it with the rest of the world's music. It's just such a powerful force and it's so energetic, you just have to tap your feet. It's so lively that it crosses all musical boundaries."

That contention was borne out almost 250 years later, in 1991, when an album of *puirt-a-beul* with afro/pop underpinnings by Mouth Music, the duo of Scotsman Martin Swan and American-born Talitha MacKenzie, spent 17 weeks on Billboard's World Music chart. MacKenzie departed after that first album, but Swan continued on his experimental way with a new line-up through the '90s.

The most famous writer of songs from the Lowlands, and one of Scotland's most well-known citizens internationally, is the beloved poet Robert Burns, who wrote *Auld Lang Syne*, synonymous with New Year's celebrations around the world and one of the best-known songs ever written. It is only one of the many songs that became national treasures — who has not heard *Comin' Thro' The Rye* and *Flow Gently Sweet Afton* — and have been given new life by artists like Jean Redpath and Dougie MacLean, two of the finest modern day interpreters of Burns' songs. MacLean's version of the Burns classic, *Scots, Wha Ha'e*, is a highlight of his 1995 Tribute CD.

*Scots, Wha Ha'e*

*Scots, wha hae wi' Wallace bled,*
*Scots, wham Bruce has aften led,*
*Welcome to your gory bed*
*Or to victorie!*

*Now's the day, and now's the hour:*
*See the front o' battle lour,*
*See approach proud Edward's power —*
*Chains and slaverie!*

*Wha will be a traitor knave?*
*Wha can fill a coward's grave?*
*Wha sae base as be a slave? —*
*Let him turn, and flee!*

*Wha for Scotland's King and Law*
*Freedom's sword will strongly draw,*
*Freeman stand or freeman fa',*
*Let him follow me!*

*By oppression's woes and pains,*
*By your sons in servile chains,*
*We will drain our dearest veins*
*But they shall be free!*

*Lay the proud usurpers low!*
*Tyrants fall in every foe!*
*Liberty's in every blow!*
*Let us do or die!*

— Robert Burns

Burns, an avid collector of Scottish traditional songs who undoubtedly saved many of them from extinction, died at the age of 37 in 1796 and is remembered annually on his birthday, January 25.

Dougie MacLean is full of admiration for those of his own craft who have gone before. "The *people* wrote these songs," Dougie MacLean emphasizes.

"There was no music industry and there were no record charts and there were no genres of music like folk, blues, or rock'n'roll. They just made music, and if it didn't have the magic in it, it would never have survived. These were genuine songs written about genuine subjects with genuine passion in the writing of them. I'm in awe of some of the older songs. If we manage to grab magic from about here, then they grab magic from way up here somewhere. I don't know how we'll ever get to find that, but you keep trying."

One place to find this magic is in the history of the Scots. The Viking invasions of Scotland, or Alba as it was then known, began late in the 8th Century and brought major change to the region. The Norse presence is still to be found in the names of thousands of islands and coastal place names and, less obviously, in the set of famous chess pieces found in Uig, on the west coast of the Isle of Lewis during the winter of 1830-31. These chess pieces became the inspiration for the song *Marching Mystery*, the title track to a CD by Dougie MacLean, released in 1994.

"The Isle of Lewis is very wild and remote," relates MacLean, who has spent a lot of time on the island. "In the early 1800s, there was a big storm that washed away part of a sand dune to reveal this little stone box which contained a hundred little ivory chess pieces, all beautifully carved. Being superstitious, the locals, thinking they had uncovered a nest of gnomes and goblins, fled for their lives. When the archaeologists made their examination, they dated the box and its contents from something like the 11th century, though nobody knows why they were buried where they were in this stone box.

"I bought a replica set of these and I kept them on my kitchen table. One night I was sitting there with all these guys lined up . . . and they're really miserable looking. They've got this real gaunt look on their faces and the Queen actually has her head in her hands. There was a kind of weird sadness about them and I began imagining these little characters marching up the beach where they were found. What was their purpose? Where were they headed to? That's how the song *Marching Mystery* came about. It's fun because it presents a picture of what the local people would have thought when they discovered them."

*Marching Mystery*

*From ship to shining shore*
*Out of an age when time was young*
*Across the silver ocean's floor*
*Their endless battle has begun*

*Chorus:*
And they burn upon the open hand blinding all who see
They feast upon the desert land marching on
They burn upon the open hand blinding all who see
They feast upon the desert land
Marching, marching, marching mystery

She holds her weary head
Her heavy horsemen stand alone
It's for the living and the dead
To search their fortune far from home

*Chorus*

There is majesty, there is tragedy all in its place
Rank and file ever turning and moving the space
On paths of black and gold
They come with tales too dark to speak
But the fascination holds
Compels us on to search and seek

— Dougie MacLean

Buzzby MacMillan of the Scottish group Old Blind Dogs asserts that folk music of any stripe isn't a trend. "It's not a fashion that comes and goes," says Macmillan. "It seems quite rooted in people. It reminds them of something timeless. It's an identity, and you can't just write it off as a pretty melody. There's more to it than that. It's about the people and it comes from a whole culture. It doesn't need much to set these sympathetic strings ringing within people."

"These songs were originally made up for storytelling purposes," notes vocalist Ian Benzie, lead vocalist and guitarist with Old Blind Dogs. "Those old ballads, that run to 100 verses, told one big story. They were the public records of the time. Now music is churned out for the immediate ear to last just over two minutes. It's very instantaneous and very disposable. When these songs were written, there wasn't the same sort of media coverage and there wasn't the same accessibility to music."

If the number of musical instruments, like the triple pipes, drums, and harps, displayed on the standing stones scattered across the Scottish landscape is any indication, music has played an integral part in the life of the inhabitants of Scotland since its earliest history. An 8th-century Pictish stone-carving from Nigg is the oldest known depiction of a triangular-framed harp anywhere in the world, though other stones from places like Monifieth and Dupplin, dated between the 8th and 10th centuries, also display harps with straight arms and pillars and long strings. The Scottish harp (*clarsach*) has found its contemporary champions in artists like Alison Kinnaird as well as Mary McMaster and Patsy Seddon of the duo Sileas.

Somerled, one of Celtic Scotland's greatest leaders, died in 1164. His legacy was in part to have rid Scotland of the Vikings, but in a wider historical view, he was the progenitor of the Lords of the Isles who ruled the Western Isles of Scotland and parts of the west mainland until the early 16th century. During this period, music flourished as the courts of the nobles supported professional bards and musicians who played the *clarasch* (harp) and *piob mhor* (bagpipes). By this time, the chiefs of the day had also established the hereditary position of clan piper. The most notable of these are The MacCrimmons, who were the hereditary pipers to the Chief of Clan MacLeod.

Until the Middle Ages, the bagpipes, in their various forms, had been popular throughout most of the known world. By the early 19th century, the bagpipes were almost exclusively to be found in Scotland, known as the Highland bagpipe and the Lowlands or Border bagpipe. The Border pipes, which had traditionally accompanied dance, died out as the fiddle gained in popularity, while the Highland bagpipes became associated with military activities as part of the Highland regiments and their associated military tattoos and competitions.

Violins began to appear in Scotland during the mid-17th century, as the Scots who had traveled to Italy to study began to bring back the instruments made by renowned Italian manufacturers like Amati and Guarnerius. These designs were subsequently copied by Scottish craftsmen, and, by the close of the 17th century, the violin had gained great popularity throughout the country. Martin Martin, who wrote about the Western Isles during this period, notes, "They are great lovers of Musick; and when I was there I gave an account of eighteen men who could play on the Violin pretty well, without being taught."

The popularity of the violin also brought the dance forms for which the Highlands are renowned — strathspey, jig, reel, and hornpipe — into fashion. A golden age of the fiddle in Scotland came in the mid-18th century with the emergence of the composers and masters of the instrument like the legendary Niel Gow and his son Nathaniel, Robert Mackintosh, William Marshall, and Captain Simon Fraser, most of which had aristocratic patrons. Niel Gow, one of Scotland's first professional fiddlers, wrote more than 80 tunes for the fiddle during his lifetime and is still revered for his unique style and the timelessness of his compositions.

Following a period of relative disinterest by the public, traditional fiddle music made a comeback in the late 19th century with the emergence of Scott Skinner, who came to be known as "The King of the Strathspey." Considered the last of the great fiddle composers with over 600 pieces published, he is the only early legend of the fiddle to have been recorded.

Today, all of these instruments have found a new audience as part of the worldwide interest in Celtic music. The bagpipes, in all their forms, have suddenly found themselves back in the heat of the action as an integral part of the sound of traditional Scottish groups like Alba, the Battlefield Band, Ossian, and Runrig. The Piping Centre in Glasgow, which was founded in essence to promote "a national musical instrument with international appeal," has become a recognized performance venue in Glasgow for traditional music. In a recent newsletter, John Drysdale, the Centre's director of administration, thumbnailed the Centre's current view on the world of piping. "We have no axes to grind," states Drysdale. "We recognise, for example, that ceilidh piping is part of a total piping scene. And the broader the base, the higher the mountain. Out of any group, some will want to take things further. We will help people whatever their preferences because that is how the tradition will survive and thrive."

### Will Ye Gang To The Hielands, Leezie Lindsay?

*Will ye gang to the Hielands, Leezie Lindsay?*
*Will ye gang to the Hielands wi' me?*
*Will ye gang to the Hielands, Leezie Lindsay,*
*My bride and my darling to be?*

*To gang to the Hielands wi' you, sir,*
*I dinna ken how that may be;*
*For I kenna the land that you live in,*
*Nor ken I the lad I'm gaun wi'.*

*O, Leezie, lass ye maun ken little,*
*If sae ye dinna ken me?*
*For my name is Lord Ronald MacDonald,*
*A chieftain of high degree.*

*She has kilted her coats o' green satin,*
*She has kilted them up to her knee;*
*And she's off wi' Lord Ronald MacDonald,*
*His bride and his darling to be.*

— Old Scottish Ballad

Back on the London to Inverness train, the early morning wake up call comes, well, early. There's a sharp rapping on the sleeper cabin door, and in pops the steward bearing a breakfast tray laden with an assortment of breakfast fare that includes a steaming pot of freshly-brewed coffee that fills the cabin with a heady aroma that keens the sleep-deprived senses.

Sliding the window blind up, I'm greeted by a Celtic dawn of breathtaking beauty. The drama of the Highland landscape — of mountain, loch, and moor — is heightened by the panoply of autumn colors that gleam and glitter in tartan shades under the glare of the rising sun. Over breakfast, I spend the last portion of the trip transfixed by the ever-changing panorama outside my window as the train descends from Dalwhinnie, the highest village in the Highlands, and wends its way along the River Spey valley, through Newtonmore, Kingussie, and Aviemore into Inverness. We're almost 12 hours and 600 miles from London in terms of time and distance, but a world away in terms of heritage and music culture.

Inverness, the historic capital of the Highlands, is situated on the Moray Firth nestled at the foot of an encircling ring of mountains. In this, Scotland's northernmost city, you'll find Balnain House, a restored Georgian mansion on the banks of the River Ness, known as "the home of Highland music." Within its walls, the development of traditional Highland music is charted using videos, listening points, displays, and hands-on demonstrations during which visitors are encouraged to pick up and play the bagpipes, fiddle, guitar, bhodran, and harps. There's a cafe and a shop that complements the exhibition and the performance and education programs with a wide selection of tapes, CDs, instruments, and music books. Throughout the year, Balnain House hosts concerts, ceilidhs, informal music sessions, and annual events like the Highland Harp Festival in May and the Highland Fiddle Festival in the fall while promoting tours by musicians in the Highlands and Islands.

Balnain House is also committed to developing relationships with other regions and countries in the areas of performance and education. The Canada Room marks the strong musical link between the Highlands and the music and dance of Cape Breton. This geographical and cultural connection that had its beginnings in history a few miles east of Inverness on the battlefield at Culloden Moor. Here, on April 16, 1746, Prince Charles Edward Stuart — the Bonnie Prince Charlie of legend — and his Jacobite forces were routed, ending the House of Stuart's hope of regaining the throne. In the aftermath of the defeat, life changed drastically for the Highlanders whose clan system was decimated; land was seized from the Jacobite chiefs by the new landlords who began evicting their tenants. This became known as the Highland Clearances, a black period in Scottish history, that incredibly lasted until the late 1800s, during which time many of those dispossessed of their land and livelihood immigrated to the four corners of the earth, in particular, the island of Cape Breton.

"The clusters of ruined homes which litter the Highlands and islands are an eloquent reminder of the people's experience at the hands of the landlords," writes Rob Gibson, who has compiled a guide to the movement of the Scottish population during that period titled *Highland Clearances Trail*. "Improvement by the lairds were for their profit so inevitably most of the people became surplus to the requirements of the sheep and deer forest economy. Even when townships were deprived of their lands to such an extent that the people found it in their interests to leave and so clearances were effected without exciting much public attention or without causing any great outcry, the weight of evidence provides lessons for us today. Whether in writing, in song or in the memories of the dispossessed these lessons of the Clearances relate directly to the condition of the battered little nation which Scotland is today. The removal of so many Highlanders from their homeland was not only the destruction of Gaelic Scotland but as Neal Anderson has put it, 'one of the grand crimes of modern Europe.'"

In 1755, 51 percent of the Scottish population of Scotland was in the north or The Highlands; 37 percent lived in central Scotland (Glasgow and Edinburgh); and 11 percent in the south. The 1981 census revealed that the distribution of population had radically changed. Only 21 percent of the people lived in the north, while 74 percent of the population was now living in the center of Scotland, and only 5 percent to the south. Thousands chose to emigrate from their home land. "And much was lost in that time, much of the Highland race, with all their songs and verse and pluck and resourcefulness and ability and gaiety, who vanished overseas into new continents and other cultures," declares John MacLeod in his enjoyable and often controversial book, *Highlanders: A History of the Gaels*. "In places such as Nova Scotia they arrived in such volume that they created a new Gaelic culture. One startling figure shows how vast and sweeping the work of clearance had been. In 1901, 250,000 Scots spoke Gaelic. In Nova Scotia, Canada, there were that year a million Gaelic speakers."

MacLeod tells of seeing a young woman from Cape Breton, of Hebridean descent, performing Gaelic songs one evening in the Harris Hotel near his home in the Outer Hebrides. "Though she had never seen the Hebrides until that week, and her family had been Canadian for five generations, she had only to start a song for her Harris audience immediately to join in the chorus. But there were one or two Harris songs she sang which no one knew. The words and tunes had vanished to Canada with her lost kinsmen, 160 years before."

My Heart's In The Highlands

My heart's in the Highlands,
My heart is not here;
My heart's in the Highlands
A-chasing the deer;
Chasing the wild deer,
And following the roe,
My heart's in the Highlands,
Wherever I go.

Farewell to the Highlands, farewell to the North,
The birthplace of valour, the country of worth!
Wherever I wander, wherever I rove,
The hills of the Highlands for ever I love.

Farewell to the mountains high cover'd with snow,
Farewell to the straths and green valleys below,
Farewell to the forests and wild-hanging woods,
Farewell to the torrents and loud-pouring floods!

— Robert Burns (1790)

Alasdair Fraser, one of Scotland's greatest traditional fiddlers, lives these days in Nevada City, California, where he spends the little time he has when he's not touring solo or with his group Skyedance, running his own music company, Culburnie Records, directing the 50-member Scottish Fiddlers Orchestra, and running summer music camps in northern California and on the Isle of Skye in Scotland. A few years ago, Fraser invited the noted Cape Breton fiddler Buddy MacMaster to one of his Isle of Skye workshops, in part to stimulate an exchange of ideas about fiddling from the two regions and to compare them.

"I've been playing Scottish fiddle music for many years since I was a young boy, and over the years I gradually became aware that a lot of the music was missing in Scotland, that there was something not quite right," Fraser told Peter Murphy, who traveled to Scotland with Buddy MacMaster to shoot the trip for his documentary film, *Buddy MacMaster: The Master of Cape Breton Fiddle*. "I started looking into the history of the fiddle and, in particular, through the history of dance. There's lots of old paintings and woodcuts showing fiddlers and cello players playing for a dance, and nowadays, you hardly ever hear that, if ever. I got the feeling that there was a mystery here and it needed some explanation.

"I was always playing concerts in Scotland and doing tours and things and I started to play more and more of the old tunes that I had heard from Cape Breton — and this is where it gets interesting. People would say, 'Oh, it's that Canadian music that you're playing' and I had to say, 'Well, no, hang on a minute. These tunes came from Lochaber, Knoydart, Moidart or Skye. You'll find them in the old Niel Gow or Skye or Simon Fraser collections,' but, of course, these collections weren't available in Scotland.

"It's sad that the folks had to leave here to go to the eastern seaboard of the North American continent, but, in a way, it has been a good thing because it meant a lot of the culture was preserved. The Cape Bretoner is very tenacious — or has been very tenacious — about the culture and has held on to the old Gaelic ways of playing and the old Gaelic ways of thinking and expressing yourself. Somehow, they knew it was important. There's a set of tools that a fiddle player can use to play, especially playing for a dance — the good rhythm in your playing and excitement. That was lost in Scotland. There were lots of fiddlers playing the tunes but not really focusing on the rhythm, the old ideas, the old ornaments, the old scales, so hopefully we're just expanding the Scots set of tools again so that they can decide to play in a rhythmic Highland/Cape Breton style, or decide to play in a Northeast style like Scots kind of play. They have to make that decision. The main thing I'd like to see happen is all the tunes come back again.

Tunes like *King George*, the Old King's Reel. I have never heard these tunes in Scotland. The list is endless of great, old fiddle tunes, not just pipe tunes, that were never heard in Scotland. If you can get them back again to Scotland and have them swimming around in the repertoire, then I think we will have achieved a lot.

"The whole circle is being completed. Bringing Buddy [MacMaster] back for a week of solid immersion in Highland fiddle music and for Scottish fiddlers to be interested in it, is gratifying. Ten years ago, they wouldn't really have been into it. The climate wasn't right; the time wasn't right. The time is right now and the Scots are discovering the same thing I did years ago, because I had to leave to find this out, that we had been missing something."

Suggests Dougie MacLean, "No culture is ever pure anymore. If a culture is growing and developing, it's pulling in influences all the time from various sources. I'm not a great believer in capturing it [culture] in a little box and turning it into a museum piece. Sometimes people will say, 'Oh, that's not the way to play the fiddle. That's not the way they played it 300 years ago.' And your reply is, 'No, but I've been listening to Irish fiddle players and American fiddle players and . . .' I mean, every time you hear something, you add it on to the layers of things that you use to make your own personal music."

Alasdair Fraser, though he's a great supporter of preserving Scotland's musical heritage, is in full accord with MacLean. "Scotland's music is so rich. It can speak to every mood and emotion, from wild, raucous dance tunes to plaintive airs. But it's crucial that it not be regarded as a museum piece, or finished product. What keeps the music alive is that each player puts a personal spin on it. You have to make the music your own."

Robin Morton, a former member of The Boys of the Lough and, since 1980, manager of the Battlefield Band whose slogan is "Forward to Scotland's Past," assessed the current state of Scottish traditional music in speaking with Steve McGrail of *Scottish Life* magazine. "It's in fine shape. There's a pile of talent around, a power of good ideas. Over 30 years, a band [Battlefield Band] sees a lot, naturally. We ourselves have kept ahead by innovating, whilst keeping our feet firmly on the ground. We've followed our instincts, trusted audiences, a formula that's worked.

"We've kept faith with the essence of Scottish music, but not as a sacred cow. It's got to be about enjoyment, or it's nothing. For instance, we positively like our audiences to get up and dance if they want to — and they do, grannies and ravers alike. That, I reckon, is Scottish music at its best!"

THERE'S SO MUCH HAPPENING AT

BALNAIN
HOUSE

*Aly Bain &*
*Phil Cunningham*

*Old Blind Dogs*

The Battlefield
Band

Runrig
(with Bruce Guthrie)

115

Deaf Shepherd

Kathryn Tickell

**Janice and Charles Soane**
*The Ardyne — St. Ebba Hotel*
*Rothesay, Isle of Bute*

# INVERNESS WELCOMES THE ROYAL NATIONAL MOD

## 10-17 OCTOBER 1997

An Comunn Gaidhealach extends an invitation to you to visit Inverness, capital of the Highlands, to attend the Royal National Mod in October 1997. This Mod is the centenary celebration of the 1897 National Mod and we confidently expect this Royal National Mod, the largest festival of Gaelic music, song and dance held annually, to be the best attended yet.

Inverness is well served by road, rail and air and offers good accommodation and excellent hospitality.

*For further information contact:*

Ann Souter, Inverness Royal National Mod Convenor, 15 Green Drive, Inverness IV2 4EX, Scotland. Tel. 01463 232406

## AN COMUNN GAIDHEALACH

*Organisers of the Royal National Mod*

An Comunn Gaidhealach was founded in 1891 and promotes the Gaelic language and culture through the everyday use of the language and encouraging the tradition of music, song, folklore and literature. If you wish to play your part in the continuing development of the Gaelic language, music and culture you can help by joining An Comunn Gaidhealach. Annual Membership is £10 (£3 for Senior Citizens and £1 for Juniors) and Life Membership is £200. For further information contact An Comunn Gaidhealach at:

109 Church Street, Inverness IV1 1EY. Tel. 01463 231226 e-mail: acginv.demon.co.uk.

*Ar Cànain 's Ar Ceòl*

the Glasgow Royal Concert Hall

celtic connections

120

# Chapter Five

# Ceilidh Trail: Cape Breton & The Rankins

with

Ashley MacIsaac ❀ Archie Neil Chisholm ❀ Mary Jane Lamond ❀ Emily Butler ❀ John Allan Cameron ❀ Buddy MacMaster ❀ Frank Ferrel ❀ Joella Foulds ❀ Natalie MacMaster ❀ Jennifer Wrigley ❀ Paddy Moloney (The Chieftains) ❀ Doug Pringle ❀ Frank Davies ❀ Deane Cameron ❀ Bill Anderson ❀ Mary Black ❀ Ian Tyson

❀ Kilted, bearded, wild-eyed, bushy-haired and with nostrils flaring, Ashley MacIsaac, the "Mad Fiddler of Creignish," made his entrance on to the Celtic Colours International Festival stage like one of those fearsome Celtic warriors of legend, the very sight of which had once caused the mighty Roman legions to flee in terror. MacIsaac is having a similar influence on the older members of the audience tonight during the fiddle-fueled finale to the festival, although under the assault of the ear-splitting sound, the blinding light show and MacIsaac's "devil in the kitchen" demeanor, the effect is communal catatonia as many sit frozen in their seats in case they catch MacIsaac's eye and he decides to attack. The set runs over an hour and there are some folks who don't flex a muscle until the house lights are up and MacIsaac has left the building.

MacIsaac's brand of Celtic punk or "fiddle grunge" has been given locals the horrors since their home boy apparently abandoned his traditional Scots / Irish music roots for a career in the alternative regions of rock. "It's not the fiddling I do in the dance hall at Mabou that got all this going," MacIsaac told the *Globe & Mail*'s Ray Conlogue early in his career. "It's the bastardized stuff I do that has caught the attentions of the labels.

"I want to be loyal to the original music, I want to live here and play square dances. I like it that our fiddling is different from Québec or Cajun music, that it's ours. But . . . fiddlers are a dime a dozen around here, it's fiddleville! And we can say what we want to keep thing traditional, like they did about people speaking Gaelic.

"But look what happened with that. It got so strict that people lost interest, and now only about 200 people are left that speak Gaelic. We could kill fiddle music too."

MacIsaac's attitude hadn't changed much following the release of his first album for A&M Records. "There are people in the actual music scene that drive me crazy," he moaned, referring to those who would accuse him of abandoning his roots for the greener pastures of commercial success. "People tend to forget that if you learn to work on a car and, the next year, you learn how to work on a truck, you haven't forgotten how to work on a car. I'm brought up in more of a traditional sense than any of the kids today who are learning to play the fiddle. I heard disco and said, well hey, that's 120 beats per minute. That bass drum sounds like my foot when I'm playing; I can play fiddle over this, and I went out and learned *Stayin' Alive* on the fiddle. It was really in disco and dance music that I first thought about finding a different way to present the music I had been brought up with. Six to eight months later, I met a few musicians who were actually pop musicians and had a Cape Breton connection. I put a band together, and early on, we did a show over in Newfoundland that was attended by some music industry people and all of a sudden we had record company people saying, hey now we know how to sell him because he plays *Stayin' Alive* on the fiddle."

MacIsaac, who recently toured Japan and China with The Chieftains, is an enigma. He continues to pay tribute to his mentor, Cape Breton fiddle legend Buddy MacMaster, who is traditional to the core, and his pride in his island heritage is unquestioned, but he marches to the beat of a different drummer, personally and musically. MacIsaac, who claims that his favorite holiday is Hallowe'en, has already walked the media plank for some alleged sexual activities outside the mainstream and within nine months of the Celtic Colours concert, he will part ways with his long-suffering manager, Sheri Jones, following an apparent mix-up in greetings of welcome from the stage during a series of tour dates. Dropping his usual "Hi™how are you today?/Fine® . . . thank you very much" salutation, he reportedly invites the audience to "Fuck™ off!" and "Stick® it up your ass!"

The ten-day Celtic Colours International Festival, organized to showcase the best in Celtic music from Cape Breton and around the world, also coincides with the spectacle of the changing colors of the leaves around the island, which has been a long-time tourist attraction, as well as the Canadian Thanksgiving, a feast that dates back some two thousand years to the ancient Celts whose celebration of the end of the harvest season was one of the most important of the year.

The concept for a festival of this kind originated with Joella Foulds and Max MacDonald of Sydney, Nova Scotia-based Rave Entertainment, who were behind the formation of the Celtic Colours Festival Society. The stated mission of this society is "to promote and maintain the Celtic cultures of Cape Breton, the Gaelic language, music, arts and crafts; and to heighten national and international awareness of the natural beauty of Cape Breton Island by, but not solely by, the creation and presentation of an international festival celebrating our Celtic heritage and music, to be held annually during the beauty of the autumn colours at various venues around the island."

"Like ancient genetic matter suspended in amber, Gaelic culture and language are preserved on the tiny island of Cape Breton," as *Time* magazine travel writer Michael Creadon so poetically put it, and over a ten-day period in October, Cape Bretoners and visitors to the island are treated to a series of concerts headlined by some of the biggest names in Celtic music from home and away, as well as workshops, square dances, ceilidhs, theater, dance, a lecture series, Gaelic language events, visual arts, exhibits, and demonstrations.

And there's much to showcase as far as music and culture in the area is concerned. Over the past decade, this small island has not only become a major contributor to the world of Celtic music, but also to the pop music mainstream with home-grown artists like Rita MacNeil, The Rankins (formerly The Rankin Family), Ashley MacIsaac, Natalie MacMaster, the Barra MacNeils, Mary Jane Lamond, and Bruce Guthro, now the lead singer for the traditional Scottish group, Runrig, as well as a solo singer/songwriter in his own right, among others.

The island was given its first major profile boost in the 1970s and '80s by John Allan Cameron, the singer/guitarist/storyteller who's often referred to as the 'godfather' of the Cape Breton music scene. He toured the world with Canadian singing legend Anne Murray, and, in the process, widened the audience for some of the traditional music that made up a good part of his repertoire.

Singer/songwriter Rita MacNeil, a native of Big Pond, Cape Breton, who for a short period was also associated with Anne Murray's Balmur Ltd. management company, has not only become one of Canada's most recognized faces on television, given the success in recent years of her own variety series and a number of one-off specials, but also one of the country's foremost singing stars internationally. Influenced by the traditional Celtic music of her native Cape Breton — there's a Celtic version of the Anne Murray standard, *Snowbird*, on her latest album — as well as forms as disparate as rock, gospel, folk, and country, she made her recording debut in 1987 with the album FLYING ON YOUR OWN. The title track was covered by Anne Murray and the success of the song brought MacNeil her first major recognition at home and abroad. In the years since, she has being honored as a member of the Order of Canada, as well as with the top Canadian music trophies, including a mantle full of Junos, Canadian Country Music Association (CCMA), and East Coast Music Association (ECMA) Awards. She has topped the charts, not only in Canada but in the U.K. and Australia, and her world tours have seen her sell-out concerts in places as far afield as Sweden, Japan, Australia, and the U.K., a frequently cited highlight of which was her 1991 show at the Royal Albert Hall in London.

When MacNeil is off the road, you can often find her greeting the many customers and fans who, each summer, drop by Rita's Tea Room, a former one-room schoolhouse in Big Pond, Cape Breton, to sample MacNeil's own brand of tea and to see the many awards and mementos from her career on display.

In the mid-to-late 1980s, it was time for the family groups to make an impression as The Barra MacNeils of Sydney Mines debuted with a self-titled album in 1986, which hinted at the wide-ranging musical talents of siblings Sheumas, Kyle, Stewart, and Lucy, who have since become one of the most widely-traveled and respected groups in the field of Celtic music. The late-1980s saw the release of the self-titled debut album from The Rankin Family (now known as The Rankins) from Mabou, on Cape Breton's west coast. Within a couple of years, Cookie, Heather, Jimmy, John Morris, and Raylene Rankin were being courted by the major record labels, ultimately signing with EMI Music Canada. The group's career exploded then as their subsequent CDs FARE THEE WELL LOVE, NORTH COUNTRY, and ENDLESS SEASONS brought them widespread acclaim not only in the Celtic music world, but also in pop and country music circles where they regularly found themselves at the top of the charts. The group's popularity, marked by the unprecedented sales of their CDs and sold-out concert tours, not only instigated the '90s traditional music boom in Canada, but also helped to stimulate interest in the genre internationally.

Outside of Scotland, Cape Breton is the only area in the world where Gaelic continues as a living language. The Gaelic culture and traditions have been handed down here for well over two hundred years, through seven generations.

The earliest Scottish settlers arrived in Canada at an area on the east coast known as New Scotland or Nova Scotia in 1622 and 1623, with the first settlement established in 1629. That presence was short-lived, however, as the French domination of the area forced the abandonment of the Scots colonies by 1632. These French settlers, who became known as "Acadians" before being forced by the British south to Louisiana where they became known as "Cajuns," settled Cape Breton Island in the mid-1700s, and their communities are still to be found on the Island's west and southeastern shores. Before the Scots or the French, though, Cape Breton was home to the Mi'kmaq people, the original settlers, whose culture still thrives in First Nations communities on the island.

The aftermath of the Battle of Culloden in Scotland in the mid-18th century saw the systematic dismantling of Gaelic social and political life. The Gaelic language was outlawed. Chieftains were replaced by landlords and throughout the Highlands and Islands, the crofters were evicted from their ancestral homes. A mass exodus to the New World took place, and, at the close of the 18th century, The Highland Clearances saw thousands of Gaelic speaking Scots make the treacherous voyage across the Atlantic to establish thriving pioneer communities throughout Cape Breton and eastern Nova Scotia. Extraordinary times always give rise to remarkable stories of human accomplishment and courage in the face of adversity. In this regard, the names of Reverend Norman MacLeod and Angus William Rudd MacKenzie have become legendary in Cape Breton.

Reverend MacLeod, an austere, fundamentalist minister of the Presbyterian church, emigrated to Pictou, Nova Scotia in the early 1800s after falling out with the church elders in Scotland over what MacLeod felt were their increasingly humanist attitudes to the faith. He would find much the same religious outlook in Pictou, and in the end the charismatic

MacLeod and his small band of loyal followers built their own ship in the summer of 1819. The following spring they set out for the American midwest via the eastern seaboard, the Gulf of Mexico, and the Ohio River. As it turns out, the voyage was extremely short as the unpredictable Atlantic weather forced them to seek shelter in a Cape Breton inlet known as St. Ann's Bay. It was here that he established his church, and over the next few years, a significant Highland Scots community developed in the area.

This small colony thrived until the middle of the 19th century when the Great Famine hit the area. Despairing at the hardships being endured by his congregation, MacLeod once again inspired his band of followers to put their last ounce of energy into the building of a ship sturdy enough to carry them around the world to New Zealand and what he hoped would be more prosperous surroundings. Using the last of their meager resources, a seaworthy vessel was built, and in October of 1851 they set out for the Antipodes, ultimately arriving at their planned destination and establishing a colony near Aukland that survives to this day.

There's a real irony in the fact that the Cape Breton legacy of Norman MacLeod, who certainly had no time for secular music and dance, lived on in A.W.R. MacKenzie, a later emigrant from Portree, Scotland via the United States, Montréal, and Spencerville, Ontario, whose dream was to preserve the Scottish tradition in North America. Inspired by MacLeod's epic saga and against tremendous odds, MacKenzie, pastor of the Knox Presbyterian Church in Baddeck, founded the Gaelic College of Celtic Arts in 1939 at St. Ann's on the scenic Cabot Trail in Cape Breton. It has been the center of the island's Gaelic culture for close to 60 years.

Subsequent waves of immigrants joined the original surge of settlers, with most forming communities similar to their places of origin in Scotland. In this environment, localized Gaelic dialects, music, song and dance traditions were kept alive and thrived for the next hundred years. "They came out here in ship loads," the late Cape Breton fiddler and educator Archie Neil Chisholm, for whom the first annual Celtic Colours International Festival was dedicated, told Peter Murphy, producer of the video *Buddy MacMaster: The Master of Cape Breton Fiddle*. "I would say the largest group of any of them that came out, came with one purpose in mind; to find freedom. They were being coerced and tyrannized by their landlords, so they looked to America as the land of the free. Some of them did go to Australia and New Zealand, but a great many of them landed in Nova Scotia and in Cape Breton, and out of the woods they hewed and cleared the land and built their homes. It is their descendants who are now the backbone of the Scottish population in Cape Breton.

"Without their music and culture, God knows what would have happened. They had nothing. A few of the early Scots who came out here were able, under pain of death, to smuggle the musical instruments out, but only rarely. The rest had to make their own instruments, but music and singing and story-telling played an enormous part in their early lives. Their early parties were danced to what they call *puirt-a-beul* or mouth music and then, whenever a fiddler appeared, he was like a visit from the Almighty and he was looked up to. Then, gradually, the younger people began to realize the respect with which fiddlers were held. In addition to their natural inclination for music, they would want to have some of that respect and some of that boosting that went with the musician and they began to follow it until now we have an army of musicians."

The Old World traditions were kept alive at community events called *ceilidhs*, where the talents of local singers, musicians, and dancers were showcased as well as at the communal "milling frolic." At most of these evening gatherings, the oral tradition, for which the Celts are famous, would blossom, and the music, song, and storytelling would continue into the night. Neighbors would share their collective knowledge. Fiddle bowing styles and fingering techniques or the history behind a story or a song, the meaning and nuances of a particular word or line, were discussed or even debated.

"A lot of the people who are tradition bearers in Gaelic culture have an incredible love of language and poetry and music and very high standards support all of these art forms including storytelling," states Cape Breton singer Mary Jane Lamond. "We lost some of our best storytellers in recent time, people like Joe Neil MacNeil and Donald Angus Beaton, but there are still others in Cape Breton who can relate Fenian stories and ballads that date back to the 13th century. The stories of the Fenians appear in ancient Irish tales. The Irish began moving into Scotland around 500 AD and over the next 1000 years, Scottish Gaelic developed. Even though the language changed, and through all the social upheavals in Scotland and the ultimate immigration of people to Cape Breton 200 years ago, you still find the same stories, so it's an amazing culture in that way."

In the foreword to a collection of songs from the area, compiled and edited by musician/composer/publisher Matthew Patrick Cook, under the title *The Night in the Kitchen Collection*, Emily Butler talks about the real music heritage of the island. "In Cape Breton, it has always been said that music is 'in the blood' — almost as though anyone fortunate enough to have been born on this island arrives tapping the feet, with tunes coursing through the veins. But I think it is more accurate to say that, in Cape Breton, music is in the heart. It defines our moods. It punctuates our social events. It adds seasoning to our daily chores. It also fortifies us against the economic hard times that have always been a fact of life here. In Cape Breton, it is also said that the kitchen is the 'heart' of the home. It is natural, then, that much of the music begins there: at a mother's knee or around the kitchen table with a pot of tea. Over the years, we have been fortunate enough to have had many ceilidhs at our home: in the living rooms and in the dining room. But the last music of the night — and some might say the best — is always in the kitchen, right where it began."

Guitarist, singer, and raconteur John Allan Cameron recalls growing up in this tight-knit musical community. "Of course, we had the radio but for the most part we made our own entertainment. I consider myself exceedingly lucky to have grown up in a society, and in a community, where music was such an important part of life, where you're sitting in a kitchen session or at a party with fiddlers and singers and step-dancers who were your family or neighbors. In contemporary society, sometimes you have to call up and make an appointment if you are going to visit somebody. When I was growing up, neighbors just dropped in. It was a wonderful way of being neighborly, and if Jezebel MacNeil had baked some extra biscuits, she would bring some along and the kids would bring their guitars or fiddles. My sisters played the piano, my brother played the fiddle, as I did a little bit, and the visit turned into an impromptu music session. That was the type of social structure that I grew up with and I think it is sadly lacking in contemporary society." On his 1998 CD GLENCOE STATION, Cameron includes two such sessions, *The Parlour Session* and *The Kitchen Session*, described in the liner notes as "tunes . . . by some of my favorite Cape Breton composers" and including "Father John Angus Rankin" by Jerry Holland, "Hair Of The Dog-Reel" by Piper Alan MacLeod, "Cameron/Walker-Reel" by Brenda Stubbert, and the traditional Irish "Dillon Brown-Reel."

Ashley MacIsaac has similar memories of those kitchen and parlor sessions. "The whole island is pretty much a music community. The main source of entertainment, besides sports and things like that, is fiddle music. When I was five years old, I started taking step-dancing lessons, and before that, my father played the fiddle and there were parties around the house. My cousin Wendy also plays and my next door neighbor was the mother of Daniel MacDonald who has a lot to do with the Cape Breton Fiddler's Association. I can remember music always being in the house and me, at three years old, sitting on the piano and my brother taking piano lessons from this person by the name of Candy Lane. She was teaching him some fiddle tunes on the piano and then the local parish priest would start coming over and playing fiddle tunes at the house with my father and it just really developed. I took dancing lessons when I was five, and, by the time I was eight and a half, I was step-dancing in concerts a lot. I had been around fiddle music every weekend for a couple of years, and when the opportunity to take fiddle lessons came up when I was nine, that's when all of this started."

Raylene Rankin of The Rankins recalls her childhood in Mabou, just up the highway from where MacIsaac grew up on the west coast of Cape Breton. "Our parents had a real appreciation for music and for the live musical tradition and by that I mean people dropping in to your house on a Friday evening. If somebody was home from 'away', they would drop in and maybe play some fiddle. When John Morris was younger, none of us really played instruments. John Morris had started playing when he was eight or nine, and fiddlers would drop in and he would chord with them and then he would play a couple of tunes for them and somebody would chord with him, so their was a rich musical tradition in the community that we grew up in and in other communities in Cape Breton."

As the organ made its first appearance in the New World, followed soon after by the piano, the kitchens and parlors of Cape Breton rang with the sound of the fiddle with keyboard accompaniment that often featured distinctive fingering techniques and chord progressions that would have bemused the maestros of European classical music. Tracey Dares of Marion Bridge is one of a new generation of piano accompanists who's carrying on the tradition. As Ashley MacIsaac remarks, "I took piano lessons for about six months and that taught me how to read a bit. I still use it now when I'm learning to play fiddle tunes. I took some chording lessons from a fellow by the name of Gordon MacQuarrie. I guess it all worked to make me a better fiddle player."

At the time of the Highland Clearances, the fiddle was reaching its peak of popularity in Scotland. The bagpipes had more or less replaced the harp as a favorite instrument during the 16th and 17th centuries. Now the fiddle, in turn, was rivaling the pipes. As the Highlanders landed on the shores of Nova Scotia, the fiddlers brought with them these traditional instruments, their talents, and their status as highly valued members of their communities.

John Allan Cameron recollects that when he was growing up in Glencoe Station, Cape Breton, in some circles the term "music" and "fiddle" were synonymous and inseparable. "As far as my mother was concerned, the fiddle was the real music. I remember there was a time when some people came to her house and they were singing some songs and this and that. Well, after about an hour, there was a short break, and my mother piped up: 'Okay boys, now let's have some music.' She meant she wanted one of the fiddlers to get up and play."

For the recent generation of Cape Breton fiddlers, one of the maestros to whom they looked for inspiration was Buddy MacMaster from Judique on the island's west coast. The documentary *Buddy MacMaster: The Master of Cape Breton Fiddle* is a fascinating look at the life and times of MacMaster and his influence on the fiddling community, not only in Cape Breton, but in Scotland as producer Peter Murphy accompanies him to one of Alasdair Fraser's workshops on the Isle of Skye. Influenced by fiddlers like Dan R. MacDonald, Dan Hughie MacEachern, and Bill Lamey, who were frequent visitors to his family's home in Judique, MacMaster tells Murphy that he was a good listener and could pick up a tune very quickly.

"They played well and I tried to imitate them and play as correct as I could by ear," remembers MacMaster. "I really don't know, but I always seemed to want to put my own touch to it, you know. From that time on, I guess I started playing for school dances and our parish hall up there and I picked up a few dollars."

And, what a surprise, MacMaster's parents also had an ear for a good tune. "My mother was very fond of music. She didn't play herself but she really loved it. She could jig tunes for us kids to dance to, you know. I was about eleven when I started to play. My father's fiddle was in his trunk, so I discovered the fiddle in the trunk and I took it downstairs. I remember it was minus one string but I did get part of a tune, the *Rock Valley Jig*, that day. That encouraged me to keep at it."

At the age of 18, MacMaster began working in telegraphy at various railway stations around Nova Scotia, often on the night shift. "I was away from playing for dances during that time. I usually had the fiddle with me and, on some of the night jobs, there wasn't very much business and I'd have time to play. Occasionally, I'd even play in the station before the train would depart. I'd play a tune or two for the passengers and they'd go away happy. In 1949, I came from Antigonish to Mabou and got a permanent job and right away I started to play for dances, so I've been going pretty well full tilt since. I was more interested in learning to play than to make money at that time. To see people enjoying the music made you feel you were making people happy. That was rewarding. If you have a good crowd and good dancers, they're lively and a lot of fun."

The late Archie Neil Chisholm pays tribute to MacMaster's style. "They say that imitation is the most sincere form of flattery. There are dozens of players, especially among the young ones today, who would try to imitate Buddy's style of playing. They want to be miniature Buddys and that has led them to struggle and fight to be as good as he is and this has done a tremendous amount for music."

John Allan Cameron says he grew up listening to Buddy MacMaster, who is not much older than he is, as well as Winston "Scotty" Fitzgerald. "Now, that man, if he was living today, God rest his soul, would be on top of the world because of the renewed interest in Celtic music worldwide. He had such flair. When he got on the stage and performed, you couldn't keep your eyes off him, he had that kind of magic about him. He performed every type of music. He even played fiddle for Hank Snow way back before Snow became an icon in country music, but he stayed in Cape Breton to be close to his roots.

"One of the things I love about Cape Breton and the fiddle players here is that they place a great importance in developing their own styles and giving the music self-expression. It's great to see some of the fiddlers just digging in and playing from the heart, not just reading out of a book and doing it mechanically. When you listen to Donald Angus Beaton playing the fiddle, as soon as he touches the strings you know it's Donald Angus. The same with Dan J. Campbell, Bill Lamey, and Scotty Fitzgerald, who all developed their own styles."

Adds Ashley MacIsaac, "There's Willie Kennedy in Mabou, who wears a baseball cap and plays the fiddle from his soul. And maybe he doesn't play with as much technical accuracy as Buddy McMaster, but you've still got that same depth of feeling there, and many times, that's what makes the music really good. I don't want to worry about playing technically, and sometimes you forget about thinking altogether, and just let the emotion flow."

Natalie MacMaster is Buddy McMaster's niece and an international pop and Celtic music star in the making. "I didn't actually take lessons from Buddy. He was extremely busy and still is. It's incredible the schedule that he keeps. But, of all the music that was in our house, he was probably played the most frequently. That's not only the way it was in our household, but I think that's the way it was in most households in Cape Breton. He is the most popular, or the most commonly recorded, fiddle player, and the most easily accessible. He plays so much and is so gracious in giving his time that his music is very familiar to all of us."

MacMaster, who hails from Troy in Cape Breton, says she was nine when she started to play the fiddle, but her introduction to fiddle music probably began when she was in the womb. "Our house was always filled with fiddle music, mostly on the tape recorder," she recalls. "Mom would always have some kind of tape playing. A lot of the tapes that I grew up with were party tapes or tapes recorded at an impromptu ceilidh or from a dance hall somewhere. They weren't necessarily studio tapes or professional recordings but I heard a wide variety of fiddle music being played the way it was supposed to be. I always say that by the time I was nine, I actually had nine years of experience because I knew a lot of the tunes in my head."

"In the history of both sides of my family, there's a lot of music there — fiddlers, singers, step-dancers, and jiggers of the music, which could be termed mouth music. My grandmother did a lot of that. That's how she taught my mother to dance and all the rest of her brothers and sisters, through jigging the tunes. Mom learned how to dance through that and she taught me how to dance. Just on my mother's side alone, there's a long line of players and music lovers. On my dad's side, of course there's my uncle Buddy, who is a great fiddler, but my dad's other brothers and sisters, they sing and step-dance and all the rest of it. Just in that sense alone, it's in the blood and, of course, with the upbringing that I had, there are so many summer concerts where the organizers always rely on local talent to perform, so I totally grew up with it."

MacMaster says that though she can read music, she doesn't depend on it to pick up new material. "I'm more comfortable listening to tapes of impromptu ceilidhs and sessions and just picking tunes from there that I like. That's a great way to pass on the music because you are hearing what the older style fiddlers did and you obviously pick up on that. There are actually a lot of the old tunes that are transcribed to paper and a lot of great old books out there you can just flip through that contain these old tunes from just years and years ago, and that's great too."

Frank Ferrel, a noted fiddler in the Celtic tradition from New England on the east coast of the United States, has had a long-time connection with Cape Breton and its traditional music community. In 1995, Ferrel traveled to Cape Breton to record with his old friend J.P. Cormier and Hilda Chaisson for Rounder Records. He returned to the island in the fall of 1997 to take part in the first annual Celtic Colours Festival. Ferrel characterized the events of that week as "Fiddler's Heaven" in documenting his experiences during the festival. His observations, from the perspective of a "fiddler from away," as Cape Bretoners would say, are insightful.

"I'm listening to a tape. Filtered through the underlying shuffle of dancing feet, whoops, yells, and percussive step dancing is the amplified, slightly distorted blast of a Cape Breton fiddler in full swing, ripping out a dance set. I had the momentary clarity of mind to grab my little cassette recorder and push the record button just in the nick of time before I was jerked back to reality. It's my proof that I was there. Many wouldn't believe me. It's the stuff of pure science fiction, being transported to another world. You see as a musician, I'm convinced that Cape Breton Island is another world altogether.

"It's a world where over the years, Cape Breton's Scottish, Irish and French cultures have nourished a unique musical tradition, one which has remained relatively intact to this day. In recent years, the music of Cape Breton has spread, and today you can find people playing and listening to Cape Breton music from Texas to Ireland.

"This is a story about a fiddler going to fiddle heaven. And if you're looking for a fiddler's heaven, then Canada is as good a place as any to find it.

"Canada's love affair with the fiddle as popular culture goes back at least as far as the 1950s when a fiddler from New Brunswick named Don Messer began broadcasting a program of mostly fiddle music from Charlottetown, Prince Edward Island. The show went national, and over the next three decades, the Canadian Broadcasting Corporation (CBC) broadcast the show weekly, first on radio, then television, making Don Messer the Canadian equivalent of Lawrence Welk with a fiddle. That interest in the instrument carries over to today's pop culture, where Cape Breton's own Ashley MacIsaac has recordings that go platinum in Canada, and he's touted in the headlines of a Cape Breton tabloid as the island's first millionaire fiddler. Or take the example of Donnell Leahy, an Ontario fiddler with roots in Cape Breton, whose music video *Call To The Dance*, featuring fiddle and step-dancing, is at the top of Canada's CMT: Country Music Television chart.

"I first thought I'd gone to fiddle heaven when I got the call inviting me to perform at the festival. And they'd pay me and everything. Not to mention that it was taking place right at the height of — no, not the fall colors or Canadian Thanksgiving — but the height of the fall salmon run in the Margaree River. Needless to say, I packed both my fiddle and my fly rod.

"Over the years, I've brought numerous Cape Breton musicians to American festivals and had a hand in getting many of them recorded. And if I were to consider for a moment such metaphysical concepts as karma or divine intervention, I'd qualify this as one of the two at work. I've always tried to combine my interests in fiddling and fishing in my travels. It's kind of a concept I've been working on over the years. At first there were these cultural enrichment tours where I got a state arts grant to perform in rural Indian schools, which, coincidentally, were most located at the mouth of salmon-bearing rivers, where, coincidentally, I was able to . . . well, you know, fish. Then there were the two summer tours I did as a special guest artist with the Scottish-based band, the Boys of the Lough, where we toured outlying Scottish villages which were, coincidentally, located on or near prime fishing waters. And what with their fiddler Aly Bain's shared passion for the two Fs . . . well, you know, we fished. Now this.

"For a fiddler, names like Jerry Holland, Brenda Stubbert, Alex Francis MacKay, J.P. Cormier, Dougie MacDonald, Dave MacIsaac, and Carl MacKenzie are the stuff of legend. And to be asked to perform with them is the stuff of dreams. As I said before, I packed my two Fs along with some extra clothes, rosin, flies, and a box of fiddle recordings for easy listening on the way up. I chose the traditional method of travel, an '87 Mazda pick-up truck sporting 173,000 miles on its ticker, and 14 hours of driving. Leaving early Friday morning, I arrived at the Big Pond Fire Hall just in time for the sound check Saturday afternoon.

"The Fire Hall was a lot smaller than I'd expected, and set up in the traditional manner with tables crowded around a small dance floor, the bar open at one end, and the stage in the middle. Despite my misgivings, the estimated crowd that night was well over 300 people. Each of us got 12 minutes of three sets of tunes. In some cases the three sets of tunes stretched to 20 minutes, what with the tendency on the part of Cape Breton fiddlers to play as many as 20 tunes in a set. A tune a minute. It's the law; live with it!

"By the time Dougie MacDonald got up to play, the crowd was sufficiently in their cups to find the prospect of staying seated just too much to bear. With Dougie's first note, most of the crowd bounded to the floor and began to dance. Dougie is a younger player, a dance player, and one of my favorites. When he's not fiddling, he runs his own pulpwood logging operation. Before logging, he spent 10 years away, working the mines in Ontario. I guess it keeps your fingers nimble. There were still a number of performers left on the lineup when Dougie started his riot. Fiddler Carl MacKenzie was the MC for the night, and in a gesture of frustration, threw up his hands and was heard to comment, 'Well, so much for the concert, the crowd's running the show now!' Dougie had the common courtesy to end this set before things went totally wild, and Carl was able to get the rest of us up to play.

"One of my favorite memories of the week was not a wild session or a hot concert performance, but a quiet Sunday drive ending up in an old fiddler's farmhouse sharing tunes in the shadow of an old wood-fired cook stove. On Thanksgiving day, pianist Dougie MacPhee took pity and invited me out to the Delta Hotel in Sydney for their big annual Thanksgiving luncheon buffet. Once we'd put a good dent in their larder, including heaping portions of what Dougie referred to as the 'mortal sins,' we set out in his aging but sturdy Lincoln town car for the west side of the island, a drive that took us most of the afternoon, to Mabou, Port Hood, Judique, a visit with fiddler Buddy MacMaster, and finally ending up in Kingville, at Alex Francis MacKay's farm, another legendary, but perhaps lesser known site of Cape Breton fiddling.

"Alex Francis and his wife Jessie has just returned from the Piper's Gathering that afternoon up at St. Ann's. Alex Francis is one of the great older players, a Gaelic speaker, and keeper of a style of music fast becoming extinct in Cape Breton. He is a real old-time sound, his playing laced with Gaelic and speaking to Cape Breton's rich Celtic heritage. With Dougie at the ready on the piano stool, Alex Francis got out his fiddle and kept up for a good while, playing the old marches, strathspeys, and reels he's kept for so many years.

"Alex Francis has recently been introduced to the world of recording. Rounder Records has just released a collection of his music, recorded over the past three years by Cape Breton collector and musician, Paul MacDonald. Sitting in his wood-paneled parlor, I felt a real connection to this music, sitting where fiddlers have sat over the years, filling the room with that ancient order of notes, aging the wood with tradition. An aging formal portrait of his cousin, fiddle in hand, hangs on the wall by the piano. It's none other than the legendary Cape Breton composer, Dan Rory MacDonald. Talk about your tradition! Before we left, nothing would do but to move us out into the old farm kitchen and have tea. A time to socialize, chat, tell the odd story, and give ample time to leave gracefully.

"Following my evening with Alex Francis, I was slated to be part of the concert the next night on the other side of the island in the French Acadian fishing community of Cheticamp, about a two-hour drive from Sydney. If you stop you can to drool at the salmon pools along the way where the Margaree River comes within casting distance of the road. Following a traditional Acadian dinner in the local parish hall, I had the good fortune to perform with my good friends J.P. Cormier and Hilda Chiasson, along with fiddler Donny LeBlanc, the Andre Marchand Trio, Eddy Arsenault, and the Prince Edward Island-based group, Barachois. At the parish hall soiree following the concert, I also got a chance to meet the next generation of LFITs — that's 'Legendary Fiddler In Training.' Mark Boudreau is his name and someday I'll say, 'Why, I heard him when he was only 12 years old, and playing like Winston Fitzgerald even then.' Well, what do you expect, after all he's been playing now for two whole years!

"The other highlights of the festival for me was the chance to get to know and play with some of the musicians I'd heard about, but had never met. Musicians like Prince Edward Island fiddler and fisherman Eddy Arsenault, along with his family of musicians. Evolving out of kitchen sessions at the Arsenault home came the group Barachois, meaning loosely 'a quiet pool of water.' Anything but! These folks bombard the audience with Acadian song, music and humor, utilizing their feet, fiddles, pump organ, piano, guitar, harmonica, spoons, carpenter's saw, knives, a double-bitted axe, and a unique Barachois invention, the cardboard Co-Op box drum kit. Watching them do a stepping routine while sitting down and playing is better than Riverdance any day! And then there's the Irish performer Frankie Lane, who smokes more cigars in a day than most of Havana, has a penchant for American hillbilly music, favors wearing ultra tight Mariachi pants on stage, and plays great Irish music on the dobro. Frankie's association with the infamous Irish band The Fleadh Cowboys brought him on stage with groups like The Pogues, U2, and Bob Dylan. Not to mention his partner in crime, Eamonn Coyne, a Dubliner armed with a killer banjo and a Ph.D in biophysics. Not only does Eamonn have a great repertoire of Irish music, but seems to know every Cape Breton fiddle tune ever played as well.

"Following an evening of music in Cheticamp, I was finally able to get out on the Margaree River for a day of fishing. A good balance to nights full of music, wading a classic salmon river in shirtsleeves and giving the salmon a proper scare. Following my day on the river, my time at the festival came to an end with the evening concert and dance at the Barn, a famous venue out back of the old Normaway Inn, nestled in the hills above the Margaree Valley."

*Come From Away*

*What's that name, dear? I've never heard it 'round here.*
*And what's that you say, you've come from away?*
*But where is your home, and what makes you roam?*
*Have you come for a while, or come here to stay?*

*Born in the mountain, raised on the plains,*
*I've travelled the country, its cities and lanes*
*Like your father's forefathers who came on the sea,*
*The island of islands has called out to me.*

*Chorus:*
*Come from away. Come, come to stay*
*So take what I offer and all that it means,*
*My love and my labor, my hopes and my dreams.*
*We all come from somewhere, sometime, so it seems,*
*And it's here that I'm longing to stay.*

*There are places to come from, there are places to go,*
*There are places to struggle, and places to grow,*
*But the place that you choose to live out your days*
*Is the one that can hold your heart with a gaze.*

*There's a place I call home where the sea and the foam*
*Toss Cape Islanders far from the hills on the shore.*
*Not the place of my birth, mot a measure of worth,*
*But a peace that is greater than any on Earth.*

*Come from away. Come, come to stay*
*Like the child that is chosen when birth is denied,*
*The love keeps on growing with each rising tide.*
*For home is a feeling I hold deep inside*
*And it's here that I'm longing to say.*
*For home is a feeling I hold deep inside*
*And it's here that I'm longing to stay.*

— Joella Foulds

🌀 Over the years, the traditional songs of 18th and 19th century Scotland brought to Cape Breton by the early settlers have continually had new life breathed into them by successive generations of local musicians and singers. Today, most repertoires are comprised of a selection of the Old Country standards as well as songs more recently composed in that tradition on this side of the Atlantic.

John Allan Cameron, a latter-day troubadour, has carried the music of Cape Breton, specifically, and the Celtic music tradition, in general, to the four corners of the globe. During the course of those travels, though, he has often found himself the proverbial musical square peg testing a round hole's adaptability. On May 16th, 1970, he was the first — and no doubt the only artist — ever to play Nashville's Grand Ole Opry wearing a kilt. Incredibly, he received a two-minute standing ovation from an audience that either thoroughly enjoyed his performance that evening or admired his guts in risking a lynching by showing up at the shrine of traditional country music wearing a skirt.

At the peak of his international career in the 1970s, John Allan worked closely with Canadian superstar and fellow Maritimer Anne Murray, with whom he toured extensively as her opening act. A regular stop on tour was always a lengthy stint at one of the big Las Vegas show rooms, as Cameron recalls. "I'm not a Las Vegas act, and when I returned home people would, almost apologetically, ask me, 'When you were in Las Vegas, did you play your Cape Breton type of stuff.' I'd always tell them, 'Yes, and I did it with pride.'"

My Cape BReTon ShoRe

I left Glencoe on a wing and a prayer
They were young and wondrous times
But the spirit of the Celts I could not leave behind
Now I close my eyes everytime I feel alone
And the sailing ships and the memories take me home

Chorus:
Oh how I long to be in her arms again
Oh how I long to see those waves come rolling in
And I will leave her never more
My bonnie, my Cape Breton shore

Sometimes the bloom of youth can lead your heart astray
But the miles and the years just wake you up one day
So close your eyes everytime you feel alone
And the sailing ships and the memories take you home

ChoRus:
Oh how I long to be in her arms again
Oh how I long to see those waves come rolling in
And I will leave her never more
My bonnie, my Cape Breton shore.

— John Allan Cameron, J.K. Gulley, Tom Messenger

Ashley MacIsaac's praise for John Allan is high. "People call him the Godfather of Cape Breton music, and that's true because 25 years ago, there weren't people going out and promoting the music from Cape Breton. At that point, only if you really liked fiddle music or you were brought up with it, was there any real connection to the music. John Allan was out there beating the paths and eventually playing in Las Vegas opening for Anne Murray. I looked at the albums of him wearing his kilt and presenting his 'Celticness'. That's pretty pop, you know, wearing a kilt and playing guitar. He's one of the reasons I like to wear a kilt now. There's no doubt he opened the doors for a lot of us."

Cameron says he started out playing the fiddle but soon became intrigued by the guitar. "In 1946, I was going to a Glencoe Station school and there was a guitar player there. That's when I decided I wanted to give it a shot and I kept bugging my father to get me one. There was one day my father came home from Port Hastings. He got off the train, walked into the house, and handed me a guitar. He said, 'John Allan, I got this — he called it a cartar — I got this cartar for 14 dollars and 75 cents. If you don't learn her, I'm gonna sell her.' I was totally self-taught on the guitar and probably doing all kinds of things mechanically wrong, but it worked and still works for me. I developed my own style. I had this great love for Celtic music and I started picking out tunes on the guitar. I still love playing the Celtic stuff on the guitar."

Cameron hadn't always had music in mind as a full-time career. He was in the seminary for almost seven years and then there was six months ordination in the priesthood when he left. He then went back to university and subsequently taught high school. "Through all of it, I came to the realization that the whole process of education is to find out what you're good at and what you enjoy doing," states Cameron. "If you can get paid for that, it's a bonus. My revelation was that I loved being on stage and I liked playing the guitar and the fiddle and entertaining people. I found that out when I was attending St. Francis Xavier University in Antigonish, Nova Scotia. I was in a winter carnival variety show and the student body gave me three encores. They didn't expect it, this poor, humble folk singer from Cape Breton doing his stuff, but it went over well. At that point, I said to myself, there's something to this and I kinda like it. My friend, the late Stan Rogers, said sometimes it takes courage to be awkward, and I was certainly a little awkward when I first started playing in the lounges wearing my kilt, playing my guitar and fiddle, and singing Gaelic songs."

Along the way, Cameron has seen the traditional music scene in Cape Breton blossom with a new generation of singers, musicians, and dancers. "I remember The Rankin Family when they were very young. My mother sold them their first piano and she used to go over and sing Gaelic songs in their kitchen. To show you how everyone is a link in the chain, I remember listening to the Rankins being interviewed by Peter Gzowski on his old show and one of the girls mentioned that the first album she heard with Gaelic on it was mine. I was so flattered by that. My personal hero was fiddler Scotty Fitzgerald and he was a link in the chain back then. There are others down the line who are going to carry on and find a new way of expressing the music. We're just part of an oral tradition. My son Stuart, who plays guitar with Ashley MacIsaac, is a wonderful guitar player and I can't do a lot of what he does on the instrument. I was one of the first to play Celtic tunes, which were meant for the fiddle, on the guitar. Now there are a number of young guitar players here in Cape Breton, like Dave MacIssac and Gordie Sampson, who are great Celtic guitar players."

*A young man comes home from college in Boston and drops by an inn in Baddeck, Cape Breton for a drink.*

*As he stands at the bar, an old man asks him how he is in Gaelic.*

*"I'm fine, thank you," answers the college student in English.*

*The old man persists, but the young man continues to answer him in English.*

*"Have you no Gaelic left in you?" the old man finally asks.*

*"Oh yes," says the young man. "I can understand it, but I can't speak it."*

*The old man pauses for a moment. "Ay," he says. "I have a dog like that back home."*

I'm not sure who told that joke but I certainly wouldn't be surprised if it was Mary Jane Lamond, who allows no sacred cows to graze in her field of endeavor — traditional songs sung in the original Gaelic. During her appearance at the Celtic Colours Festival, she gave the following introduction to a song sung in the ancient tongue: "The next song is a Gaelic love song. Almost all Gaelic love songs are of unrequited love. The first time I ever sang a song in public it was a Gaelic love song, and after I finished singing it, an old fella came up to me and he said, 'That's the way it is with these Gaelic songs. They're always singing to the girl, and she's never there.'" Lamond also jokes, when she's performing, that you could do a whole record of Gaelic songs and call it "More Songs About Death and Drowning."

Don't mistake Lamond's levity for disrespect. This ex-punk rocker has an abiding affection bordering on awe for the language and its heritage. Besides, the ancients weren't adverse to a little humor themselves. "There's a great tradition of satirical songs here as well," explains Lamond. "Actually, in the Celtic tradition, satirists and poets were greatly feared because they believed that satire could actually have a physical effect on you and that you could actually become ill from a poet satirizing you. For example, there's a satirical song written by a man who wasn't invited to a certain wedding. I wanted to record the song because I really liked it. I phoned a friend of mine, who I knew had the song, and he said, 'You can't record that because it still causes bad feeling between the two families involved' — and this song is probably more than 50-years old.

"People often say to me that the music moves them spiritually and is a great inspiration, but I'm always a little amused by that because Cape Breton culture is very — as they would say here — close to the floor. It's very no nonsense with no expressed idea of it being in any way spiritual. The music is part of people's lives and definitely part of their artistic expression as a community. I'm thinking about some of the people I learned some of my songs from, and if you told them they were spiritual leaders, they'd look at you like you had two heads. I think about myself that way. Though people talk to me about the music being spiritual and inspiring, it seems pretty down to earth to me."

It's certainly down to earth enough to top the charts. A few years ago, Lamond, in collaboration with Ashley MacIsaac, joined the likes of Enya, Clannad, and Capercaillie in a select circle of artists who can claim to have had a chart-topping hit with a song performed in Gaelic. The name of the song was *Sleepy Maggie*, and in the wake of its success, Lamond toured with MacIsaac and his Kitchen Devils on the same bill as artists like Melissa Ethridge, The Chieftains, and Crash Test Dummies.

Lamond recalls the genesis of the song. "I got a call from guitar player Gordie Sampson who told me that he and Ashley were working on a song and would I come down. I went to his house and listened to the song and I picked out a little of the strathspey. The middle is just a straight forward traditional reel. The only part I really wrote was the chorus and the harmonies on it. That was just to create the bridge. It's just a simple little line that says, 'I will not be sad when the fiddler arrives tonight.' For us, it seemed like a very unusual song at the time. I thought it was kind of a lark, sitting in Gordie's basement and working on this tune just for fun. It became a song that ruled my life."

Adds Ashley MacIsaac, "Gordie Sampson came up with the idea to take a fiddle tune called *Sleepy Maggie* and put it in a dance groove. I was coming home from New York where I was hanging out in clubs all the time and I was looking for something with a dance vibe. It was basically four chords, like in a pop groove, around a fiddle tune and from that a beat was put behind it. Eventually, he and Mary Jane put together lyrics in English and then she translated them into the Gaelic. It's a typical disco song really. Dance, dance, listen to the fiddler, and dance some more."

Lamond's grandparents, on her father's side, who are from outside of Sydney towards Louisburg, spoke Gaelic, so she was first introduced to the language as a child. "We lived for a time in Cape Breton and spent all of our summers with our family down there. I didn't get introduced to the songs until much later. I knew about Gaelic songs, but I hadn't really heard any traditional singers until I attended a traditional milling frolic in North River, which is up towards St. Ann's Bay. I was just blown away by the songs I heard them sing, and I knew I just had to learn those songs. There was a real power to them. It wasn't that everybody was really a terrific singer or anything, it was just that rhythm produced by people hitting this blanket on the table and singing these songs along to it."

That experience sparked her interest and prompted her to really pursue the language, which she realized had to be the first step in learning the songs. "When I started performing the songs I wanted to do them as traditionally as possible," explains Lamond, who released her first album BHO THIR NAN CRAOBH (FROM THE LAND OF THE TREES) before she graduated with a degree in Celtic Studies at Saint Francis Xavier University in Antigonish, Nova Scotia. "I have an incredible respect for both the people that have kept these songs going and for the tradition itself. When you finally come to understand the depth of this culture, it makes you feel very small in comparison, and so you feel it's a gift for you to be able to sing these songs. For that reason, I didn't want to change anything very much, but when I began performing with Ashley MacIsaac, I was being accompanied by acoustic guitar and piano. I soon realized that even those instruments, a microphone, and stage were really taking it way beyond what's traditional. It's no longer a sharing of the songs, it's a performance of the songs, but adding more instrumentation was really about trying to add a soundscape that would create textures and express the emotion I felt for these songs. My philosophy in recording the album was that if you took away all the instrumentation, you'd still have a decent rendition of a traditional song. These songs stand on their own beautifully and you don't need to change them to make them better. It's really a question of accompanying the song and letting the song dictate what happens with it."

In any discussion of the traditional music to be found in Cape Breton, the subject of its unique rhythmic character is always raised. "The Gaelic language is so rhythmic and in Cape Breton fiddle music, your foot is going all the time," states Lamond. "But beyond just the rhythmic way people sing things, there's also an inherit rhythm in the language that kind of lulls you. The vowel sounds are what causes rhyme, not the rhyming word at the end of the line like in English poetry. In Gaelic, it's the vowel sounds within a line that determine the rhythm of the melody."

Ashley MacIsaac explains that there are certain places in Cape Breton, like Mabou, where the music is very rhythmic. "It's very Gaelic and language oriented and it's more about the drive and that beat . . . the pulse. That's some of the best music. It might not be as technically accurate but people just play it from their soul. It's about rhythm and the dancing is connected to that."

"Jigging" is a term used to describe the way that someone sings or hums a tune or melody meant for the fiddle or any other instrument, using only their voice. "Because there are no words, it doesn't sound like a regular song," explains Natalie MacMaster. "If you are a good jigger though, there's a lot of life in it and a lot of similar phrasing as there would be in the fiddle tune. It's very much connected to the Gaelic language and its rhythmic feel. A lot of the tunes I play on the fiddle have Gaelic words and those words would be sung out to the tune of the fiddle for that melody. That required a lot of vocal usage and throaty sounds.

"I started dancing before I started playing. I was five when my mom taught me a few steps and I have thrown that into my live shows just because it's very entertaining. I am there just to help people relax and enjoy the music, so I throw that in because dancing is a fun way to do that as well as being a very important part of the music. The feel of the Cape Breton fiddle style is very rhythmic with a strong pulse and a strong sense of timing to it. That comes from the years of fiddlers playing for square dances and step dances. You have to have a real steady solid driving rhythm and you can still hear that in the music."

☙

Much of the credit for the current boom of interest in the traditional music of Cape Breton and the rest of Atlantic Canada lies with The Rankins, who helped to thrust Celtic music into the mainstream in the early 1990s. At the outset, in their home town of Mabou, as the members of the group graduated from university, thoughts of international success were far from their minds. In fact, they had all but given up the idea of pursuing a musical career much further than playing the odd club date or "Pig and Whistle" gig.

"There were people who were very encouraging to us in those early days, like the local CBC affiliate and the Cape Breton Summertime Review Society," recalls Cookie Rankin of the group. "They were very instrumental in us carrying on. The summer we graduated, they approached us and asked if we were interested in doing a production ourselves and calling it 'The Mabou Jig.' We did a little dancing and a little singing and, by the fall, we had all these songs that we had put together, so we decided it wouldn't be such a bad idea to try a record. This was something unknown to us. We weren't sure we could afford it, and, to be honest, we were somewhat sceptical of anything coming of it."

The members of the group had saved up enough money through the summer to fly to Toronto where they recorded their self-titled debut album over a two-week period. That was in 1989 and, by the summer of 1990, they had become much in-demand on the folk festival circuit, where they began selling their tapes at their shows. A year later, they recorded their sophomore album, FARE THEE WELL LOVE, and, through TV, radio, and concert appearances, managed to sell over 70,000 copies of the two albums, independently.

"The first year they held the East Coast Music Awards, we won a couple of awards, and I think that's when the record companies first heard of us, but we didn't hear anything that following year," says Cookie Rankin. "We played a lot of Celtic music and most of the reps who flew down to Halifax that year and saw us were basically into rock 'n' roll. The connection was finally made when someone who had a connection with Cape Breton and who also worked for EMI Music Canada took our tapes to them. They called us right away with interest in what we were doing."

The group subsequently had their CDs hit the multi-platinum sales level. In layman's language, that's hundreds of thousands of albums. Suddenly, Celtic music in Canada became very, very hip, and Cape Breton and Atlantic Canada in general became the favored destination for record company executives looking for the next Rankins.

"Each member of the group is connected to the island in a different way," states Raylene Rankin. "John Morris, through his fiddle music, is very connected in that a lot of tunes that he plays come from the Cape Breton fiddling tradition. We all try to keep in touch with the Gaelic tradition with the songs we sing. When we research the songs, we try to find songs that have some kind of connection with the Gaelic culture in Cape Breton. Jimmy, when he writes his songs, a lot of them have some kind of reference to Cape Breton, whether it be geographically, the weather or the sea or the ocean; there's always a mention of that in a lot of the songs that he sings. Even in *You Feel The Same Way Too*, which is more of a country/rockabilly kind of song, he has mentioned in interviews that he was thinking about the dance hall tradition in Cape Breton which we grew up with. We played at what they would call 'Pig & Whistles' in our teens and some of the music that we play comes directly from that tradition."

*Feel The Same Way Too*

*Hey hey sweet darling*
*Let's go dancing tonight*
*My clock has been ticking*
*It tells me the timing is just right*
*Well I woke up this morning*
*With a feeling I call lonesome and blue*
*And there's no need asking, 'cause I know*
*You feel the same way too.*

*Hey hey sweet darling*
*Let's lay the whole thing down*
*This world if you let it*
*Will drive you into the ground*
*I got twenty dollars and I know*
*That it should get us by the door*
*When the band starts playing*
*How can they ask for more.*

*We may do the bump and grind*
*Shake around our little behinds*
*Do some things that you normally do*
*On a Saturday night and that's alright*
*We may drink a little too much*
*We may lose our fancy touch*
*And step outta line with reality*
*That's the way it should be*
*And there's no need asking, 'cause I know*
*You feel the same way too.*

*Hey hey sweet darling*
*A lot of words have been unkind*
*But that was yesterday*
*Why don't we leave the past behind*
*You know that I'll always be true*
*And there's no need asking, 'cause I know*
*You feel the same way too*

— Jimmy Rankin

Cape Breton's current status as a major center in the traditional music universe means different things to different people. Jennifer and Hazel Wrigley are sisters from Orkney in Scotland who play fiddle and guitar, respectively, and who, as a duo, have lately been garnering critical acclaim for their work in fusing their own Orcadian influences with a wide range of musical styles. In a cover story on The Wrigleys that appeared in *Folk Roots* magazine, writer Colin Irwin casually commented on the pool of talent thrusting Cape Breton into the world music spotlight of late. The reaction from Jennifer Wrigley surprised even Irwin. "I don't understand how Cape Bretoners can use the whole image of Scotland and present Cape Breton music as this pure-bred form of Scottish traditional music. How can they say that when the music has traveled all the way to Cape Breton? It obviously changed a lot during that time. It's so different to Scottish music and what is going on in Scotland right now. I can't think of anybody like Natalie MacMaster or people who play the fiddle and dance at the same time in Edinburgh.

"Yet there are a lot of people, a lot of Scottish people, who believe that the most important thing in Scottish music is what is happening in Cape Breton. They're trying to say that what's happening in Cape Breton is what everyone else should be doing now but that can't be right. Cape Breton has a strong tradition but it's Cape Breton music, and that is very different to Scottish music. I don't feel we have to sound like Cape Breton musicians to make it work . . . and we don't have to sound like Aly Bain or Tom Anderson either. There's room for all kinds of fiddle music and we have our own, with nice tunes and good stories, and we're very proud of that."

John Allan Cameron remembers playing a folk festival in Chicago a few years ago where he ran into a newspaper man from Scotland who asked him about "this Celtic stuff." As Cameron recalls, "I told him that the most important thing for its future, as in anything, is the kids and their love of it and what they bring to it as part of their own personal expression. You hold on to your roots but there are different expressions of music out there and they're all valid. I'm so happy with The Rankins who brought Gaelic music to another level. Their singing and harmonies are pristine pure and I'm happy to see their international success. And God bless the Ashley MacIsaacs of this world. They've found another way of reaching hundreds of thousands of people who never would have heard the word 'Celtic.' Same with Natalie MacMaster and her boundless energy on stage as she jumps around and plays the fiddle with reckless abandon — but it's controlled reckless abandon. That type of thing fires up an audience and I like it. Ashley, Natalie, The Barra MacNeils and Mary Jane Lamond, Cape Bretoners all. It's amazing."

He may well have added the youthful group Slaine Mhath (pronounced Slawncha Vah) of Sydney Mines, which features two of the younger brothers of the members of the Barra MacNeils, Ryan and Boyd. The five-piece group, which also includes Highland bagpipes, has that "next big thing" potential, judging by their rousing performance at the Celtic Colours Festival and the subsequent demand I witnessed for their records by a bus-load of out-of-towners at one of the bigger record outlets in Sydney the following day.

"The quality of music that's happening in this part of the world, and the whole of Canada as far as I'm concerned, is just incredible," Paddy Maloney of The Chieftains declared as he completed recording sessions in Halifax, Nova Scotia, with a number of artists from Cape Breton and the rest of Canada for the CD that would become FIRE IN THE KITCHEN. "All these young musicians getting in there, I wouldn't want to go into competition with any of them now. They're just amazing. It's a dream come true for me to come here to record with them. In the mid-'70s, we were over here touring. We did the Maritimes and places like St. John's and I heard the music. It reminded me of so much of the south and the rural part of Ireland with the little parish halls. It wasn't the thing to do to record with them in those days. We played with some of the musicians here but I swore that some day we'd come back and do some recording."

The FIRE IN THE KITCHEN CD features various members of The Chieftains and Canadian artists like The Rankins, Ashley MacIsaac, Rita MacNeil, Natalie MacMaster, Mary Jane Lamond, and the Barra MacNeils from Cape Breton; Leahy, from Lakefield, Ontario; La Bottine Souriante from Québec; Great Big Sea and The Ennis Sisters from Newfoundland; and Nova Scotia's Laura Smith, whose version of the song, *My Bonnie*, was reportedly one of the early inspirations for producer Paddy Moloney in the creation of this project, as was a radio show he did with the Barra MacNeils.

The rambunctious lads of Newfoundland's Great Big Sea traveled to Murphy's Pub in Kilarney, Ireland with The Chieftains to shoot the video for *Lukey/Lukaloney*, their contribution to the CD. One thing they could be assured of, the video's going to get a lot of play, not only on the influential Canadian-based music video network MuchMusic, but also on the Canadian version of CMT: Country Music Television, the country music video network. This, of course, is in stark contrast to CMT in the U.S. where groups playing bodhrans, tin whistles, pipes, and other Celtic paraphernalia aren't likely to get a sniff.

In the years that followed, not only did Celtic music artists from the rest of Atlantic Canada get a boost from the added exposure and subsequent presence on the Canadian country charts, there was a significant rise in the number of traditional artists emerging from all across Canada. From Atlantic Canada, came the trad folk/rock group Figgy Duff, led by the late Noel Dinn that produced singer Pamela Morgan, as well as Rawlins Cross, Ron Hynes, Evans & Doherty, The Irish Descendants, Anita Best, The Ennis Sisters, The Celtic Connection, Lennie Gallant, MacKeel, McGinty, Modabo, and The Punters, to name a few. Québec's contribution to the nationwide ceilidh is La Bottine Souriante, whose eclectic blend of traditional music forms carries enough Celtic influence to be included here. Fast-rising groups like Leahy from Ontario and promising newcomers like The Paperboys from Vancouver, the home of the Celtic flavored folk/rock group Spirit of the West, and Calgary's Scatter the Mud, have all followed the first wave.

Keeping the traditional ballads alive is John McDermott, who came to Canada from Scotland with his family in the mid-1960s and developed his voice at St. Michael's Choir School before acquiring an avid interest in traditional songs of the British Isles. His debut album, DANNY BOY, for Angel/EMI in 1992, which was originally recorded as a 50th anniversary gift for his parents, became a best-seller in Canada, the U.K., Australia, and New Zealand, where it even knocked fellow Canadian Bryan Adams from the top of the charts. McDermott's latest CD, his fifth, is WHEN I GROW TOO OLD TO DREAM.

In the summer of 1998, McDermott had one of the lead roles in *Needfire*, a celebration of Canada's Celtic culture, which opened at the Princess of Wales Theatre in Toronto. The three million dollar Mirvish production also featured Nova Scotia-born Denny Doherty, best-known as a founder of the '60s pop group, The Mamas and The Papas; singers Mary Jane Lamond, John Allan Cameron, and Jim Fiddler; The Irish

Descendants and The Ennis Sisters from Newfoundland; pipers Sandy and Rob Campbell; multi-instrumentalist Duncan Cameron; 13-year-old fiddler Jeffrey Gosse; and a chorus line of step dancers.

The acceptance of Celtic music into the mainstream in Canada can be traced, in part, back to scheduling decisions made by radio programming executive Doug Pringle of RAWLCO Communications. He was involved in the launch of the above-mentioned Canadian country video network, originally known as NCN: The New Country Network, as well as Canada's largest country radio station, Toronto's CISS-FM. NCN came on the scene at approximately the same time that The Rankin Family were emerging, and Pringle had no qualms in adding what he considered to be a traditionally Canadian form of music to the station's program schedule. "People forget that Canada's country traditions were unfolding parallel to what was going on in the U.S., they just weren't as high profile," Pringle stated at the time, as he opened the playlists to not only country artists in the Nashville tradition, but also Canadian artists in the Celtic music tradition, which, after all, was at the root of all country music originally.

Noted music publisher, Frank Davies, whose company TMP-The Music Publisher has offices in both Toronto and Nashville, has long recognized the close relationship between the traditional music of Atlantic Canada and country music. "A lot of the music from the east coast is a hybrid and certainly isn't country music as the Americans see it, but it is something very strong and identifiable with Canada," stated Davies. "Really, it's folk music and we have an incredible history of traditional/roots folk music."

Deane Cameron, the president of EMI Music Canada, the record company that signed The Rankin Family, adds, "Canadian ethnic music, whether it be Acadian-based or Maritimes-based, is a mixture of folk and some traditional Celtic music. The Celtic folk music mixed with black music is country music; which is in abundance in this country. The problem is, I find some of the existing organizations in the country music area just so entrenched in Nashville. People begin to think that if it doesn't look and sound like Nashville, it's not country, and that's wrong."

Radio broadcaster Bill Anderson, who was recently inducted into the Canadian Country Music Association's Hall of Honour, lived and worked in the Maritimes of Canada in the 1970s, early in his radio career. "Anybody who has spent any time on the east coast of Canada knows there is a rich musical heritage there," said Anderson. "When we lived in Sydney in

Cape Breton, we used to joke that there wasn't that much public entertainment, so you had to make your own. The house party (*ceilidh*) was big
and everybody played an instrument. That was part of the Scottish/Irish
heritage and those Scottish/Irish settlers, who ended up in the Ozarks
rather than in the Maritimes, took their music with them and that was the
beginning of American country music."

The Rankin Family, in fact, have recorded extensively in Nashville.
Their ENDLESS SEASONS album was produced by John Jennings, who had
previously worked with country singer/songwriter Mary Chapin Carpenter.
Carpenter performed with The Rankins on the CD's title track.

"When Irish people left Ireland in the last century and immigrated to
America, they brought with them their tunes and their songs and their
music," notes Irish singer Mary Black. "That in turn has influenced much
of American folk music, particularly country music, which can be very
closely connected with traditional Irish music as well as Appalachian and
Cajun music, all of which have strong Irish influences. Then it kind of
came back around full circle and Ireland is listening to what's happening
in America and listening to female singers like Emmylou Harris, Joan Baez,
Joni Mitchell, and Bonnie Raitt, among others. It somehow becomes an
exchange of ideas rather than anything else."

When the Scotch/Irish arrived in America at the end of the 18th century, most found that most of the prime real estate along the Atlantic tidal
plains had already been claimed by the aristocratic families who comprised
the landed gentry in those days. They were forced inland where they settled
in the Appalachian mountain range that stretches from Vermont in the
north to Georgia in the south. It was here that many of these early immigrants put down roots. The music of the Appalachians — that "High
Lonesome Sound" of legend — developed from the rich cultural heritage
of these new settlers, who not only brought with them their religious hymns
and melodies, but also music of a more secular nature — their beautiful ballads and rousing reels, jigs, and strathspeys played on the fiddle, guitar, lute,
dulcimer, bagpipes, and banjo. They also brought the family recipe for a
particularly potent form of combustible liquid known as "moonshine
whiskey," which was usually produced in a still hidden deep in the woods
away from the prying eyes of the authorities.

Subsequent waves of immigrants crossed the mountains and moved
into the wide open spaces of America where their music came into contact with other cultures and heritages. In the north, a French and
Scandinavian influence produced the songs of the lumberjacks, or the
shanty boys as they came to be known — from the French word *chanter*,

to sing. The sea shantys became the songs of those settlers who took to the sea to make their living. The Acadian French from the province of Nova Scotia in Canada migrated to Louisiana in the southern United States. Here, where the Acadians became known as "Cajuns," another fusion of music cultures took place. In the west, the music mingled with that of the Spanish settlers whose primary instrument was the guitar. Here, where the cowboy was king, those old ballads of love and longing struck a real chord among those whose lives were spent in solitude on endless cattle drives with only a horse for companionship.

Canadian singer/songwriter Ian Tyson, a second generation Welshman whose father, in true pioneer spirit, had originally settled in the Canadian west, is primarily known for his work as one half of the '60s folk duo Ian & Sylvia, for which he wrote the hit song *Four Strong Winds*. But over the last two decades, he has become one of the leading exponents of cowboy music and its culture, having recorded a series of highly-acclaimed albums for Stony Plain Records in Canada, including the best-selling COWBOYOGRAPHY.

A former rodeo rider and still a working rancher in southern Alberta, Tyson reckons that his move from folk to cowboy songs was not much of a journey. "The old songs of America's cattle country were based on traditional Scots-Irish ballads with an infusion of frontier wit, Mexican vaquero lingo and the rhythms of freed black slaves, who joined the cattle drives north," he told Jane and Michael Stern in a 1995 profile which ran in *The Atlantic Monthly*. "The Old World strains became cowboy folks songs." These songs — and cowboy culture as a whole — are celebrated annually at an event called the Cowboy Poetry Gathering in Elko, Nevada. "In this crowd," the Sterns contend, "Ian Tyson is a living god at the summit of his creative power. To write a song with him in 1995 is like what it might have been to riff with Charlie Parker in 1950 or Elvis in 1956 or Dylan in 1965."

Today, Tyson is sitting in front of an old stone cabin, originally built by Scottish crofters who had come to this area more than a century ago, that has become a sanctuary on his sprawling ranch in the foothills of the Canadian Rockies. With the horses grazing in the foreground and with a range of the snow-capped Rocky Mountains as a breathtaking backdrop, we're chatting about this Celtic-cowboy connection. "It's amazing really," says Tyson, idly picking at the vintage Martin guitar on his lap. "David Wilkie, who is a fine musician from this area, has been doing research in Ireland. There was a song that Ian & Sylvia recorded in the '60s called *Spanish Is A Loving Tongue*. The words to that song were written by an old cowboy poet by the name of Charles Badger Clark and nobody knew who wrote the melody. People actually began attributing it to me, but I didn't write it. Lo and behold, David Wilkie was over in Ireland this year and found the melody, which is hundreds of years old. It came over with those Celts. They first went to Kentucky and Tennessee and the Carolinas and they drifted into Texas and went west and brought their long rifles and their sad songs with them."

If country music represents the tidemark of Celtic music in America, then what of its contemporary connection with the broad category of World Music? For the answer to that, we need to re-cross the Atlantic and return to the regions in Europe, Africa, and the British Isles where the ancient Celts left the strongest traces of their culture hundreds of years ago.

Rita MacNeil

John Allan Cameron

*Rawlins Cross*

*The Irish*
*Descendants*

Spirit of the West

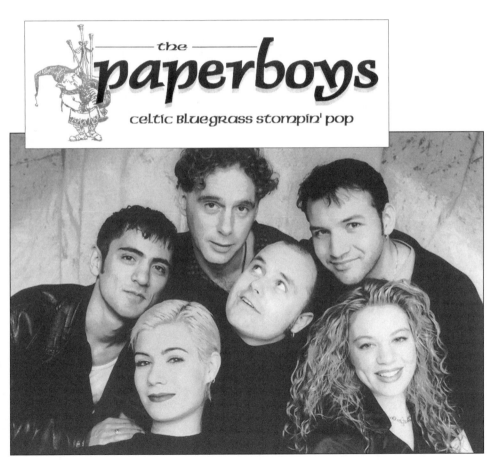

The Paperboys

*Mary Jane Lamond*
*waulking at Milling Frolic, Christmas Island Fire Hall, Cape Breton*

# CHAPTER SIX

# Beyond The Ninth Wave: World Music & Loreena McKennitt

with

Frank Delaney ⊕ Thomas Raine Crowe ⊕ Philip Sweeney ⊕ Maire Brennan (Clannad) ⊕ Davy Cattanach (Old Blind Dogs) ⊕ Seamus Egan ⊕ Alan Stivell ⊕ Steve Winick ⊕ Paddy Moloney ⊕ Sean O'Casey ⊕ Ken Russell ⊕ June Tabor ⊕ Ashley Hutchings

⊕ With banners waving, thousands of determined men and women set out to march on London in a crusade for more independence for another Celtic nation — Cornwall.

Relatives from all over the world flew in to join the protest, to proclaim their roots — and their ancient rights.

With Wales and Scotland looking forward to devolution and their own assemblies, Cornwall boasts a Celtic tradition as strong as any, but the county has been bypassed in the devolution debate.

And to supporters of the Cornish nationalist party Mebyon Kernow, this is another example of their nationhood being overlooked by "them up-country."

— International Express (May 28, 1997)

"I hate the English," the Cornishman declared to no one in particular as he drained his glass and returned it with a thud to the table.

We'd been chatting over a pint in the Nelson Bar of Penzance's Union Hotel in Cornwall, a distinctly Celtic enclave on the southwestern tip of England, and I had let it drop that I was born about a mile from where we were sitting. That revelation had no doubt lowered the barriers of reserve and out popped the aforementioned epithet.

This utterance was made within hallowed halls. It was at this very spot where news of Nelson's glorious victory at Trafalgar — and of his own demise — first reached English shores and was relayed back to London. I glanced over at the dimly-lit doorway, half expecting to see the apparition of the Lord Admiral himself hovering like Marley's ghost, glowering menacingly at such a blasphemy. My Cornish acquaintance would recant the statement later, explaining that he wasn't actually anti-English, but rather pro-Cornish, yet his earlier broad-stroke declaration was one that I had heard repeated like a mantra in moments of patriotic ardor as I traveled through the Celtic world.

"Patriotism," Irish-born author George Bernard Shaw once suggested, "is the conviction that your country is better than all others because you were born in it." It's a reasonable perspective on the subject, but reason and nationalism are rarely found in the same mixing bowl when preparing a meal of peace, love, and harmony. After a relatively short history as the oppressors of Europe, including the Romans and Greeks, the Celts and their kin have had a long history of oppression by imperialist powers like the Romans themselves and the Brits, and in this regard their collective memory has proven to be elephantine.

The Romans long ago declined and fell, while the British more recently saw the sun set on their glorious Empire. These days, as England consolidates her own future within the European community, most of her long-time dependents are loudly re-iterating their demands for greater autonomy. The Celtic regions of Scotland, Wales, Cornwall, and even Northumbria have been clamoring for self-rule, while across the Irish Sea, Northern Ireland seeks to find a perfect balance between her mainland Irish reality and her historical links to Britain, for the sake of future peace and prosperity. Needless to say, the lot of the Celts have always been closely tied to their fortunes as oppressors and the fortunes of their oppressors.

In tracking the Celtic migrations from eastern Europe to Galicia and Asturias on the European continent and to Cornwall, Wales, the Isle of Man, Scotland, and Ireland, we are accepting the historically-correct journey of the Celts through the ages. But can there be absolute certainty attached to a people's history given its antiquity and the myriad possibilities of their movements in times of crisis or simply in the restless spirit of exploration. Of late, many historians and Celtic music artists have discovered, through new archaeological evidence and through the more instinctive medium of musical exploration, that in all likelihood, the Celts also migrated through North and West Africa before arriving in western Europe and the British Isles.

With the fall of the Roman Empire, a long and bloody struggle ensued for control of the British Isles. The Celts regained control for a short period, during which they established the early Celtic Christian church. They were soon displaced as the pagan tribes of Angles, Saxons, and the Jutes poured into Britain. Another effect of the collapse of the Roman Empire was to prompt a number of the Gallo-Roman provinces across the channel to declare their sovereignty. One of these provinces, known as Amorica, saw a wave of immigration by Brythonic tribes who introduced their dialect to the area. The area today is called Brittany, located in the northwest of France, where the language is Breton, spoken in four dialects.

Until recently, this Celtic diaspora was unified, in part, by language. The Celtic languages fall into two groups: the Brythonic (British), which includes Breton (Brittany or Breizh), Cornish (Cornwall or Kernow), and Welsh (Wales or Cymru); and the Goidelic (Gaelic), which includes Irish (Ireland or Eire), Scottish Gaelic (Scotland or Alba), and Manx (Isle of Man or Maninn). But it isn't language that defines the Celtic character at the dawn of the 21st century. In searching for clues to the contemporary existence of the Celtic character, Frank Delaney, author of *The Celts*, notes their fierceness in battle when tested in recent wars "and always the music — no notation, no formal structure, just rampant imagination, embellishment, individual ornamentation."

In this context, note the introductory comments of American critic Thomas Rain Crowe to a remarkable collection of poetry from the Celtic world titled *Writing the Wind: A Celtic Resurgence*. "When the tide of Franco/English conquest rolled in across western Europe, it left little of the Celtic language cultures intact," Crowe states. "Not unlike the case in the last half of this millennium in North America of the European genocidal treatment of the native tribal cultures on this continent, so Celtic Europe became a forced community of homogeneity. When the tide ebbs, as we know it must by the very dictates of our observations of relative nature, we will see the Celtic tribes still standing and largely a result of the resilience of their writers, poets, and bards."

Today, music is surely the common language, and in listening to the music and commentary from the artists of various Celtic regions, there is no doubt that the contemporary Celtic character has been shaped by a shared heritage, the common elements of mythology and the elemental Celtic landscape with the temperamental sea at its door.

In some circles, and certainly the ones that matter in the recording industry, this music is, with good reason, now often referred to as World Music.

⟳

World Music was given definition in the summer of 1987 by a group of music business executives who were trying to capitalize on the growing interest in African music. The problem was, they were finding resistance at local record stores because the managers didn't know whether to stock it under existing categories like ethnic, folk, international or some other equivalent.

Philip Sweeney, author of *The Virgin Directory of World Music*, was at this meeting, and in the introduction to his book, he explains how the ubiquitous term found life. "After a good deal of discussion the term chosen was 'World Music', other contenders such as 'Tropical Music' being judged too narrow of scope," writes Sweeney. "Within months, the term was cropping up in the British press, within a year it had crossed the Channel and was rivalling the existing 'sono mondiale', coined three years earlier by the fashionable Paris glossy *Actuel* and its broadcasting subsidiary Radio Nova, and within three years it was in regular mainstream music industry use in Britain, the United States and northern Europe. No better short phrase has yet been proposed, and thus the term World Music has taken on a quite sturdy life of its own, which is one of the reasons it forms the title of this book. The clinching reason is its nearest rival. The Virgin Directory of World Popular & Roots Music From Outside the Anglo-American Mainstream is somewhat lacking in elan." The Celts, whose named derived from the ancient Greek word meaning "outsiders," would seem to fit Sweeney's definition to perfection.

But perhaps there's some reality reflected in placing Celtic artists under the World Music banner if you buy the reasoning that the Anglo-Americans represent the mainstream and an ancient Gaelic melody sung in the *sean nos* style from Connemara is likely to fall a little short of the *Top of the Pops*. You may, of course, get an argument from Mouth Music, Enya, Loreena McKennitt, Clannad, and other Celtic music artists who've had hits with records that hardly fit the traditional sound of the American or British Top 40 chart.

Following the chart success of Clannad's *Harry's Game*, the group arrived in England to perform on the long-running *Top of the Pops* TV show. "During an interview, somebody asked, 'Well, what's it like writing a commercial song and being in the commercial world?,'" Maire Brennan of the group recalls. "I just looked at him and said, '*Harry's Game* is no more commercial than the man in the moon,' because if you wrote that thinking of it as being a commercial product, you wouldn't have written something like *Harry's Game* and you certainly wouldn't have written it in Irish if you had wanted to be on Top of the Pops."

Brennan adds, "we know that Irish music has always been strong around the world and it's getting even stronger. If you take America, for instance, everything is put into categories, so our recordings in America would have been put into folk music. And then there was a new category developed, New Age music, basically for people that didn't know where to put certain types of music, and you'd sometimes find anything from Joni Mitchell to Miles Davis to us in that category. New Age music to me can be quite boring. Now there's a new category which is World Music and that's where Irish music slots in and that's why it's got a new audience, a new field and so has all the other cultural music in the world."

For further evidence of the 'world' character of Celtic music, check out recordings by the Afro Celt Sound System, Martin Okasili (THE INVISIBLE HISTORY OF THE BLACK CELTS), or even chat with Scottish traditional group Old Blind Dogs, whose percussionist Davy Cattanach uses an array of African drums. "I decided not to use a conventional drum kit because I didn't think it really suited the music," explains Cattanach, who once played in a reggae band from Aberdeen and claims that those rhythms are the biggest influence he's had on his drumming style. "I do have a lot of critics in the traditional scene who think what I do is horrible, a complete travesty of justice."

Of late, many artists in the genre have likewise found great inspiration in exploring the music of a wide variety of exotic cultures while keeping the traditional core intact. "It's a very healthy approach for me," Maire Brennan of Clannad has stated. "When I write my own music, I like to enhance it with other kinds of influences, whether it's South African or Indian or Tibetan or from different parts of Africa, especially West Africa. I think it strengthens the whole thing because Irish music is terribly strong and it's not going to lose that strength; it's just too deep down."

For Philadelphia-born multi-instrumentalist Seamus Egan, one of the most stimulating characteristics of traditional music is its need to constantly evolve. "New ideas, new things need to happen in order for it to stay alive," explains Egan. "It's important that it doesn't become something that's protected behind glass. The people that came before us, they made it their own. It was still within the tradition, but a stamp was placed on it and it was their innovations and moving things forward that excited the next generation to start to play. It's just a natural progression."

Breton/Celtic harpist Alan Stivell, regarded by many as the godfather of the contemporary Breton music scene, and an early influence on artists like Loreena McKennitt and the accomplished Welsh triple harpist, Robin Huw Bowen, among many others, has also indulged his interest in the music of other cultures within the framework of the Celtic tradition. "When I was very young, I was passionate about Celtic music, but I soon became very curious about other styles of music as well, especially those that reminded me of Celtic music," says Stivell, whose RENAISSANCE OF THE CELTIC HARP album of 1972 is considered a landmark recording in the revival of interest in the harp, in particular, and in the whole genre of Celtic music, in general. "In listening to music from the Far East, China, music of the American Indians and even more standard American forms like the Negro spiritual, I found elements that had something in common with Celtic music. I was interested in music from all over the planet and I liked the idea of fusion. What we now call Breton music is something which has been much-influenced by standard medieval European music. At the end of the 20th century, our approach should be to adapt things from outside of Brittany, or outside of the Celtic nations, to the Breton or the Celtic sound."

Early on, Stivell drew inspiration from British traditional/folk outfits like Steeleye Span and Fairport Convention and traditional Irish groups like Planxty, Sweeney's Men, and The Chieftains, who in the mid-1980s traveled to Britanny at the suggestion of Polig Monjarret, a noted collector of Celtic tunes from the area, to record an album of traditional Breton dance tunes titled CELTIC WEDDING. More than a decade before that, Stivell had played harp, bagpipes, and Irish flute in a group with renowned Breton guitarist Dan Ar Bras, who was a member of Fairport Convention in the mid-1970s, and guitarist Gabriel Yacoub, who went on to form Marlicorne, a band highly regarded in the 1970s and '80s for their vocal harmony and a sound that melded medieval instruments like the crumhorn with synthesizers and electronic gizmos of their own design. Other ensembles followed Stivell's early lead, including Tri Yann, Gwerz, Lo Jai, L'Ange Vent, An Trickell, and Kornog, which features Scots singer, mandolin, and bouzouki player Jamie McMenamy. Also of note is Breton fiddler Christian LeMaitre, who was a member of Celtic Fiddle Festival, with Johnny Cunningham and Kevin Burke, who recorded an album and toured America in 1992 and 1994.

Steve Winick, a prolific commentator on the world of Celtic music, noted the adventurous musical spirit still alive in Brittany today in an article on the region that appeared in the magazine *Dirty Linen*. "The Breton music tradition is a constant source of amazement," he exclaimed. "Not only are there many traditional musicians performing purely traditional music, there is also a population of explorers, who look at the tradition as a grounding for their own musical explorations. The simultaneous use of tradition and innovation, of continuity and change, marks the best in contemporary Breton music."

As examples, he notes the recent recorded works of Breton artists like Alter Ego, Cabestan, Alain Pennec, Maubuissons, the duo of Jean-Michel Veillon and Yvon Riou, and Dao Dezi, Brittany's contribution to the body of recently recorded works that have successfully combined traditional music with techno/dance rhythms on projects like Mouth Music (Scotland) and Deep Forest (Central Africa), the latter of which involved the same production team as Dao Dezi.

Galicia and Asturias on the north Atlantic coast of Spain are also areas of Celtic influence. In that region, much of the musical activity has been centered in the Galician city of Santiago de Copestela, a pilgrimage site for people in the middle ages as well as an inspirational destination for artists from other parts of the Celtic world and beyond. Paddy Moloney and The Chieftains came to the area in the mid-1990s to travel the traditional pilgrims' route to the cathedral of Santiago de Compostela, recording as they gained inspiration from the various sites visited along the way. An addition to the group during this period was the young Galician recorder and Gaita (Galician pipes) player Carlos Nunez, whom Moloney had met in 1984 while performing at an outdoor festival hosted by local legends, Milladoiro. The resulting album, SANTIAGO, released in 1996, which among other gems includes the live favorite *Dueling Chanters*, featuring the rousing interplay of Moloney on uilleann pipes and Nunez on Gaita, documented the group's voyage of musical discovery through the Latin world.

"Music of the more contemporary history evolved when Galicians, like many of their Celtic cousins, emigrated in great numbers to the new world," states Moloney in the CD's liner notes. "Whether by design or necessity, they settled primarily in the south, spreading their roots from Mexico and the Caribbean through Central and South America. In our travels, we were able to sample only a taste of this exotic fare, to Cuba with Carlos and our good friend Ry Cooder and later to southern California with Los Lobos and Linda Ronstadt."

Among the Galician artists of note are the aforementioned Milladoiro, who formed at the University at Santiago de Compostela in the early 1980s and have since toured the U.S., and the adventuresome Matto Congrio. From Asturias, Llan De Cubel have become one of Spain's most renowned folk groups.

Looking across the English Channel from Britanny, one immediately encounters Cornwall, the isolated county in the southwest of England attached to the mainland by the Royal Albert Bridge across the Tamar River. Local nationalists like to call the county "one of the four nations of Britain" — the other three being the Celtic territories of Wales and Scotland along with "them up-country" or England, their Anglo-Saxon neighbor.

The Cornish, Bretons, and Welsh are known as Brythonic Celts because of the commonality of the language. During the Saxon conquest of Britain in the fifth century, many of the Celts from Cornwall fled to the north of France where they put down roots in the area now known as Brittany. The proximity of the two communities and the resulting shared heritage is evident in some of the songs and dances from the area. The Breton "Fest-Noz" has its mirror image in the Cornish "Troyl," a celebration of music, dance, and story-telling that is also a popular past-time, under different names, in other Celtic regions.

Ironically, though Breton is still alive as a language, the Cornish actually became the first Celtic territory to "lose" their language as the last remaining people with native knowledge of it died in the 19th century. As in many Celtic areas where the heritage and language had begun to fade into memory, there has been a revival of interest in not only keeping the language and customs alive but also in making these elements of culture a vital part of everyday life. Music is often at the forefront of these initiatives as is the observance of some of the old traditions.

In Cornwall, the ancient rites of Spring are still celebrated with the Furry Dance procession (May 8) to an ancient tune through the streets of Helston. And there's the May Day (May 1) celebrations in Padstow, during which the 'Obby Oss'(Hobby Horse), tied to the promotion of fertility and a fruitful growing season is paraded through streets decked out in flowers, sycamore, ash and maple boughs. The song associated with the festival, the *Padstow Hobby Horse* song or the "Padstow May Day" song, has been given a contemporary reading by English trad/folk group Steeleye Span and more recently in Cape Breton by The Rankins on their *Endless Seasons* CD. The Padstow festivities were also one of the influences on Loreena McKennitt's hit single, *The Mummer's Dance*.

*Padstow (May Day Song)*

*Unite and unite, let us all unite*
*For summer is a'coming today*
*And whither we are going, we will unite*
*In the merry morning of May.*

*Oh where are the young men that now here should dance*
*For summer is a'coming today*
*Well some there are in England and some are in France*
*In the merry morning of May.*

*Oh where are the maidens that now here should sing*
*For summer is a'coming today*
*They're all out in the meadows a flower gathering*
*In the merry morning of May.*

*The young men of Padstow, they might if they would*
*For summer is a'coming today*
*They might have built a ship and gilded it with gold*
*In the merry morning of May.*

*Oh where is St. George, oh where is he oh*
*He's down in his longboat upon the salt sea oh*
*Up flies the kite, down falls the lark-o*
*And Ursula Birdwood, she has an old ewe*
*And she died in her old park-o.*
*With a merry ring and a joyful spring*
*For summer is a'coming today*
*Oh happy are the little birds and merrily do they sing*
*In the merry morning of May.*

The traditional Morris Dance of the region and its accompanying music has been incorporated into the repertoire of a number of contemporary trad/folk artists. Ashley Hutchings' Albion Band recorded the album MORRIS ON, which brought renewed interest to the tradition on both sides of the Atlantic. More recent promoters of traditional Cornish music and dance is the family group, Anao Atao, who have appeared on festivals around the world. The late Brenda Wootton is considered the queen of Cornish traditional folksingers.

ᕉᕯ

As the ancient Greeks had done centuries before, the Saxons dubbed The Celts they encountered on their march across Britain the "foreigners" — or in the Saxon tongue, the "weahlas." As the various Celtic tribes established themselves in the mountainous areas to the west, the territory became known as "the land of the foreigners" or Wales. Likewise, "the land of the Cornish foreigners" further to the south became Cornwall.

The Welsh are internationally renowned for their love of singing, and certainly one of the enduring images of the region's culture are the male voice choirs which are still at the center of village life, despite the decimation of the mining industry. But there is another side to the Welsh music character in which the bardic tradition is kept alive by way of a competitive music, song, and dance festival called *eisteddfod*. Unique in style and content to the Welsh, the event, which results in the winner taking on the title of Chief Bard, is held alternately each year in North and South Wales. The National Eisteddfod, the culmination of many small competitions, is held in August.

Traditional folk music in Wales, known to the natives as "gwerin," had its contemporary beginnings with the acknowledged godfather of the scene, Dafydd Iwan, back in the mid-1960s and now boasts a number of instrumental and vocal artists known in international circles, including Welsh triple harpist Robin Huw Bowen; singer/harpist Sian James, dubbed "the Welsh Enya"; and Fernhill, a group comprised of noted traditional singer Julie Murphy and acclaimed musicians Jonathan Shorland, Andy Cutting, and Ceri Rhys Matthews, who play "traditional music from Wales, Brittany and England, combining the sound of European bagpipes and reed instruments with cittern, diatonic accordion, and flutes." Local heroes include the band Bob Delyn and up-and-comers, the Kilbride Bros, the siblings of Jenny and Gil Kilbride, who were active on the local folk scene during the 1970s and '80s.

🌐 The Isle of Man, which lies in the Irish Sea off the coast of Britain, unlike other parts of the Celtic world, was untouched by Roman influence and therefore managed to keep their Manx language until recent times when English predominated. There's a unique music, song, and dance culture on the island as well, which is celebrated each July as part of the Yn Cruinnaght Inter-Celtic Festival. Among those artists upholding the musical tradition on the island are Manx groups Mactullagh Vannin, The Tholtan Builders, and The Mollag Band as well as instrumentalist Peter Cubberley, Celtic harpist Charles Guard and composer/instrumentalist, Adie Evans.

🌐 Despite the adversarial air between the Celts and the Brits, if you think that England has had no part in this Celtic music uprising, think again. The boundaries are not as clearly defined as one might think.

"As Ireland isn't anything as Irish as some Gaels make her out to be, so England isn't as English as many Irish think her to be," wrote Sean O'Casey, the Irish dramatist, in the sixth and final volume of his autobiography, *Sunset and Evening Star*. O'Casey lived in the county of Devon, in the southwest of England, from just before the outbreak of the Second World War until his death in 1964. "Half of England, and maybe more, is as Keltic as Ireland itself. Listen to the pipe-playing and folk-singing of Northumberland, or to the Cumberland farmers still counting their sheep close to the way the people of Ballyvourney number their scanty flocks. Listen any night to 'Dance Them Around' . . . their band is as Irish as any Ceilidh band in any country town of Ireland. The old songs are neglected and half-forgotten today, and are no longer commonly sung in cottage or farmhouse, just as they are neglected and half-forgotten by Cahersiveen in Kerry and Cushendall in Antrim; though now there is a sleepy interest taken in holding fast to a folk-lore that has almost bidden a picturesque goodbye forever to the common song a people loves to sing."

In listening one night to a gathering in a village hall near Leamington, in Warwickshire, O'Casey heard an old woman of seventy-four, the traditional singer of the localry, giving the audience *Johnny My Own True Love*, just as he had heard his own mother sing it in the days of long ago. "It was H.G. Wells who, through *Mr. Britling Sees It Through*, voiced delight in the fact that the bigger part of England's place-names had a Keltic origin; so, what with all this, with Wales by her side and Scotland over her head, adding the Irish and their descendants, England is really more Keltic than the kilt."

The world of traditional folk music in England rings with the names of the pioneers who, through a succession of different groups with varying combinations of players, breathed new life into the form. Ashley Hutchings, Sandy Denny, Richard Thompson, Maddy Prior, David Swarbrick, Martin Carthy, Robin Williamson, Bert Jansch, John Renbourn, and June Tabor, among others, have all been instrumental in creating a contemporary audience for trad/folk music as artists in their own right and as members of groups like Fairport Convention, The Albion Band, Fotheringay, Steeleye Span, The Incredible String Band, Pentangle, Waterson: Carthy, and The Oyster Band.

And, of course, there was balladeer, songwriter, playwright, TV and radio producer and champion of the British folk song, Ewan MacColl. He had a tremendous influence on a later generation of artists, including Christy Moore, Luke Kelly of The Dubliners, and Shane MacGowan of The Pogues. Many of his own songs have become standards in the idiom, including *The First Time Ever I Saw Your Face* and *Dirty Old Town*, which became hits for Roberta Flack and The Pogues, respectively.

Director Ken Russell's entertaining and humorous documentary *In Search of the English Folk Song* is an eccentric romp through the traditional, and the not-so traditional, world of the folk song, which Russell notes was defined as "a spontaneous utterance from the unlettered classes" by turn-of-the-century song collector Cecil Sharp. (Cecil Sharp House on Regents Park Road in London is the home of the English Folk Song and Dance Society and the repository for a major collection of English folk music.) In a particularly entertaining segment of the film, Russell visits his old friend, singer June Tabor, who performs a moving rendition of the contemporary folk song *The King Of Rome* about a man of who invests all his hopes and dreams in life in the performance of the carrier pigeon he has trained.

Visibly moved by the song and Tabor's expressive performance, Russell asks Tabor what, in her opinion, gives the typical English folk song its character. Her answer is worth noting as it applies to the whole body of traditional music no matter where it is to be found. "I think it's the directness of the language of the way the story's told," suggested Tabor. "It's very simple. It's simple to the point that there is not a single word wasted in that song. You're inside the song. You're with Charlie; you're with the pigeon and you're feeling his emotions as he finds out what happens to the pigeon. I think the best of folk music has that directness. At its best, it's simple, but timeless. That song is a story but at the same time it's a metaphor for the human condition, for the unquenchable nature of the human spirit in the face of tremendous adversity. It was actually written about ten years ago but it could have been written much longer ago because of its wonderful, timeless nature."

"I love the humanity of it," interjected Russell. "You can almost picture the man, the poor, old underdog."

"Yes and the triumph of the common man over his situation," continued Tabor. "I suppose that's what appealed to many about traditional songs and what kept people singing them. You've got to have something with which you can identify. The best of the songs that have survived definitely have that, whether they're about love gone wrong, which is pretty universal and timeless and happens to us all, or something like this song in which you can feel and experience Charlie's victory with him."

During the course of the film, Russell also tracked down Ashley Hutchings for comment at the Fairport Convention's 30th anniversary celebration held as part of their annual reunion during the second weekend of August at Cropredy, Oxfordshire, England. It drew a crowd of over 20,000 people. "I think the English folk song probably died just before television and radio," says Hutchings, though he acknowledged that there is still English folk music being written with contemporary themes and viewpoints. "Modern communications make it totally different now. Folk songs could only really exist in a time when people had to make their own entertainment and had to pass on information through song and through stories and ballads. The songs and the stories were the newsprint of the time."

In some ways, the story we are telling here is a tale of revival, whether it be the English folk song or the traditional music of the various Celtic areas often performed in the original language. No artist of late has been more involved in this world-wide exploration and revival of Celtic music than Canadian singer, harpist, and composer Loreena McKennitt.

❧

"Ms. McKennitt regrets she's unable to talk today."

With apologies to Cole Porter, that is the gist of the message received from Richard Flohil, Loreena McKennitt's long-time publicist, who is fielding phone calls from the clamoring media on the occasion of the release of her seventh album, THE BOOK OF SECRETS, and the enormous popularity of one track, *The Mummer's Dance*, which has found itself in the extraordinary position of having become an international dance hit.

Loreena's on a bicycle trip in China, explains Flohil, but not to worry. She's left the phone number of nearly every hotel from Beijing to Woo knows where and communication links are being kept open.

McKennitt's friends and associates have come to take this spur of the moment wanderlust in stride. After all, this is not an isolated occurrence. Take your eye off her for one moment and there she is — gone. In recent times, you might have run into McKennitt riding the Trans Siberian Express, wandering the mountainous terrain around Bobbio, the first Irish monastery in Italy, strolling through a Moroccan marketplace or soaking up the rich, cultural heritage of Galicia, the ancient Celtic region in the northwest of Spain. Marco Polo, the 13th-century explorer who inspired the instrumental track bearing his name on THE BOOK OF SECRETS, would have been proud.

A tireless explorer in the Celtic world and beyond, McKennitt's bestselling CDs, THE MASK AND THE MIRROR, THE VISIT, and THE BOOK OF SECRETS, were all inspired by her travels to the four corners of the globe. "The eight songs contained therein," a short biographical piece accompanying THE BOOK OF SECRETS CD notes, "will lead the listener on unexpected journeys from ancient Byzantium to a puppet-maker's theater in Palermo, Sicily, from the rocky island of Skellig Michael once inhabited by Irish monks in the Dark Ages to Venice and the journeys of Marco Polo, from the stirring drama of The Highwayman and its tragic narrative to the thunder of hooves across the Caucasus and the echoes of Dante's words found, unexpectedly, in a train journey across Siberia."

The inspiration for Loreena McKennitt's million-selling THE MASK AND THE MIRROR CD of 1994 came, in part, from a visit to Galicia and in particular, Santiago de Copestela. McKennitt was moved to think about the journey of the pilgrims back to their homes in various corners of Europe carrying, as she puts it "pollen of influence." She was subsequently drawn to a piece of music that came from that period and gave it the title *Santiago*.

"A sense of journey has been a major part of what I do, but in different way and at different times," admits McKennitt, who is tenacious in exploring the physical and spiritual world of the music she has taken to her heart. "When I got interested in Celtic music, my first major trip was to go to Ireland and track it down in its more indigenous form. At that point in time, I was just following something that was really fascinating me, but I wasn't aware of myself on a quest."

It was the period surrounding the recording, touring, and promotion tied to THE VISIT project that saw the full bloom of McKennitt's adventurous spirit, which has often seen an idle whim turn into a full-blown odyssey to exotic lands halfway around the world. The photo shoot for the cover and booklet of THE VISIT CD could well have been produced locally, but a chance viewing of some photos of Portugal from the portfolio of photographer Elisabeth Feryn, who has a studio close to McKennitt's office in Stratford, Ontario, soon had the two of them packing their bags and jetting off to the Iberian Peninsula.

During that same period, there was a three-day break in a lengthy cross-Canada tour. Most artists would have coveted the rest. Not McKennitt. She had read about one of the most extensive exhibitions of Celtic artifacts ever assembled in Venice, Italy. Needless to say, there was no talking her out of the journey. "The exhibition contains many pieces that have emerged from Eastern Europe as a result of the loosening up of the political situation and have never been seen before in the west," explained McKennitt shortly before her departure. "I'll take pictures — as many as they will allow me to — because it's so much the territory of what was spinning through my head for two years in preparation for this recording [THE VISIT] and very much the door which I feel I have barely opened and about which I'm very, very curious from a musical standpoint. I'm just very curious about those earlier cultures, what the ingredients were and what we've lost along the way."

As THE BOOK OF SECRETS was being released, McKennitt looked back on that trip to Venice as a pivotal moment in her evolution as an artist and in her understanding of the pan-Celtic culture. It transformed her music. "Until I went to that exhibition I thought that Celts were people who came from Ireland, Scotland, Wales and Brittany," she told her biographer. "Seeing the unimagined riches and variety in the centuries of Celtic art gathered from as far afield as Hungary, Ukraine, Spain and Asia Minor, I felt exhilarated. It was like thinking that all there is to your family are your parents, brothers and sisters, and then you realize there's a whole stretch of history that is an extension of who you are."

One might surmise that a prime motivator for trips of this sort would be part of a greater quest to trace one's own roots. McKennitt, who says that her ancestors originally came from northern Scotland and arrived in Canada by way of Ireland, claims that really was not the case. "This is more like taking a history course — Celtic History 101. The Celts did come up through Spain and Portugal and that's why I want to see this exhibition. It has much less to do with the fact that it is my own ancestry."

The Mummers Dance, the out-of-left-field hit single, was inspired by a number of chance encounters and local customs experienced on her ramblings through the Celtic world, including the work of a marionette maker she met in Palermo, Sicily, the "hobby horse" of May Day celebrations in Padstow, Cornwall, and a Sufi order in Turkey. As McKennitt's biographer points out, "Ultimately, the months of research underpinning each track are subliminal; the experience of the music is simply sensual."

McKennitt, whose mother was a nurse and her father a livestock trader, hails from Morden, Manitoba on the Canadian Prairies where she initially became interested in Celtic-based music in the mid-1970s as a member of a folk club in the city of Winnipeg. Here she was exposed to a number of groups of the Celtic persuasion from the British Isles, including Planxty, Bothy Band, and Steeleye Span. She also recalls a particular recording by Breton harper Alan Stivell, titled THE CELTIC HARP RENAIS-SANCE.

"Once I heard that record, I was instinctively drawn to the music and really smitten by it," McKennitt has explained. "That recording enthralled me so much that I had it copied onto a reel-to-reel tape so that I could go to bed at night listening to the whole recording without having to jump up in the middle and have to turn the record over."

It wasn't until 1984 that she took up the harp as her main instrument, and, in some ways, she reckons the harp found her. "I was in hospital in London, England," she recalls, "and there was a music store across the street. Some friends of mine, who had come to visit, told me about it and let me know there was a harp in the window. The day I got out of the hospital, I walked over and bought it. That was really the beginning of all this."

She refers to that period as a homecoming of sorts, in that it brought together in one instrument all of the aspirations and interests she had in music at the time. It gave her a focus not only in her repertoire of traditional music, but also in the area of composition in the Celtic style. With ten years of classical piano training behind her, this was somewhat of a radical departure for her as a musician and for her musical direction.

"In the years just prior to that I was working at the Festival Theatre in Stratford, Ontario — the first year as a singer, the second as an actress and the third as a composer," McKennitt recalls. "Prior to that, I had been playing in lounges and been through the whole trip of putting on high heels and the whole outfit and working from nine o'clock at night until one o'clock in the morning. I had about three years of commuting between Winnipeg and Toronto playing lounges in both cities."

The experience was motivational. It wasn't long before the unsinkable Ms. McKennitt was giving thought to recording and putting together a reasonable business plan for her career. The results of her foray into the music business jungle have become somewhat legendary in independent music circles around the world. Having borrowed $10,000 from her family, and with the aid of a do-it-yourself guide to the record business by Diane Rapaport titled *How To Make Your Own Recordings*, she recorded her first album, ELEMENTAL, in 1985 and issued it on her own Quinlan Road label. The self-produced CD, which contained a sampling of her arrangements of a number of the traditional Celtic songs and melodies in her repertoire at the time as well as musical settings of poems by Yeats and Blake, was originally sold as she busked in places like the St. Lawrence Market in Toronto.

Over the next three years, she busked, promoted her own concerts, and gradually built a grass-roots following until the sales of her CDs, which now included TO DRIVE THE COLD WINTER AWAY and PARALLEL DREAMS, caught the eyes and ears of some of the major labels. When PARALLEL DREAMS sold 25,000 copies independently, McKennitt realized the dynamics of the artist/record company relationship had changed somewhat. "I felt that it was really important that, as an artist, I advance my own career to the point where it would be of some value to somebody else," McKennitt explains. "At that point, I felt I would be able to strike a deal that would be somewhat equitable." Ultimately, that deal was with Warner Music internationally.

It was actually during her previously-mentioned stint in the actor's circle that McKennitt moved to Stratford, Ontario in the early 1980s, where she rented a farm house about a mile and a half out of town that also served as her business office. She now has an office in London, England as well as headquarters on the main street of her home town of Stratford, both of which she frequents with some regularity.

Though McKennitt travels extensively, not all of her journeys are of the physical variety. Widely read, she has taken musical inspiration from her exploration of the works of writers like Dante, Yeats, Tennyson, Noyes, Blake, and Shakespeare. Tennyson's epic poem *The Lady of Shallott*, set to music by McKennitt, echoes from far-off Camelot through the mists of time. In some ways, this is McKennitt's strength as a composer — her ability to paint, with her own brush and palette of colors, a musical portrait of such contemporary and universal appeal from the words and imagery of another age and custom.

Most artists squirm when asked to categorize their music or sound. McKennitt is no different. "It's difficult to define," she has said. "I've had people suggest that there are elements of Kate Bush and of Enya in it. When that's suggested, I'm very flattered because they are artists whose work I admire, but I've tried to focus in on my own musical stamp. The other dimension of my music is that I work with musicians who work in rock and roll and in jazz and a wide range of genres so that when we work together, either in performance or on a recording as this one [THE VISIT], you'll get a lot of influences in the arrangement so people will be as likely to hear a tin whistle and an Irish pipe and the Irish harp as they will hear electric guitar and synthesizer and the tambour and the sitar, so it's a real wide cross-section of influences."

When the suggestion is made that a number of cuts on her albums might not sound terribly out of place in juxtaposition with many of the epic-proportioned Led Zeppelin tracks, especially those that reflect the Celtic and folk/acoustic interests of group members Robert Plant and Jimmy Page, she warms to the prospect that people might think that her music had a landscape of that breadth to roam in. "The real danger — and it happens here and there — is that the music becomes something terribly precious and very new age or something — and that totally misses the point because it should feel very much at home in that [Led Zeppelin] kind of territory."

"The Sufis have an expression of polishing the mirror of your soul," McKennitt explains on her video, No Journey's End, which explores the diverse influences behind THE VISIT and THE MASK AND THE MIRROR. "My voice becomes the polishing aspect, that is, it is the vehicle of expressing things that occur in a very primal and instinctive kind of way. I think that is part of the strength of what I do. You try not to have barriers. You open your soul; you open yourself up."

Perhaps this is the essence of Celtic music — primal, instinctive, open — and the reason why this music travels so far and so wide. Echoing with wonder, cloaked in mysticism, steeped in tradition, Celtic music has journeyed through the ages from the old world to the new. Through tides of glorious victory and crushing defeat, emigration and displacement, social and political upheaval, and the advent of new technologies, the Celtic legacy has survived and today flourishes with the descendants of an enigmatic people, "outsiders," for whom music, dance, and storytelling are often treasured as highly as life itself.

Back in Nashville, St Patrick's Day gives way to the encroaching gloom of a mild March night. Right now, Dublin, Inverness, and Mabou — Cornwall, Brittany, Galicia — all seem so very far away, in time if not in space. Time to pack and head out for supper and a quick night cap before turning in. God, I only hope they've run out of green beer.

# Celtic Music Discography

⊕ This discography was compiled from various sources including my own record collection, record stores, record companies, artists, managers and other reference works. We would welcome any corrections or updates for future editions of this book and other planned reference works. Contact Martin Melhuish, c/o Quarry Music Books, P.O. Box 1061, Kingston, Ontario, Canada K7L 3A6, e:mail: info@quarrypress.com, tel: (613) 548-8429, fax: (613) 548-1556.

❧

**KEY** — (**Acc**) - Accordion. (**Ag**) - Acoustic Guitar. (**Bacc**) - Button Accordion. (**Bal**) - Balalaika. (**Ban**) - Bandura. (**Bbo**) - Bass Bombarde/Piston. (**Bla**) - Basola. (**Bg**) - Bass Guitar. (**Bj**) - Banjo. (**Bk**) - Biniou-koch [Brittany]. (**Bl**) - Blarge. (**Bo**) - Bombarde/Breton Oboe. (**Bod**) - Bodhran. (**Bon**) - Bones. (**Bp**) - Bagpipes. (**Bps**) - Bowed Psaltery. (**Bsn**) - Bassoon. (**Bz**) - Bouzouki. (**Ceh**) - Celtic Harp. (**Cel**) - Cello. (**Cg**) - Congas. (**Ch**) - Crumhorn. (**Cha**) - Chromatic Harp. (**Cit**) - Cittern. (**Cl**) - Clarinet. (**Con**) - Concertina. (**d**) - Drums. (**Dar**) - Darabuka. (**Db**) - Double Bass. (**Dd**) - Didgeridoo. (**Dh**) - Diatonic Harp. (**Dj**) - Djembe. (**Dul**) - Dulcimer. (**Dum**) - Dumbek. (**Ec**) - English Concertina. (**Eg**) - Electric Guitar. (**Fi**) - Fiddle. (**Fif**) - Fifes. (**Fl**) - Flute. (**g**) - Guitar. (**Ha**) - Harp. (**Hd**) - Hammered Dulcimer. (**Hmc**) - Harmonica. (**Ho**) - Hammond Organ. (**Hp**) - Highland Pipes. (**Hw**) - Harmony Whistle. (**Jh**) - Jew's Harp. (**k**) - Keyboards. (**Lw**) - Low Whistle. (**m**) - Mandolin. (**Ma**) - Mandola. (**Mc**) - Mandocello. (**Mel**) - Melodeon. (**Mg**) - MIDI Guitar. (**Mh**) - Medieval Harp.

(**Mo**) - Mouth Organ. (**Np**) - Northumbrian Pipes. (**Ob**) - Oboe. (**Oc**) - Ocarina. (**p**) - Piano. (**Pan**) - Pandeireta. (**Pc**) - Percurssion. (**Pi**) - Pipes. (**Pic**) - Piccolo. (**Pw**) - Penny Whistle. (**Rec**) - Recorder. (**Req**) - Requinta (Galician Flute). (**Ri**) - Reed Instruments. (**Sd**) - Step Dancing. (**Sg**) - Steel Guitar. (**Shk**) - Shakuhachi. (**Sp**) - Small Pipes. (**Spo**) - Spoons. (**Sw**) - Swayne Whistle. (**Sx**) - Saxophone. (**Syn**) - Synthesizer. (**Tab**) - Tabla. (**Tro**) - Trombone. (**Tru**) - Trumpet. (**Tw**) - Tin Whistle. (**Up**) - Uilleann Pipes. (**v**) - Vocals. (**Vdg**) - Viola da Gamba. (**Vla**) - Viola. (**Vln**) - Violin. (**Wo**) - Woodwinds. (**Zev**) - Zeta Electric Violin. (**Zi**) - Zither.

Labels listed are from North America and the United Kingdom except for artists whose appeal is regional. In that case, local labels are noted.
(*) An asterisk prior to the label designation indicates a contemporary re-issue. The name of the original label(s) follows. [1974] Square brackets containing a designated year indicate the year of a group's formation or the year of a record's release.

**AFRO CELT SOUND SYSTEM**
Ireland/West Africa. **Simon Emmerson**
(Producer); **Jamie Reid** ('Co-conspirator');
**Iarla O Lionaird** (v); **Davy Spillane** (Up);
**Ronan Browne** (Up); **James McNally** (Tw);
**Ayub Ogada** (nyatiti); **Kauwding Cissokho**;
**Massamba Diop**; **Jo Bruce** (k).

**Volume 1 Sound Magic** (Real World) [1996]

**THE ALBION BAND**
England. [1976] Also known as The Albion
Country Band, The Etchingham Steam
Band, and the Albion Dance Band, which at
various times included **Ashley Hutchings**
(Bg) with **Shirley Collins** (v); **Simon Nicol**
(g); **Richard Thompson** (g); **Roger Swallow**
(d); **Martin Carthy** (g); **Sue Harris** (v);
**John Kirkpatrick** (v, Con); **Steve Ashley**
(Hmc); **Dave Mattacks** (d); **Linda
Thompson** (v); **Sue Draheim** (v, Fi, Bj);
**Royston Wood** (v, Con); **Ian Holder** (Acc);
**Terry Porter** (Hmc); **Ashley Reed** (Vln);
**Christine White** (v); **Ric Sanders** (v); **Julie
Matthews** (v) et al.

BLASTA!
THE IRISH TRADITIONAL MUSIC SPECIAL

**No Roses** (Pegasus) [1971] as Albion
Country Band
**Battle Of The Field** (B.G.O./Island) [1976]
as Albion Country Band
**The Prospect Before Us** (Harvest) [1977] as
Albion Country Band
**Rise Up Like The Sun** (Hannibal/Harvest)
[1978]
**Albion River Hymn March** [1979}
**Lark Rise To Candleford: A Country
Tapestry** (Virgin/Charisma) [1980]

**Light Shining** (Albino) [1982]
**Shuffle Off** (Making Waves (1983)
**Under The Rose** (Spindsrift) [1984]
**A Christmas Present From The Albion
Band** (Fun) [1985]
**Stella Maris** (Making Waves) [1987]
**The Wild Side Of Town** (Celtic Music)
[1987]
**I Got New Shoes** (Making Waves) [1987]
**Give Me A Saddle, I'll Trade You A Car**
(Topic) [1989]
**Albion Band 1990** (Topic) [1990]
**Songs From The Shows, Vol. 1** (Road Goes
On Forever) [1992]
**Songs From The Shows, Vol. 2** (Road Goes
On Forever) [1992]
**BBC Radio I Live In Concert** (Windsong)
[1993]
**Albion Heart** (Multi Media/HTD) [1995]
**Acousticity** (Multi Media/HTD) [1996]
**Best Of 1993-1997** (HTD) [1997]
Also:
**Captured** (Magnum/HTD)
**Demi Paradise** (HTD)
(Also see Ashley Hutchings)

**ALTAN**
Donegal, Ireland. **Mairead Ni Mhaonaigh** (v,
Fi); **Ciaran Curran** (Bz); **Daithi Sproule** (g);
**Ciaran Tourish** (Fi); **Dermot Byrne** (Acc);
**Jimmy Higgins** (Bod). Alumnus: **Frankie
Kennedy** (Fl, Tw), died on Sept. 19, 1994.

**Albert Fry** (Gael-Linn) [c1980] as Mairead
Ni Mhaonaigh & Frankie Kennedy
**Ceol Aduaidh** (Gael-Linn) [1983] as
Mairead Ni Mhaonaigh & Frankie Kennedy
**Altan** (Green Linnet) [1987]
**Horse With A Heart** (Green Linnet) [1989]
**The Red Crow** (Green Linnet) [1990]
**Harvest Storm** (Green Linnet) [1991]
**Island Angel** (Green Linnet) [1993]
**Ceol Aduaidh** (Green Linnet) [1994]
**First Ten Years 1986-1995** (Green Linnet)
[1995]
**Blackwater** (Virgin) [1996]
**Best Of Altan** (Green Linnet) [1997]
**Runaway Sunday** (Virgin) [1997]

**ANAM**
Dublin Ireland/Edinburgh, Scotland. **Brian o
hEadhra** (v, g, Bod); **Aimeé Leonard**

(v, Bod); **Treasa Harkin** (Bacc); **Neil Davey** (m, Bz).

**Anam** (Ceirnini Anam) [1994]
**Saoirse** (Ceirnini Anam) [1995]
**First Footing** (JVC) [c1996]
**Riptide** (JVC) [1998]

## ANAO ATAO
Cornwall, England. **Kyt Le Nen Davey** (m, Acc, Bo, Tw); **Soazig Le Nen Davey** (g, Pc); **Sterenn Le Nen Davey** (Fl); **Maela Le Nen Davey** (Cl, Bo, Pc). ALSO LIVE: **Andy Davey** (Bp, Fi, Acc, m); **Neil Davey** (m, Fi, Bz, Acc).

**The Hole In The Harper's Head** (Plant Life) [1982] under the name Bucca
**Esoteric Stones** (Kesson) [1994]
**Poll Lyfans** (Kesson) [1998]

## AN TRICKELL
Brittany, France. **Pol Quéffeléant**; **Hervé Quéffeléant**.

**La Harpe Celtique** (Le Chant du Monde) [1990]
**Rowen Tree** (Keltia Musique) [1992]

## DAN AR BRAS
Guitar/vocalist. Brittany, France.

**Stations** (Thélème)
**Irish Reels, Jigs, Airs & Hornpipes** [c 1975]
**Douar Nevez** (Hexagone/Musidisc) [1977]
**Allez dire à la ville** (Hexagone/Musidisc) [1978]
**The Earth's Lament** (Hexagone/Musidisc) [1979]
**Musiques pour les silences à venir/Music For The Silence To Come** (Keltia) [1985]
**Septembre Bleu** (Keltia) [1988]
**Songs** (Keltia) [1990]
**Frontières de sel/Borders Of Salt** (Keltia) [1991]
**Les iles de la mémoire: Compilation** (Keltia) [1992]
**Reve de Siam (Original Film Soundtrack)** (Keltia) [1992]
**Xavier Grall chanté par Dan Ar Braz** (Keltia) [1992]
**Acoustic** (Green Linnet) [1993]

**Songs** (Keltia) [1994]
**Theme For The Green Lands** (Keltia) [1994]
**Kindred Spirit** (Keltia) [1995]
**Islands Of Memories** (Keltia) [1996]
**Music For The Silences To Come** (Shanachie) [1996]
**L'Héritage des Celtes** (Columbia) [1997]
Also:
**L'Héritage des Celtes Live** (Columbia)
**L'Essential en 3 CD** (Keltia)

## ARCADY
Ireland. [c1988] **Johnny "Ringo" McDonagh** (Bod, Pc); **Niamh Parsons** (v); **Patsy Broderick** (p); **Brendan Larrisey** (Fi); **Nicolas Quemenar** (g); **Conor Keane** (Acc). Alumni: **Sharon Shannon** (Acc); **Frances Black** (v); **Paul Doyle**; **Peter O'Hanion**; **Louise Costello**; **Tommy McCarthy**; **Derek Kickey**; **Sean Keane**; **Gerry O'Connor**; **Cathal Hayden**; **Jackie Daly** (Acc).

**After The Ball** (Shanachie/Dara)
**Many Happy Returns** (Shanachie/Dara) [1995]

## ALY BAIN
Fiddle. Lerwick, Shetland Islands, Scotland.

**Aly Bain** (Whirlie)
**Lonely Bird** (Whirlie) [1992]
**Aly Bain and Friends** (Greentrax)
**Aly Bain Meets The Cajuns** (Lismor Folk)
**The Pearl** with Phil Cunningham (Green Linnet) [1995]
**Lonely Bird** (Green Linnet) [1996]
**Follow The Moonstone** (Whirlie) as Aly Bain & the Scottish Ensemble

## BARACHOIS
Prince Edward Island, Canada. **Albert Arsenault** (Fi, Bon, p, v, Pc); **Hélène Bergeron** (Fi, k, g, v); **Louise Arsenault** (Fi, Hmc, g, v); **Chuck Arsenault** (g, v, Tru).

**Barachois** (Iona/House Party Productions)
**Party Acadien** (House Party Productions) [1995]

## THE BARRA MACNEILS
Sydney Mines, Cape Breton, Nova Scotia,

Canada. **Stewart MacNeil** (v, Acc, k, Tw, Fl, g); **Sheumas MacNeil** (p, k, v); **Kyle MacNeil** (Fi, g, m, v); **Lucy MacNeil** (v, Bod, Ceh, v, Vla, Fi).

**The Barra MacNeils** (*Mercury/Celtic Aire) [1986]
**Rock In The Stream** (*Mercury/Celtic Aire) [1989]
**Timeframe** (*Mercury/Celtic Aire) [1991]
**Closer To Paradise** (Celtic Aire/Mercury) [1993]
**The Traditional Album** (Celtic Aire/Mercury/Iona) [1994]
**The Question** (Celtic Aire/Mercury) [1995]
**Until Now** (Celtic Aire) [1997]

### BATTLEFIELD BAND
Glasgow, Scotland. **Alan Reid** (k, v, Ha); **John McCusker** (Fi, m, Cit, Tw, Pw, k); **Mike Katz** (Bp, Pw, Tw, Pi, Bg, g); **Davy Steele** (v, g, Cit). Alumni: **Brian McNeill** (Fi); **Alistair Russell** (g, v); **Iain MacDonald** (Hp, Fl, Tw, Pw).

**Battlefield Band** (Temple) [1977]
**At The Front** (Temple) [1978]
**Stand Easy & Preview** (Temple) [1979]
**Home Is Where The Van Is** (Temple/Flying Fish) [1981]
**The Story So Far...** (Temple/Flying Fish) [1982]
**There's A Buzz** (Temple) [1982]
**Anthem For The Common Man** (Temple) [1984]
**On The Rise** (Temple) [1986]
**Music In Trust V. 1** (Temple) [1986] with Alison Kinnaird
**After Hours — Forward to Scotland's Past** (Temple) [1987]
**Celtic Hotel** (Temple) [1987]
**Music In Trust V. 2** (Temple) [1988] with Alison Kinnaird
**Home Ground - Live From Scotland** (Temple) [1989]
**New Spring** (Temple) [1991]
**Quiet Days** (Temple) [1992]
**Stand Easy & Preview** (Temple) [1994]
**Battlefield Band** (Temple) [1994]
**At The Front** (Temple) [1994]
**Threads** (Temple) [1995]

**Across The Borders** (Temple) [1997]
**The Sunlit Eye** (Temple) [1997] Alan Reid solo album
**Live Celtic Folk Music** (Munich) [1998] 1980 Live Concert at the Winterfolk Festival

### DEREK BELL
Harp/multi-instrumentalist. Belfast, Ireland. Member of The Chieftains.

**Carolan's Receipt** (Shanachie/Claddagh) [1975]
**Carolan's Favourite, Vol. 2** (Claddagh) [1980]
**Derek Bell Plays With Himself** (Claddagh) [1981]
**Derek Bell's Musical Ireland** (Shanachie/Claddagh) [1982]
**From Singing To Swing** (Ogham) [1984]
**Ancient Music for The Irish Harp** (Claddagh) [1989]
**The Mystic Harp: Music In The Celtic Tradition by J. Donald Walters** with J. Donald Walters (Crystal Clarity) [1996]
**A Celtic Evening with Derek Bell - Live At The Mountain View Center For The Performing Arts** with Mairéid Sullivan (Clarity Sound & Light) [1997]

### MARTYN BENNETT
Fiddle/Pipes. Newfoundland, Canada/Kingussie, Scotland.

**Martyn Bennett** (Eclectic Records) [1996]
**Bothy Culture** (Rykodisc) [1997]

### MARY BERGIN
Tin whistle. Ireland.

*Feadoga Stain*: **Traditional Music On The Tin Whistle** (Gael Linn)

### FRANCES BLACK
Vocalist. Dublin, Ireland.

**The Black Family** (*Rego/Dara) [1986] with The Black Family
**Time For Touching Home** (Dara) [1989] with The Black Family
**Frances Black & Kieran Cross** (CBM) [1992]
**Talk To Me** (*Celtic

Heartbeat/Atlantic/Dara) [1994]
**All The Lies That You Told Me** (Dara EP) [1994]
**The Sky Road** (*Celtic Heartbeat/Atlantic/Dara) [1995]
**The Sky Road** (Dara EP) [1995]
**Once You Said You Loved Me** (Dara EP) [1995]
**The Smile On Your Face** (Dara) [1997]
**Stranger On The Shore** (Dara EP) [1997]

## MARY BLACK
Vocalist. Dublin, Ireland.

**General Humbert** (Dolphin) [1975]
**General Humbert II** (Dolphin) [1978]
**Mary Black** (*Gift Horse/Dara) [1982]
**Collected** (Dara) [1984]
**Without The Fanfare** (*Gift Horse/Dara) [1985]
**The Black Family** (*Rego/Dara) [1986] with The Black Family
**By The Time It Gets Dark** (Dara) [1987]
**No Frontiers** (Curb/Grapevine) [1989]
**Babes In The Wood** (Curb/Grapevine) [1991]
**The Collection** (Grapevine) [1992]
**The Holy Ground** (Curb/Grapevine) [1993]
**Looking Back** (Curb) [1995]
**Circus** (Curb/Grapevine) [1996]
**Shine** (Curb/Grapevine) [1997]
Also:
**The Best Of Mary Black** (Curb)
**Uncollected** (Gift Horse)

## LUKA BLOOM
Singer/songwriter. Newbridge, County Kildare, Ireland. Née Barry Moore.

**Treaty Stone** (Mulligan) [1978] as Barry Moore
**In Gronigen** with Eamon Murray [1980] as Barry Moore
**No Heroes** (Ruby/WEA/Warner) [1982] as Barry Moore
**Luka Bloom** (Mystery) [1988]
**Riverside** (Reprise) [1990]
**Acoustic Motorbike** (Reprise) [1992]
**First Bloom** (Blue Knight) [1992] Live Swedish radio show
**Turf** (Reprise) [1994]

## BOHINTA
Malvern, England. **Martin Furey** (v); **Aine Furey** (v).

**Sessions** (aarde) [1997]

## THE BOTHY BAND
Ireland. **Paddy Keenan** (Up); **Triona Ni Dhomhnaill** (v, k); **Micheal O'Dhomnaill** (v, g); **Matt Molloy** (Fl); **Donal Lunny** (g); **Kevin Burke** (Fi). Alumni: **Tony MacMahon** (Acc); **Paddy Glackin** (Fi); **Tommy Peoples** (Fi).

**Bothy Band 1975** (*Green Linnet/Mulligan) [1975]
**Old Hag You Have Killed Me** (*Green Linnet/Mulligan) [1976]
**Out Of The Wind, Into The Sun** (*Green Linnet/Mulligan) [1977]
**After Hours — Live In Paris** (*Green Linnet/Mulligan) [1979]
**Best Of Bothy Band** (*Green Linnet/Mulligan) [1981]
**Live In Concert** (Green Linnet/Windsong) [1994]

## BOURNE & MCLEOD
Canada. **Bill Bourne; Alan McLeod**.

**Dance & Celebrate** (Attic)
**Moonlight Dancers** (Attic)

## BOYS OF THE LOUGH
Scotland/Ireland. [1967] **Aly Bain** (Fi);

Cathal McConnell (Fl, Tw, v); **Dave Richardson** (m, Cit, Ec, Bacc): **Brendan Begley** (Acc); **Garry O'Briain** (g, Mc, p). Alumni: **Tom Anderson; Willie Johnson; John Coakley** (Fi, Acc); **Christy O'Leary** (Up, Tw, Mo, v); **Chris Newman** (g); **Mike Whelans** (g, v); **Dick Gaughan; Robin Morton; Tich Richardson** (g).

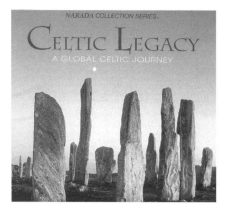

**Boys Of The Lough** (Shanachie/Trailer) [1972]
**Second Album** (Rounder/Trailer) [1973]
**Live At Passim's** (Philo/Transatlantic) [1974]
**Lochaber No More** (Philo/Transatlantic) [1976]
**The Piper's Broken Finger** (Philo/Transatlantic) [1976]
**Good Friends - Good Music** (Philo/Transatlantic) [1977]
**Wish You Were Here** (Flying Fish/Transatlantic) [1978]
**Regrouped** (Flying Fish/Topic) [1980]
**In The Tradition** (Flying Fish/Topic) [1981]
**Open Road** (Flying Fish/Topic) [1983]
**To Welcome Paddy Home** (Shanachie/Lough) [1985]
**Far From Home - Live** (Shanachie/AUK) [1986]
**Farewell and Remember Me** (Shanachie/Lough) [1987]
**Sweet Rural Shade** (Shanachie/Lough) [1988]
**Live At Carnegie Hall** (Sage Arts/Lough) [1992]
**The Fair Hills Of Ireland** (Sage Arts/Lough) [1992]
**The Day Dawn** (Lough) [1994]
**A Midwinter's Night Dream** (Blix Street Records) [1996]
**The Boys Of The Lough** (Philo/Rounder) [1997]

**PAUL BRADY**
Singer/songwriter/guitar/piano. Strabane, County Tyrone, Northern Ireland.

**Andy Irvine/Paul Brady** (*Green Linnet/Mulligan) [1976]
**Welcome Home Kind Stranger** [1978]
**Hard Station** (Mercury) [1981]
**True For You** (Mercury)
**Back To The Centre** (Mercury)
**Primitive Dance** (Mercury)
**Trick Or Treat** (Fontana/Mercury) [1991]
**Songs And Crazy Dreams** (Fontana/Mercury) [1993]
**Spirits Colliding** (Mercury) [1995]

**BRAKIN' TRADITION**
Nova Scotia, Canada. **Cyril MacPhee** (v, g); **Doug Sampson** (g); **Scott MacDonald** (v, Bg, g, d).

**Music Man** [1992]
**Powerfolk** [1993]
**Presence In The Past** [1995]
**Matthew's Voyage** [1997]

**KEVIN BURKE**
Fiddle. London, England/Ireland.

**Sweeney's Dream** (Folkways) [1977]
**If The Cap Fits** (Green Linnet) [1978]
**Promenade** with Micheal O Domhnaill (Green Linnet) [1979]
**Eavesdropper** (Green Linnet) [1981]
**Portland** with Micheal O Domhnaill (Green Linnet) [1982]
**Up Close** (Green Linnet) [1984]
**Funny Reel** (Shanachie) [1985]

**JOHN ALLAN CAMERON**
Guitarist/vocalist/storyteller. Glencoe Station, Cape Breton, Nova Scotia, Canada.

**Here Comes John Allan Cameron** (Apex/Arc) [1969]
**Minstrel of Cranberry Lane** (Apex/Arc) [1973]

Get There By Dawn (Columbia) [1975]
**Weddings, Wakes & Other Things**
(Columbia) [1976]
**Lord Of The Dance** (Columbia) [1977]
**Free Born Man** (Glencoe) [1987]
**Good Times** (Freedom) [1990]
**Wind Willow** (Margaree Sound) [1991]
**Classic John Allan, Vol. 1** (Margaree
Sound) [1991]
**Classic John Allan, Vol. 2** (Margaree
Sound) [1991]
**Classic John Allan, Vol. 3** (Margaree
Sound) [1995]
**Glencoe Station** (Margaree Sound) [1996]

## CAPERCAILLIE
Oban, Scotland. **Karen Matheson** (v);
**Manus Lunny** (Bz); **Charlie McKerron** (Fi);
**John Saich** (Bg); **Donald Shaw** (k, Acc).

**Cascade** (Taynuilt/Etive) [1984]
**Crosswinds** (Green Linnet) [1984]
**The Blood Is Strong** (Survival) [1988]
**Sidewaulk** (Green Linnet) [1989]
**Delirium** (Survival) [1992]
**A Prince Among Islands** (Survival - EP)
[1992]
**Get Out** (Survival/Green Linnet) [1992]
**Secret People** (Survival/Green Linnet)
[1993]
**Capercaillie** (Survival) [1994]
**To The Moon** (Survival/Green Linnet)
[1995]
**The Dreaming Sea** (Survival) [1996] Karen
Matheson solo album
**Beautiful Wasteland** (Survival) [1997]

## MARTIN CARTHY
Guitarist, vocalist. Hatfield, Hertfordshire,
England.

**Skin and Bone** with Dave Swarbrick (Green
Linnet/Topic) [1992]
**The Collection** (Green Linnet) [1993]
**Life And Limb** with Dave Swarbrick (Green
Linnet)

## PAULINE CATO
Northumbrian pipes. Northumberland,
England.

**The Wansbeck Piper** (Cato) [1992]
**Changing Tides** with Tom McConville
(Cato) [1994]

## THE CELTIC CONNECTION
Newfoundland, Canada. [1992] **Glen
Harvey** (g, v); **Scott Graham** (g, v); **Jennifer
Trainor** (g, v); **Barry Kenny** (Bg); **Shawn
Sullivan** (d).

**Calvert's Dream** (Independent) [1994]
**Forever** (Quality Music) [1995]
**Celtic Connection** (Popular/Warner) [1997]

## CEOLBEG
Scotland. **Rod Patterson** (v, g); **Peter Boond**
(Fl, Tw, Cit, v); **Mike Katz** (Hp, Tw, Bg);
**Colin Matheson** (k, g, Acc, m, v); **Wendy
Stewart** (Ha, Con, v); **Jim Walker** (d, Pc).
Alumnus: **Davy Steele** (v, g, Bz, Bod); **Gary
West** (Hp).

**Not The Bunnyhop** (Greentrax) [1990]
**Seeds To The Wind** (Greentrax) [1992]
**An Unfair Dance** (Greentrax) [1993]
**Ceolbeg 5** (Greentrax) [1996]

## CHERISH THE LADIES
New York, U.S.A. [1985]. **Joanie Madden**
(Fl, Tw, v); **Mary Coogan** (g, m, Bj); **Mary
Rafferty** (Acc, Hw); **Donna Long** (p, Tw,
Hw); **Siobhan Egan** (Fi, Bod, Hw); **Aoife
Clancy** (v, g, Bod). Alumni: **Cathie Ryan;
Winifred Horan; Maureen Doherty
Macken.**

**Cherish The Ladies** (Shanachie 79053)
[1985]
**Fathers And Daughters** (Shanachie 79054)
[c 1986]
**The Back Door** (Green Linnet 1119) [1992]

Out And About (Green Linnet 1134)
[1993]
New Day Dawning (Green Linnet 1175)
[1996]
Live! (Big Mammy) [1997]
One And All: The Best Of Cherish The
Ladies (Green Linnet 1187) [1998]
Threads Of Time (BMG Classics/RCA)
[1998]

## THE CHIEFTAINS
Dublin, Ireland. **Paddy Moloney** (Up, Tw);
**Martin Fay; Sean Keane** (Fi); **Derek Bell**
(Ha, p); **Kevin Conneff** (Bod, v); **Matt
Molloy** (Fl). Alumni: **Sean Potts** (Tw);
**Barney McKenna; Larry Tracey** (v); **Paidi
Ban O Broin** (Fl, Sd); **Michael Tubridy** (Fl);
**Davy Fallon** (Bod); **Peader Mercier** (Bod);
**Michael O'Halun** (Tw).

The Chieftains 1 (Shanachie/Claddagh)
[1963]
The Chieftains 2 (Shanachie/Claddagh)
[1969]
The Chieftains 3 (Shanachie/Claddagh)
[1971]
The Chieftains 4 (Shanachie/Claddagh)
[1974]
The Chieftains 5
(Island/Shanachie/Claddagh) [1975]
The Chieftains 6-Bonaparte's Retreat
(Island/Shanachie/Claddagh) [1976]
Barry Lyndon Soundtrack (Warner Bros.)
[1976]
The Chieftains Live!
(Island/Shanachie/Claddagh) [1977]
The Chieftains 7 (Columbia/Claddagh)
[1977]
The Chieftains 8 (Columbia/Claddagh)
[1978]
The Chieftains 9-Boil The Breakfast Early
(Columbia/Claddagh) [1979]
The Chieftains 10-Cotton-Eyed Joe
(Shanachie/Claddagh) [1981]
The Year Of The French w/The RTE
Concert Orchestra (Shanachie/Claddagh)
[1982]
The Grey Fox Soundtrack (DRG) [1984]
The Chieftains In China [Claddagh] [1985]
Music From 'The Ballad Of The Irish
Horse' (Shanachie/Claddagh) [1986]
Celtic Wedding (RCA Victor) [1987]

James Galway and The Chieftains In
Ireland [1987]
Irish Heartbeat: Van Morrison & The
Chieftains (Mercury) [1988]
The Tailor Of Gloucester w/Meryl Streep
[1988]
A Chieftains Celebration (RCA Victor)
[1989]
Over The Sea To Skye - Celtic Connection
w/James Galway (U.K. - RCA) [1990]
Another Country (RCA Victor) [c 1991]
Bells Of Dublin (RCA Victor) [1991]
Reel Music: The Film Scores (RCA) [1991]
The Chieftains & Friends: An Irish
Evening - Live At The Grand Opera
House, Belfast w/Roger Daltry and Nanci
Griffith (RCA Victor) [1992]
Best Of The Chieftains (Legacy) [1992]
The Magic Of The Chieftains (MCTC)
[1992]
The Celtic Harp - A Tribute To Edward
Bunting (RCA Victor) [1993]
The Long Black Veil (RCA Victor) [1995]
Film Cuts (RCA Victor) [1995]
Santiago (RCA Victor) [1996]

## CLAN ALBA
Ireland. **Dick Gaughan; Mary MacMaster;
Brian McNeil; Fred Morrison; Patsy
Seddon; Davy Steele; Mike Travis; Dave
Tulloch.**

Clan Alba (Clan Alba Productions) [1995]

## THE CLANCY BROTHERS
Carrick-on-Suir, Ireland. **Liam Clancy; Tom
Clancy; Paddy Clancy.**
Christmas [1969]

Greatest Hits (Vanguard) [1987/1991]
Live with Robbie O'Connell (Vanguard)
[1988]
The Boys Won't Leave The Girls Alone
(Shanachie) [1989]
Tunes 'N' Tales Of Ireland with Robbie
McConnell (Folk Era) [1988/1996]
Irish Drinking Songs with The Dubliners
(Legacy) [1993]
Clancy Brothers Christmas (Sony Special
Products) [1993]
Clancy Brothers & David Hammond
(K-Tel) [1996]

Irish Folk Song Favourites (Madacy) [1996]
Christmas With The Clancy Brothers
(Columbia) [1997]

## THE CLANCY BROTHERS & TOMMY MAKEM
Ireland. **Liam Clancy; Tom Clancy; Paddy
Clancy; Tommy Makem.**

The Lark In The Morning - Liam Clancy,
Tommy Makem, Family &

Friends (Tradition) [c 1956]
Rising Of The Moon: Irish Songs Of
Rebellion (Tradition) [1957]
Come Fill Your Glass With Us: Irish Songs
Of Drinking & Blackguarding (Tradition)
[1959]
The Clancy Brothers And Tommy Makem
(Tradition) [1961]
In Person At Carnegie Hall (Columbia)
[1963]
Live At The National Concert Hall
(Shanachie) [1987]
The Makem & Clancy Collection
(Shanachie) [1987]
Tommy Makem & Liam Clancy
(Shanachie) [1987]
Two For The Early Dew (Shanachie)
[1987]
In Concert (Shanachie) [1987]
We've Come A Long Way (Shanachie)
[1987]
Hearty & Hellish (Shanachie) [1989]
Irish Folk Songs And Airs (Bescol) [1992]
Luck Of The Irish (Legacy) [1992]
Irish Songs (Laserlight ) [1993]
Irish Songs Of Rebellion (Laserlight) [1993]
Wrap The Green Flag (Legacy) [1994]
Ain't It Grand Boys: A Collection Of
Unissued Gems (Legacy) [1995]
The Clancy Brothers and Tommy Makem
(Tradition/Rykodisc) [1996]
Home To Ireland: 28 Irish Favorites
(Madacy) [1996]
28 Irish Pub Songs (Madacy) [1996]
Reunion (Shanachie)
Songs Of Ireland And Beyond (Legacy)
[1997]
Best Of The Clancy Brothers (Vanguard)
[1998]

ALSO
Spontaneous Performance (Columbia)
Irish Songs Of Drinking And Rebellion
(Bescol)
In Ireland (Columbia)
In Concert (Columbia)

## CLANNAD
Gweedore, County Donegal, Ireland. [c1968]
**Maire Ni Bhraonain/Maire Brennan** (v,
Ha); **Ciaran Bhraonain/Ciaran Brennan**
(Bg, p, v); **Noel O Dugain/Noel Duggan** (g,
v); **Padraig O Dugain/Padraig Duggan** (m,
g, v). Alumni: **Eithne Ni Bhraonain (Enya)**
(v, k); **Pol Bhraonain/Pol Brennan**
(Fl, g, Pc).

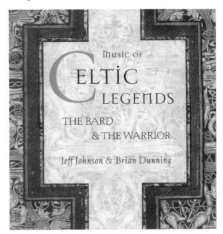

Clannad (Phillip) [1973]
Clannad 2 (*Shanachie/Gael Linn) [1975]
Dulaman (*Shanachie/Gael Linn) [1976]
Clannad In Concert (*Shanachie/Ogham)
[1978]
Cran Ull (Tara) [1978]
Fuaim (*Atlantic/Tara) [1982]
Magical Ring (RCA) [1983]
Legend (RCA) [1984]
Macalla (RCA) [1985]
Sirius (RCA) [1987]
Clannad In Concert (Shanachie) [1987]
The Collection (K-Tel) [1987]
Past Present (RCA) [1989]
The Angel And The Soldier Boy (RCA)
[1989]

**Rogha: The Best Of Clannad 1982-89**
(RCA) [1989]
**Atlantic Realm** (RCA) [1990]
**Anam** (RCA) [1990]
**Maire** (Atlantic/RCA) [1992] Maire
Brennan solo
**Banba** (Atlantic/RCA) [1993]
**Trisan** - Pol Brennan solo with Guo Yue, Joji
Hirota (Realworld/Caroline) [1993]
**Clannad Themes** (Celtic Heartbeat) [1995]
**Lore** (Atlantic) [1996]
**Perfect Time** (Epic/Word) [1998] Maire
Brennan solo

## MICHAEL COLEMAN
Fiddle. County Sligo, Ireland/U.S.A.

**Michael Coleman, 1891-1945** (Viva
Voce/Gael Linn)

## RITA CONNOLLY
Vocalist. Dublin, Ireland.

**Granuaile** - Music from Shaun Davey (Tara)
[1985]
**Rita Connolly** (Tara) [1992]
**Valparaiso** (Tara) [1995]

## J.P. CORMIER
Fiddle. Northern Ontario,
Canada/Cheticamp, Cape Breton, Nova
Scotia, Canada.

**Fiddle Album** (Independent) [1990]
**Return To The Cape** (Borealis/Main Tripp)
[1995]
**Another Morning** (Iona/Borealis) [1997]

## THE CORRS

Dundalk, Ireland. **Jim Corr** (k, g, v); **Andrea
Corr** (v, Tw); **Caroline Corr** (d, Bod, v);
**Sharon Corr** (Vln, v).

**Forgiven, Not Forgotten** (Atlantic) [1995]
**Live** (Atlantic) [1996]
**Talk On Corners** (143/Atlantic) [1997]

## THE CORRIES
Scotland. **Ronnie Brown** (g, v); **Roy
Williamson** (v, g, Con, Bod, Hmc, m) - died
on Aug. 12, 1990. Alumni: **Paddie Bell** (v);
**Bill Smith** (g, v).

**The Corrie Folk Trio with Paddie Bell**
(Elektra/Waverley) [1965] as The Corrie Folk
Trio With Paddie Bell
**The Promise Of The Day**
(Elektra/Waverley) [1965] as The Corrie Folk
Trio with Paddie Bell
**Those Wild Corries** (Fontana) [1966] as The
Corrie Folk Trio
**The Corrie Folk Trio** (Fontana) [1966]
**Bonnet, Belt And Sword** (Fontana) [1967]
as The Corries
**Kishmul's Galley** (Fontana) [1968]
**The Corries In Concert** (Fontana) [1969]
**Scottish Loves Songs** (Fontana) [1969]
**In Retrospect** (EMI Talisman) [1970] as The
Corrie Folk Trio with Paddie Bell
**Strings And Things** (Columbia/Fiesta/EMI)
[1970]
**Sound The Pibroch** (EMI) [1972]
**"Live"A Live O** (Contour) [1972]
**A Little Of What You Fancy** (EMI) [1973]
**These Are . . . The Corries** (Philips) [1974]
**These Are . . . The Corries - The Skye
Boat Song, Vol. 2** (Philips) [1974]
**Cam' Ye By Atholl** (Philips) [1974]
**Live At The Royal Lyceum Theatre,
Edinburgh** (Columbia/Fiesta/EMI) [1976]
**The Very Best Of The Corries**
(*EMI/Phonodisc) [1976]
**Peat Fire Flame** (Dara) [1977]
**Live From Scotland, Vol. 1** (Dara) [1977]
**Live From Scotland, Vol. 2** (Dara) [1977]
**Live From Scotland, Vol. 3** (Dara) [1977]
**Live From Scotland, Vol. 4** (Dara) [1977]
**Spotlight On The Corries** (Phonogram)
[1977]
**16 Scottish Favourites** (EMI) [1979]
**Stovies** (Dara) [1980)
**A Man's A Man** [1980]
**The Corries** (Ideal) [1980]
**The Dawning Of The Day** (Dara) [1982]
**Love From Scotland** (Dara) [1983]
**Scotland Will Flourish** (Dara) [1985]
**The Corries Collection** (Dara/Lismor)
[1986]
**Legends Of Scotland** [1986]
**Barrett's Privateers** (Dara) [1987]
**The Best Of The Corries** (Pickwick) [1987]
**The Corries: The Compact Collection**
(Lismor) [1988]
**The Bantam Cock Rides Again** (Dara)

Barrett's Privateers (Dara)
The Bonnie Blue (Dara)
Flower Of Scotland (BBC) [1990]
The Corries (EMI) [1991]
The Silver Collection 1966-1991
(Moidart) [1991]
Scots Wha Hae - Battle Songs Of Scotland
with Ronnie Browne (Moidart) [1993]
Bonnet, Belt And Sword (B.G.O.) [1995]
In Concert/Scottish Love Songs
(B.G.O.) [1995]
Also:
Roy Williamson - The Long Journey Home
(Moidart)
Those Wild Corries/Kishmul's Galley
(B.G.O.)
Very Best Of The Corries - 18 Fabulous
Tracks (CFP)

MARY COUGHLAN
Vocalist. County Galway, Ireland.

Tired And Emotional (WEA) [1985]
Under The Influence (WEA) [1987]
Uncertain Pleasures (WEA) [1990]
Sentimental Killer (WEA) [1992]
Love For Sale (Demon) [1993]
Love Me Or Leave Me - Best Of Mary
Coughlan
Live In Galway (Big Cat) [1996]
After The Fall (Big Cat/V2) [1997]

JOHNNY CUNNINGHAM
Fiddle. Edinburgh, Scotland.

Thoughts From Another World
(Shanachie/Highway)
Fair Warning (Green Linnet)

PHIL CUNNINGHAM
Accordion/fiddle. Edinburgh, Scotland.

Airs & Graces (Green Linnet/REL) [1984]
The Palomino Waltz (Green Linnet) [1989]

PHIL CUNNINGHAM AND
ALY BAIN

The Pearl (Whirlie) [1994]

PHIL AND JOHN CUNNINGHAM

Against The Storm (Shanachie/Highway)
[1980]

PHIL CUNNINGHAM, ANDY M.
STEWART AND MANUS LUNNY

Fire In The Glen (Shanachie) [1986]

TRACEY DARES
Piano/keyboardist. Marion Bridge, Cape
Breton, Nova Scotia, Canada.

Crooked Lake (CBC Maritimes/EMI Music
Canada/Ground Swell) [1994]

SHAUN DAVEY
Composer/Musician. Belfast, Northern
Ireland.

The Relief Of Derry Symphony (Tara)
[1990]
The Brendan Voyage: Composed by
Shaun Davey (Tara) [1991]
The Pilgrim (Tara)
Granuaile (Tara)

DEAF SHEPHERD
Scotland. Rory Campbell (Hp, Tw);
Marianne Curran (Fi); Clare McLaughlin
(Fi); John Morran (v); Malcolm Stitt (Bz,
Bp, g).

Ae Spark O Nature's Fire (Greentrax)
[1996]
Synergy (Greentrax) [1997]

DEANTA
Antrim/Derry, Ireland. Mary Dillon (v);
Clodagh Warnock (Bz, Fi, Bod); Deidre
Havlin (Fl, Tw); Rosie Mulholland (k, Fi);
Eoghan O'Brien (g, Ha); Kate O'Brien
(Fi, Vla).

Deanta (Green Linnet) [1993]
Ready For The Storm (Green Linnet)
[1994]
Whisper Of A Secret (Green Linnet) [1997]

DE DANNAN
Ireland. [1972] Alec Finn (g, Bz); Frankie
Gavin (Fi, F, Tw, p); Tommy Flemming (v);
Colm Murphy (Bod); Derek Hickey (Bacc).
Alumni: Delores Keane (v); Maura
O'Connell (v) Mary Black (v); Johnny
"Ringo" McDonagh (Bod, Bon, Pc); Charlie
Piggott (Bj, Tw, Acc); Jackie Daly (Bacc);
Mairtin O'Connor (Bacc); Aidan Coffey

(Bacc); **Brendan O'Regan** (g); **Caroline Lavelle** (Cel); **Eleanor Shanley** (v).

**De Dannan** (Polydor) [1975]
**Selected Jigs, Reels & Songs** (Shanachie) [1977]
**The Mist Covered Mountain** (Shanachie) [1980]
**Star Spangled Molly** (Shanachie) [1981]
**Song For Ireland** (*Sugar Hill/Dara) [1983]
**Anthem** (Dara) [1985]
**Ballroom** (Green Linnet) [1987]
**One-Half Set In Harlem** (Green Linnet)
**Jacket Of Batteries** (Green Linnet)
**Best Of De Dannan** (Shanachie)
**Hibernian Rhapsody** (Shanachie) [1996]

**SANDY DENNY**
Vocalist. London, England. Died April 21, 1978 at age 31.

**The North Star Grassman & The Ravens** [1971]
**Sandy** [1972]
**Like An Old-Fashioned Waltz** [1973]
**Rendezvous** [1977]

**DERVISH**
Sligo, Ireland. **Cathy Jordan** (v, Bod, Bon); **Brian McDonagh** (Ma, m, g, v); **Liam Kelly** (Fl, Tw, v); **Shane Mitchell** (Acc); **Michael Holmes** (g, Bz); **Shane McAleer** (Fi). Alumnus: **Martin McGinley** (Fi);

**The Boys Of Sligo** (Sound) [c1991]
**Harmony Hill** (Kells) [1993]
**Playing With Fire** (Kells) [1995]
**At The End Of The Day** (Kells) [1996]
Also:
**Live In Palma** (Whirling)

**PACKIE DOLAN**
Fiddle. County Longford, Ireland/U.S.A.

**Packie Dolan** (Viva Voce)

**THE DUBLINERS**
Dublin, Ireland. **Eamonn Campbell; Sean Cannon; Barney McKenna** (Bj); **Paddy Reilly; John Sheahan** (Fi). Alumni: **Bobby Lynch; Luke Kelly** (v, Bj); **Ciaran Bourke** (v, g, Tw); **Ronnie Drew** (v, g); **Jim McCann.**

**The Hoo'nanny Show** (Waverley) [1964]
**Folk Festival/Festival Folk** (Waverley) [1964]
**Irish Folk Night** (Decca) [1964]
**The Dubliners** (Transatlantic) [1964]
**In Person featuring Ronnie Drew** (Transatlantic EP) [1964]
**The Dubliners In Concert** (Transatlantic) [1965]
**The Dubliners Sampler** (Transatlantic EP) [1965]
**Mainly Barney** (Transatlantic EP) [1966]
**Finnegan Wakes** (Transatlantic) [1966]
**More Of The Dubliners** (Transatlantic EP) [1967]
**The Best Of The Dubliners** (Transatlantic) [1967]
**The New Dubliners** (Major Minor) [1967]
**Seven Drunken Nights** (EMI Starline) [1967]
**A Drop Of The Hard Stuff** (Major Minor) [1967]
**More Of The Hard Stuff** (EMI Starline) [1967]
**Drinkin' And Courtin'** (Major Minor) [1968]
**Seven Deadly Sins** (EMI Starline) [1968]
**At It Again** (Major Minor) [1968]
**Live At The Albert Hall** (Major Minor) [1969]
**A Drop Of The Dubliners** (Major Minor) [1969]
**At Home** (EMI Columbia) [1969]
**It's The Dubliners** (Hallmark) [1969]
**Revolution** (EMI Columbia) [1970]
**The Dubliners In Sessions** (Hallmark reissue) [c1970]
**The Patriot Game** (Hallmark) [1971]
**Hometown** (EMI Columbia) [1972]
**Double Dubliners** (EMI Columbia) [1972]
**Plain & Simple** (Polydor) [1973]
**The Dubliners Live** (Polydor) [1974]
**Now** (Polydor) [1975]
**Parcel O'Rogues** (Polydor) [1976]
**15 Years On** (Polydor) [1977]
**Live At Montreux** (Intercord) [1977]
**Together Again** (Polydor) [1979]
**21 Years On** (RTE) [1983]
**Prodigal Sons** (Polydor/Chyme & Ram) [1983]
**Luke's Legacy** (Chyme & Ram) [1984]

**Live In Carré, Amsterdam**
(Polydor/Kerussell) [1985]
**25th Anniversary Celebration**
(Stylus/Essential) [1987]
**The Dubliners' Dublin** (Harmac) [1988]
**Dublin Songs** (Music Collection
International) [1991]
**30 Years A'Greying** (RTE/Essential) [1992]
**The Dubliners' Dublin** (Castle
Communications re-issue) [1993]
**Original Dubliners** (EMI) [1993]
**Further Along** (Transatlantic) [1996]
**Alive Alive O** (Baycourt) [1997]

## JACKIE DUNN
Fiddle/piano/step-dancer. Antigonish, Nova
Scotia, Canada.

**Dunn To A 'T'** (Independent) [1995]

## SEAMUS EGAN
Multi-instrumentalist: flute, tin whistle,
banjo, mandolin. Hatboro, Pennsylvania,
U.S.A/County Mayo, Ireland.

**Seamus Egan: Traditional Music of Ireland**
(Shanachie) [1986]
**A Week In January** (Shanachie) [1990]
**When Juniper Sleeps** (Shanachie) [1996]

## SEAMUS EGAN, EUGENE
## O'DONNELL & MICK MOLONEY

**Three Way Street** (Green Linnet) [1993]

## SEAMUS ENNIS
Uilleann pipes. Ireland.

**Forty Years Of Irish Piping** (Green Linnet)
[1974[
**Feidlim Tonn Ri's Castle** (Claddagh) [1977]
**The Wandering Minstrel** (Green Linnet)
[1977]
**The Bonny Bunch of Roses** (Tradition)
[1997]

## ENYA
Singer/songwriter/keyboards. Gweedore,
County Donegal, Ireland. Née Eithne Ni
Bhraonain.

**Enya (The Celts)** (*WEA/BBC) [1987]
**Watermark** (Geffen) [1988]

**Shepherd Moons** (WEA) [1991]
**The Christmas EP** (Warner) [1994]
**The Memory Of Trees** (Warner) [1995]
**Paint The Sky With Stars** (Warner) [1997]

## EVANS & DOHERTY
Halifax, Nova Scotia, Canada. **Kevin Evans**
(g, v); **Brian Doherty** (g, v).
**Down The Road** (Meadowlark/Shanachie)
[1985]
**Silver Sea** (Evandoh) [1988]
**Live At The Lunenburg Folk Festival**
(Evandoh) [1988]
**Road Not Taken** (Evandoh) [1991]
**Sailors On The Asphalt Sea** (Evandoh)
[1994]
**Shine On Brighter** with Liam Clancy
(Popular) [1996]
**Galway To Graceland** (Rego) [1996]

## FAIRPORT CONVENTION
England. [1967] **Martin Allcock** (g, m);
**Dave Pegg** (Bg, m, v); **Dave Mattacks** (d);
**Simon Nicol** (v, g); **Ric Sanders** (Vln);
**Chris Leslie** (Bz, m, Vln, v). Alumni:
**Ashley Hutchings** (Bg); **Judy Dyble** (v);
**Iain Matthews** (v); **Richard Thompson** (g,
v); **Martin Lamble** (d); **Sandy Denny** (v);
**Dave Swarbrick** (Fi, v).

**Fairport Convention** (*PolyGram/Polydor)
[1968]
**What We Did On Our Holidays**

(*Hannibal/Island) [1968]
**Unhalfbricking** (*Hannibal/Island) [1969]
**Liege And Lief** (*A&M/Island) [1969]
**Full House - Live** (*Hannibal/Rykodisc) [1970]
**House Full** (*Hannibal/Rykodisc) [1970]
**Angel Delight** (Island) [1971]
**Babbacombe Lee** (Island) [1971]
**History Of Fairport Convention** (Island) [1972]

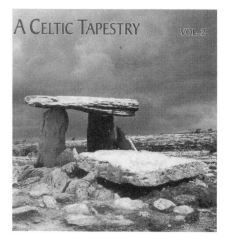

**Fairport Chronicles** [1972]
**Rosie** (Island) [1973]
**Nine** (Island) [1973]
**Live Convention - A Moveable Feast** (Island) [1974]
**Rising For The Moon** (Island) [1975]
**Gottle O'Geer** (Island) [1976]
**Bonny Bunch Of Roses** (Vertigo) [1977]
**Tippler's Tales** (*B.G.O./Vertio) [1978]
**Farewell, Fairwell** (Simons/Terrapin) [1979]
**Encore, Encore** [1979]
**Moat On The Ledge: Live At Broughton Castle** (Woodworm) [1981]
**Gladys' Leap** (*Varrick/Terrapin) [1986]
**Expletive Delighted** (*Varrick/Woodworm) [1986]
**Hey Day: The BBC Radio Sessions 1968-69** (*Hannibal/Rykodisc) [1987]
**In Real Time: Live 87** (Island) [1987]
**The Best Of Fairport Convention** [1988]
**Red And Gold** (Multimedia/New Routes) [1989]

**The Five Seasons** (New Routes) [1990]
**The Woodworm Years** (Woodworm) [1992]
**The 25th Anniversary Concert** (Woodworm) [1994]
**Jewel In The Crown** (Green Linnet/Woodworm) [1995]
**Old. New. Borrowed. Blue.** (Green Linnet/Woodworm) [1996]
**Who Knows Where The Time Goes?** (Woodworm) [1997]
**The Cropredy Box** [1998]
**Birthday Party** [1998]

### FRANK FERREL
Fiddle. Boston, Massachusetts, U.S.A.

**Fiddle Tunes** (Voyager) [1976]
**Down East, Out West** (Voyager) [1980]
**Sage Flower Suite** (Centrum) [1984]
**Yankee Dreams** (Flying Fish) [1990]
**Moxie** (EthnoDisc) [1994]
**Boston Fiddle** (Rounder) [1996]

### FIGGY DUFF
Newfoundland, Canada. [1974] **Noel Dinn** (d, Bod, Dul, p); **Pamela Morgan** (v, g, Tw, k, Syn); **David Panting** (v, m, g); **Derek Pelley** (Bg, v). Alumni: **Arthur Stoyles**; **Philip Dinn**.

**Figgy Duff** (Phonodisc) [1981]
**After The Tempest** (Boot) [1984]
**Weather Out The Storm** [1990]
**Figgy Duff** (Hypnotic/A&M) [1991]
**Downstream** [1993]
**Figgy Duff: A Retrospective 1974-1993** (Amber Music) [1995]

### RAY & ARCHIE FISHER
Scotland. Ray Fisher (v); Archie Fisher (g, v).

**Far Over The Forth** (Topic EP) [1961]

### THE FISHER FAMILY
Scotland. **Archie Fisher** (g, v); **Ray Fisher** (v); **Cindy Fisher** (v); **Joyce Fisher** (v); **Audrey Fisher** (v); **Cilla Fisher** (v).

**Traditional & New Songs From Scotland** (Topic) [1965]

## ARCHIE FISHER
Vocalist/guitarist. Scotland.

**Archie Fisher** (*Celtic Music/Transatlantic) [1968]
**The Fate O'Charlie** with Barbara Dickson and John McKinnon (Trailer) [1969]
**Thro' Recent Years** with Barbara Dickson (Decca) [1970]
**Ofreo** (Decca) [1970]
**Will Ye Gang, Love** (*Green Linnet/Topic) [1976]
**The Man With A Rhyme** (Folk Legacy) [1976]
**Off The Map** (Snow Goose) [1986] as Archie Fisher & Garnet Rogers
**Sunsets I've Galloped Into** (Red House/Greentrax/Snow Goose) [1995]

## RAY FISHER
Vocalist. Scotland.

**The Bonny Birdie** (Trailer) [1972]
**Willie's Lady** (Folk Legacy) [1982]
**Traditional Songs Of Scotland** (Saydisc) [1991]

## CILLA FISHER & ARTIE TREZISE
Scotland/U.S.A. **Cilla Fisher** (v); **Artie Trezise** (g, v).

**Cilla Fisher & Artie Trezise** (Autogram) [1976]
**Balcanqual** (Trailer) [1976]
**For Foul Day & Fair** (Folk Legacy) [1978]
**Cilla & Artie** (Topic) [1979]
**Reaching Out** (Kettle) [1986]
**Scotch Broth** with Jane Fisher & Gary Coupland (Kettle) [1986] as The Singing Kettle
**The Big Green Planet** with Jane Fisher & Gary Coupland (Kettle) [1991] as The Singing Kettle

## FOTHERINGAY
England. **Sandy Denny** (v); **Trevor Lucas** (g, v); **Jerry Donahue** (g); **Gerry Conway** (d); **Pat Donaldson** (b).

**Fotheringay** (Hannibal) [1970]

## FOUR MEN & A DOG
Ireland. [1990] **Cathal Hayden** (Fi); **Gino**

**Lupari** (Bod, Bon, v); **Kevin Doherty** (g, v); **Gerry O'Connor** (Bj, Fi); **Conor Keane** (Acc); **Arty McGlynn** (g). Alumni: **Brian McGrath** (Bj, m); **Mick "Black Dog" Daly** (v); **Donal Murphy** (Acc); **James Blennerhassit** (Bg); **Rod McVeigh** (p).

**Barking Mad** (Green Linnet/Cross Border Media) [1991]
**Shifting Gravel** (Green Linnet/Special Delivery) [1993]
**Doctor A's Secret Remedies** (Transatlantic) [1995]
**Long Roads** (Transatlantic) [1997]

## ALASDAIR FRASER
Fiddle. Clackmannon, Scotland/Nevada City, California, U.S.A.

**Portrait Of A Scottish Fiddler** (*Culburnie/Brownrigg-Canada) [1984]
**Skyedance** with Paul Machlis (Culburnie) [1986]
**The Driven Bow** with Jody Stecher (Culburnie) [1988]
**The Road North** with Paul Machlis (Sona Gaia/Narada) [1989]
**Dawn Dance** (Culburnie) [1995]
**Way Out To Hope Street** with Skyedance (Culburnie) [1997]

## THE FUREYS (aka THE FUREYS AND DAVEY ARTHUR)
Ballyfermont, Dublin, Ireland. **George Furey** (v, g, Ma, Ah, Tw); **Finbar Furey** (v, Up, Bj, Tw, Fl); **Eddie Furey** (g, Ma, m, Hmc, Fi, Bod, v); **Paul Furey** (Acc, Mel, Con, Tw, Bon, Spo, v); **Davey Arthur** (various, v).

**The Cisco Special** [1960]
**Songs Of Woody Guthrie** [1961]
**I Ain't Got No Home** [1962]
**The Dawning Of The Day** (*B.G.O.) [1972] as Finbar and Eddie Furey
**The Sound Of The Fureys And Davey Arthur** (PolyGram Ireland) [1981]
**When You Were Sweet Sixteen** (*Castle Classics) [1982]
**Steal Away** (*Castle/Ritz) [1983]
**In Concert** (Ritz) [1984]
**Golden Days** (K-Tel) [1984]
**At The End Of A Perfect Day** (K-Tel) [1985]

born hothouse flowers

The First Leaves Of Autumn (Ritz) [1986]
The Fureys' Finest (*Castle/Telstar) [1987]
as TF&DA
The Scattering (BMG/Ariola) [1989]
The Fureys Collection (Castle) [1989]
Love Letters (BMG/Ariola) [1990] as Finbar
Furey
The Very Best Of The Fureys And Davey
Arthur (Music Club) [1991]
The Best Of The Fureys And Davey
Arthur (K-Tel) [1991]
Winds Of Change (*Shanachie/Ritz) [1992]
Steal Away (Castle) [1992]
The Best Of The Fureys And Davey
Arthur (Music Club) [1996]
Celtic Collections (K-Tel) [1997] as
TF&DA
Finbar & Eddie Furey/Lonesome Boatman
(*Essential/Castle) [1997]
Also:
May We All Someday Meet Again as The
Fureys
The Collection as TF&DA (Castle)
The Spanish Cloak - Best Of (Pulse) as The
Fureys
Live At Dublin National Stadium
(Emporio)
Best Of Finbar Furey (Entertainment UK)
Traditional Finbar Furey (K-Tel)
Wind And Rain (Nora/K-Tel) as Finbar
Furey
Collection (Castle) as Finbar & Eddie Furey
Finbar & Eddie Furey (K-Tel)

Best Of The Fureys (Telstar)
Seven Claddagh Road (Premier) as The
Fureys

GABERLUNZIE
Scotland. [c1973] Robin Watson; Gordon
Menzies et al Alumni: Jimmy MacDonald;
Robbie Menzies.

Brave Words 'N' Fighting Talk
Gaberlunzie
Freedom's Sword
Scots Wha Ha'e
Wind And Water, Time And Tide
Scotland Again
The Travelling Man
Superstition
Legends
Take The Road
Half Cut In The Highlands
Highland Lines (Lochshore)
Gaberlunzie Live (Lochshore)
Summer Storms
For Auld Lang Syne (Lochshore)
Full Circle
Twa Corbies (Lochshore)

LENNY GALLANT
Singer/songwriter. Rustico, Prince Edward
Island, Canada.

Breakwater (Revenant) [1989]
Believing In Better (Sony Music
Canada/Revenant) [1991]
Land Of The Maya (Oxfam) [1992]
The Open Window (Sony Music Canada)
[1995]
Lifeline (Independent/Tidemark) [1997]

DICK GAUGHAN
Vocalist. Scotland.

No More Forever (Trailer) [1972]
The Boys Of The Lough
(*Shanachie/Trailer) [1973]
The Bonnie Pit Laddie (Topic) [1975]
Kist O'Gold (Trailer) [1976]
The Second Folk Review Record
(Folksound) [1976]
Five Hand Reel (*Black Crow/Rubber)
[1976]
Coppers And Brass (*Green Linnet/Topic)
[1977]

For A' That (*Black Crow/RCA) [1977]
Songs Of Ewan MacColl (Rubber) [1978]
Gaughan (Topic) [1978]
Earl O'Moray (RCA) [1978]
Folk Friends 2 (Folk Freak) [1981]
Handful Of Earth (*Green Linnet/Topic)
[1981]
Parallel Lines with Andy Irvine
(*Appleseed/Folk Freak) [1982]
A Different Kind Of Love Song (Celtic
Music/Folk Freak) [1983]
Songs For Peace (Rounder/Folk Freak)
[1983]
Out Of The Darkness (Fire On The
Mountain) [1984]
Fanfare For Tomorrow (Impetus) [1985]
Live In Edinburgh (Celtic Music) [1985]
True And Bold [1986]
Call It Freedom (Celtic Music) [1988]
Clan Alba (Clan Alba Productions) [1995]
Sail On (Greentrax) [1996]

PADDY GLACKIN
Fiddle. Ireland.

The Whirlwind (Shanachie) [1995]

Rabharta Ceoil In Full Spate (Gael Linn)
[1995]
Straight From The Heart (Gael Linn)
[1995]

GREAT BIG SEA
St. John's, Newfoundland, Canada. [1991]
Bob Hallett (Bacc, Fi, Tw, m, Ma, v); Sean
McCann (g, Tw, Bod, Pc, v); Darrell Power
(Bg, v); Alan Doyle (v, g, m, Bz).

Great Big Sea (Independent) [1992]
Great Big Sea (Warner Music) [1995]
up (Warner Music) [1996]
Play (Warner Music) [1997]

BRUCE GUTHRO
Singer/songwriter. Sydney Mines, Cape
Breton, Nova Scotia, Canada. Also vocalist
for Scottish group Runrig.

Sails To The Wind (Independent) [1994]
Of Your Son (EMI Music Canada) [1998]

GWERZ
Brittany, France. Erik Marchand (v);

Youenn Le Bihan (Bbo); Soig Siberil (g);
Patrick Molard (Bk); Jacky Molard (Fi);
Bruno Caillat (Pc); Alain Genty (Bg).

Musiques Bretonnes de Toujours (Dastum)
[1986]
Au Delà (Escalibur) [1988]
Gwerz Live! (Gwerz Pladden) [1993]
Fest-Noz (Escalibur) [1994] - members of
Gwerz and Kornog

MARTIN HAYES
Fiddle. Maghera, Country Clare, Ireland.

The Shores Of Lough Graney with P.J.
Hayes (Ice Nine) [1990]
Martin Hayes (Green Linnet) [1993]
Under The Moon (Green Linnet) [1995]
Stories From Ireland with Eddie Stack
(Celtic Planet) [1996]
The Lonesome Touch with Dennis Cahill
(Green Linnet) [1997]

JOE HEANEY
Sean nos singer. Carna, Connemara, Ireland.

Irish Traditional Songs In Gaelic and
English (Ossian)
The Best Of Joe Heaney: From My
Tradition (Shanachie) [1997]

NOEL HILL
Concertina. Ireland.

The Irish Concertina - Live (Shanachie)
[1982]
In Knocknagree (Shanachie) [1992]
Noel Hill & Tony MacMahon (Shanachie)
IgGnoc na Grai (Gael Linn) [1995]
Noel Hill & Tony Linnane (Shanachie)
[1996]

JERRY HOLLAND
Fiddle. Boston, USA/Cape Breton, Nova
Scotia, Canada.

Jerry Holland (Rounder) [1976]
Master Cape Breton Fiddler (Boot) [1982]
Lively Steps (Fiddlesticks Music) [1987]
Jerry Holland Solo (Cranford Publications)
[1988]
Jerry Holland (Rounder re-release) [1990]
The New Fiddle (Cho lar-Chonnachta)
[1990]

A Session With Jerry Holland (Fiddlesticks Music) [1990]
Fathers and Sons (Fiddlesticks Music) [1992]
The Fiddlesticks Collection (Green Linnet) [1995]
TBA (Green Linnet) [1998]

## HORSLIPS

Ireland. **Jim Lockhart** (k, Fl, v); **Johnny Fen** (g, v); **Barry Devlin** (Bg, v); **Eamon Carr** (d, Bod, Pc); **Charles O'Connor** (Fi, m, Con, v).

Happy To Meet, Sorry To Part (Homespun) [1972]
The Tain (Homespun) [1973]
Dancehall Sweethearts (Homespun) [1974]
The Unfortunate Cup Of Tea (Homespun) [1975]
Drive The Cold Winter Away (Homespun) [1975]
Horslips Live (Homespun) [1976]
The Book Of Invasions: A Celtic Symphony (Homespun) [1976]
Aliens (Homespun) [1977]
Tracks From The Vault (Homespun) [1977]
The Man Who Built America (Homespun) [1978]
Short Stories, Tall Tales (Homespun) [1979]
The Belfast Gigs - Live At Whitla Hall (Homespun) [1980]
Straight From The Horse's Mouth: The Horslips Story (Outlet) [1989]
Horslips (K-Tel) [1997]

## HOUSE BAND

England. **Ged Foley** (v, g, Np); **Chris Parkinson** (Acc, Hmc, Mel, k); **John Skelton** (Fl, Bo, Tw, Bod); **Roger Wilson** (g, Fi, v). Alumni: **Iain MacLeod** (m, g, v); **Jimmy Young** (Pi, Fl, Tw); **Brian Brooks** (v).

Word Of Mouth (Green Linnet) [1988]
Stonetown (Green Linnet) [1991]
Groundwork (Green Linnet) [1993]
Another Setting (Green Linnet) [1994]
Rockall (Green Linnet) [1996]
October Song (Green Linnet) [1998]

## ASHLEY HUTCHINGS

Bass guitar, vocalist. Southgate, Middlesex, England.

Morris On with Richard Thompson, Dave Mattacks et al (Hannibal) [1972]
The Compleat Dancing Master with John Kirkpatrick (Antilles) [1974]
A Favourite Garland with Shirley Collins [1974]
Son Of Morris On with Judy Dunlop (Harvest) [1976]
Rattlebone and Ploughjack (*B.G.O./Island) [1976]
Guitar Vocal with Richard Thompson [1976]
Kickin' Up The Sawdust (*B.G.O./Harvest) [1977]
An Hour With Cecil Sharp and Ashley Hutchings [1986]
By Gloucester Docks I Sat Down And Wept (EMI) [1987]
A Word In Your Ear [1991]
Twangin' 'N' A-Traddin' (Varese/HTD) [1993] as Ashley Hutchings and Big Beat Combo
Crab Wars As Remembered, Vol. 1 (Dambuster) [1994]
Crab Wars As Remembered, Vol. 2 (Dambuster) [1994]
Crab Wars As Remembered, Vol. 3 (Dambuster) [1994]
The Guv'nor, Vol. 1 (Wildcat/HTD) [1994]
As You Like It - All-Stars Live (Making Waves) [1994]
Sway With Me with Judy Dunlop (Road Goes On Forever) [1996]
The Guv'nor, Vol. 2 (Multi Media/HTD) [1997]
Collection (Mooncrest) [1998]
Also:
The View From Pa's Piano Stool
Guv'nor Big Birthday Bash (HTD)
The Guv'nor, Vol. 3 (HTD)
The Guv'nor, Vol. 4 (HTD)
The History of Ashley Hutchings (Hannibal)
Batter Pudding For John Keats (HTD)

## IAN CAMPBELL FOLK GROUP

Aberdeen, Scotland/Birmingham, England.

Ian Campbell (v); **Lorna Campbell** (v); **Dave Swarbrick** (Fi, Bj); **Dave Pegg** (Bg, m).

**Across The Hills** (Transatlantic) [1964]
**The Ian Campbell Folk Group** (Elektra) [1965]
**Coaldust Ballads** (Transatlantic) [1965]
**The Singing Campbells** (Topic) [1965]
**Rights Of Man** (Elektra) [1966]
**Tam O'Shanter** (Xtra) [1968]
**Something To Sing About** [1972]
**And Another Thing** (Celtic Music) [1995]
**This Is The Ian Campbell Folk Group/Across The Hills** (Essential/Castle) [1996]
**Something To Sing About** (Wooded Hill) [1997]
**Contemporary Campbell/New Impressions** [1998]

## THE INCREDIBLE STRING BAND
Glasgow, Scotland. [1965] Members have included **Robin Williamson; Mike Heron; Clive Palmer; Licorice McKechnie** (v, k, g, Pc); **Rose Simpson** (v, b, Vln, Pc); **Malcolm Le Maistre; Gerald Dott** (k, Fl), among others.

**The Incredible String Band** (Hannibal/Elektra) [1966]
**5000 Spirits Or The Layers Of The Onion** (Hannibal/Elektra) [1967]
**The Hangman's Beautiful Daughter** (Hannibal/Elektra) [1968]
**The Big Huge** (Elektra) [1968]
**Changing Horses** (Hannibal/Elektra) [1969]
**Wee Tam** (Elektra) [1969]
**I Looked Up** (Hannibal/Elektra) [1970]
**U** (Elektra) [1970]
**Relics Of The Incredible String Band** (Elektra) [1971]
**Be Glad For The Song Has No Ending** (Island) [1971]
**Taking Off OST** (Decca) [1971]
**Liquid Acrobat As Regards The Air** (Island) [1971]
**Earth Span** (Edsel/Island ) [1972]
**No Ruinous Feud** (Edsel/Island) [1973]
**Hard Rope And Silken Twine** (Demon/Edsel/Island) [1974]
**Seasons They Change** (Island) [1976]

**On Air - Original BBC Recordings** (Band/Joy) [1994]
**BBC Radio 1 Live In Concert** (Windsong) [1995]
**The Chelsea Sessions 1967** (Pig's Whisker/Resurgence/Blueprint) [1997]

## IN TUA NUA
Dublin, Ireland. **Leslie Dowdall** (v); **Jack Dublin** (Bg); **Ivan O'Shea** (g, v); **Paul Byrne** (d, Pc); **Martin Clancy** (g); **Lovely Previn** (Fi); **Brian O'Briain** (Up, Tw, Sx). Alumni: **Sinead O'Connor** (v, g); **Steve Wickham** (Fi); **Vinnie Kilduff** (Pi, Tw); **Aingela DeBurca** (Fi).

**Vaudeville** (Virgin) [1987]
**Long Acre** (Virgin) [1988]

## THE IRISH DESCENDANTS
St. John's, Newfoundland, Canada. [1990]. **Ronnie Power** (v, g, Tw, Bz); **Eamonn O'Rourke** (Fi, v, m, Bz, g); **Larry Martin** (v, Bg); **Con O'Brien** (g, v); **Gerard Broderick** (v, Bod, Pc). Alumni: **Kathy Phippard** (k); **D'Arcy Broderick** (Fi, Bj, g, Bz).

**Misty Morning Shore** (Independent) [1991]
**Look To The Sea** (Independent/Warner Music Canada) [1993]
**Gypsies & Lovers** (Warner Music Canada) [1994]
**Livin' On The Edge** (Warner Music Canada) [1996]
**Rollin' Home** (Warner Music Canada) [1998]

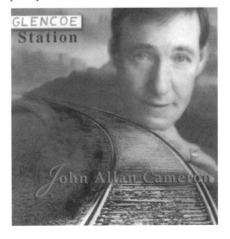

**ANDY IRVINE**
Guitar/mandolin/harmonica. London,
England/Dublin, Ireland.

**Andy Irvine/Paul Brady** (*Green
Linnet/Mulligan) [1976]
**Rainy Sundays... Windy Dreams**
(*Shanachie/Tara) [1980]
**High Kings Of Tara** (*Shanachie/Tara)
[1980]
**Parallel Lines** with Dick Gaughan (Green
Linnet) [1982]
**Rude Awakening** (Green Linnet) [1991]

**EILEEN IVERS**
Fiddle. Bronx, New York, U.S.A.

**Eileen Ivers** (Green Linnet) [1994]
**Wild Blue** (Green Linnet) [1996]
**So Far: The Eileen Ivers Collection 1979-
1995** (Green Linnet) [1997]

**THE JOHNSTONS**
Dublin, Ireland. **Luci Johnston; Adrienne
Johnston; Michael Johnston; Mick Moloney**
(m, Bj); **Paul Brady** (v, g).

**The Johnstons: The Transatlantic Years**
(Transatlantic/Demon) [1994]

**DELORES KEANE**
Vocalist. Galway, Ireland.

**There Was A Maid** (Claddagh) [1978]
**Broken Hearted I'll Wander** w/John

Faulkner (Mulligan) [1979]
**Farewell To Erin** w/ John Faulkner
(Mulligan) [1980]
**The Irish Folk Festival Tour** (Mulligan)
[1980]
**Folk Friends II** (Folk Freak, Germany)
[1981]
**Sail Og Rua** w/ John Faulkner (Gael Linn)
[1983]
**The Keane Family; Muintir Cathain** (Gael
Linn) [1985]
**Delores Keane** (Ringsend Road) [1988]
**Lion In A Cage** (Ringsend Road) [1989]
**Solid Ground** (Shanachie) [1993]
**There Was A Maid** w/the Reel Union with
Peadar Mercier & Mairtin Byrnes
(Claddagh) [1995]
**The Best Of Delores Keane** (Dara) [1997]

**DELORES KEANE &
JOHN FAULKNER**
Ireland. **Delores Keane** (v); **John Faulkner**
(Bz, Fi, g).

**Broken Hearted I'll Wander** [1979]
**Farewell To Eirinn** [1980]
**Sail Og Rua** [1983]

**SEAN KEANE**
Fiddle. County Galway, Ireland. Member of
The Chieftains.

**Gusty's Frolics** (Claddagh) [1975]
**Jig It In Style** (Claddagh) [1977]
**Sean Keane** (*Shanachie/Ogham) [1981]

**SEAN KEANE**
Vocalist. Ireland.

**All Heart, No Roses** (Shanachie) [1993]
**Turn A Phrase** (Kells Music) [1996]

**PADDY KEENAN**
Uilleann pipes. Ireland.

**Poirt a' Phiobaire** (Gael Linn) [1983]
**Paddy Keenan**

**PADDY KEENAN & PADDY GLACKIN**
Ireland. **Paddy Keenan** (Up); **Paddy Glackin**
(Fi).

**Doublin'**

## BRIAN KENNEDY
Vocalist. Belfast, Ireland.

The Great War Of Words (RCA) [1990]
Brian Kennedy (RCA)
A Better Man (RCA) [1997]

## KEVIN BURKE'S OPEN HOUSE
Kevin Burke (Fi); Paul Kotapish (g, Cit, m); Mark Graham (Hmc, Cl, v); Sandy Silva (Sd); Tim O'Brien (m, Bz).

Open House (Green Linnet)
Second Story (Green Linnet) {1994]
Hoof and Mouth (Green Linnet)

## KILBRIDE BROS.
South Wales, U.K. Daniel Kilbride (g); Bernard Kilbride (Fi); Gerard Kilbride (Fi).

Kilbride (Fflach Tradd) [1997]

## ALISON KINNAIRD
Harp. Scotland.

The Harp Key (Crann Nan Teud) —
Alison Kinnaird Plays The Scottish Harp
(Temple) [1978]
The Harper's Gallery (Temple) [1980]
The Harper's Land (Temple) [1983]
The Scottish Harp Played By Alison
Kinnaird (Flying Fish/Temple) [1988]

## ALISON KINNAIRD & CHRISTINE PRIMROSE
Scotland. Alison Kinnaird (Ceh); Christine Primrose (v).

The Quiet Tradition — Music Of The
Scottish Harp, Songs Of The Scottish Gael
(Temple) [1990]

## THE KITCHEN DEVILS
Cape Breton, Nova Scotia, Canada. Ashley MacIsaac's backing group. Scott Long (Bp); Stuart Cameron (g); Ed Woodsworth (Bg); Adam Dowling (d); Andrew Craig (k). Alumnus: Joel Chiasson (k).

## KORNOG
Britanny, France. Christian Lemaitre (Fi); Jean-Michel Veillon (Fl); Soig Siberil (g); Jamie McMenamy (v, Bz).

Première - Live (Green Linnet) [1984]
Ar Seizh Avel (Green Linnet) [1985]
Fest-Noz (Escalibur) [1994] - members of
Kornog and Gwerz

## MARY JANE LAMOND
Kingston, Ontario, Canada/Glendale, Cape Breton, Nova Scotia, Canada. Vocalist.

Bho Thir Nan Craobh/From The Land Of
The Trees (B&R Heritage Enterprises)
[1994]
Suas e! (turtlemusik/A&M) [1997]

## L'ANGE VENT
France. [1991]. Bruno Revillé (Cha. Dha, Bo, Tw, v); Christophe Archan (d, Pc, Tw, v); Eric Vasse (v, Ag); Daniel (Bg); Stéphane Archan (Eg, Ag, Mg, m, v).

Le Sang des Hommes
(Celtirock/Ethnea/Musidisc) [1995]
Les Armes de Bretagne [1997]

## LEAHY
Lakefield, Ontario, Canada. Julie Leahy (v, p, m, Sd); Siobheann Leahy (Bg, p, Fi, v, Sd); Donnell Leahy (Fi, Sd); Maria Leahy (g, p, Fi, Sd, m, v); Frank Leahy (d, Fi, Sd); Agnes Leahy (Sd, p, Fi, v); Doug Leahy (Fi, Sd, Sx); Erin Leahy (p, Fi, Sd, v); Angus Leahy (Fi, Sd, p).

Leahy (Independent) [1996]
Leahy (Virgin) [1997]

## LINDISFARNE
Newcastle, England. [c1969] Billy Mitchell (v); Rod Clements (Sg, m, Fi, Bg); Ray Laidlaw (d); Dave Denhom (g); Marty Craggs (v, Sx); Ian Thomson (Bg). Alumni: Ray "Jacka" Jackson (v, Hmc); Si Cowe (g); Alan Hull (g, v).

Nicely Out Of Tune (Charisma/Virgin)
[1970]
Fog On The Tyne (Charisma/Virgin) [1971]
Dingly Dell (Charisma/Virgin) [1972]
Lindisfarne Live (Charisma) [1973]
Roll On Ruby (Charisma) [1973]
Happy Daze (Warner Bros.) [1974]
Finest Hour (Charisma) [1975]
Back And Fourth (Mercury/Castle) [1978]

Magic In The Air (Mercury/Castle) [1978]
The News (Mercury/Castle) [1979]
Singles Album (Charisma [1981]
Sleepless Nights (LMP/Castle) [1982]
Lindisfarntastic (LMP) [1983]
Dance Your Life Away (LMP) [1984]
C'mon Everybody (Stylus) [1987]
Amigos (Black Crow/Castle) [1989]
Best Of Lindisfarne (Virgin) [1989]
Caught In The Act (Castle) [1992]
Buried Treasures (Virgin) [1992]
Elvis Live On The Moon (Castle) [1993]
Lindisfarne On Tap (Castle) [1994]
Peel Sessions (Dutch East India) [1995]
Another Fine Mess [1996]
Untapped And Acoustic (River City/Park)
[1997]
Run For Home (Music Club) [1997]
Lady Eleanor [1997]
Blues From The Bothy (River City EP)
[1997]
The Cropredy Concert (Mooncrest) [1997]

## LLAN DE CUBEL
Asturias, Spain. [1984] Elias Garcia (Bp);
Fonsu Mielgo (d); Marcos Llope (Fl); Flavio
Rodriguez; Xel Pereda; Simon Bradley.
Alumni: Susi Bello (g); Daniel Lombas
(Pc); Guzman Marques (Fi); J.M. Cano (g);
H. Urquhart (Pi); X.N. Esposito (Pi).

Arpa Celtica (SFA) [1985] with others
Deva (Fono Astur Fa) [1987]
Na Llende (Fono Astur Fa) [1990]
L'Otru Llau De La Mar (Fono Astur Fa)
[1992]
Llan de Cubel IV (Fono Astur Fa) [1995]
Festival InterCeltique De L'Orient- 25 Ans
(Virgin) [1995] with others
Llan de Cubel IV (Iona/Fono Astur Fa)
[1997]

## EWAN MACCOLL
Singer/songwriter/broadcaster/archivist.
Auchterarder, Perthshire, Scotland.

Black And White: Retrospective (Green
Linnet)

## ASHLEY MACISAAC
Fiddle. Creignish, Cape Breton, Nova Scotia,
Canada.

Close To The Floor (Ancient Music) [1992]
A Cape Breton Christmas with Ashley
MacIsaac (Ancient Music) [1993]
Close To The Floor (A&M) [1994]
hi™how are you today? (A&M) [1995]
fine®thank you very much (A&M) [1996]

## DAVE MACISAAC
Guitar/Fiddle/Mandolin/Dobro. Halifax,
Nova Scotia, Canada/Cape Breton, Nova
Scotia, Canada.

Celtic Guitar (Pickin' Productions) [1986]
The Guitar Souls, Live with Scott
Macmillan (Pickin' Productions) [1993]
Nimble Fingers (Pickin' Productions) [1995]

## WENDY MACISAAC
Fiddle. Creignish, Cape Breton, Nova Scotia,
Canada.

The Reel Thing (World) [1994]
That's What You Get (Lochshore) [1996]

## MACKEEL
Pictou County, Nova Scotia, Canada. [1995]
Dane Grant (Hp, Tw, v); Randy MacDonald
(d, Pc, Bod, v); Glenn Gordon (v, g); Fleur
Mainville (Fi); Kevin Brennan (g); Dave
Hoare (Bg).

Plaid (Independent) [1996]
Plaid (turtlemusik/A&M) [1997]

## TALITHA MACKENZIE
Vocalist. U.S.A.

Mouth Music (Rykodisc) [1991] - vocalist
Solas (Shanachie) [1994]
Spiorad (Shanachie) [1996]

## DOUGIE MACLEAN
Singer/songwriter. Dunkeld, Scotland.

C.R.M. [1977]
Caledonia (Plant Life) [1978]
Snaigow (Plant Life) [1979]
On A Wing And A Prayer (Plant Life)
[1982]
Craighe Dhu (Dunkeld) [1983]
Fiddle (Dunkeld) [1984]
Singing Land (Dunkeld) [1985]
Real Estate (Dunkeld) [1988]
Butterstone (Dambuster Music) [1989]

Whitewash (Dunkeld) [1990]
The Search (Dunkeld) [1991]
Indigenous (Dunkeld) [1991]
Sunset Song (Dunkeld) [1993]
Marching Mystery (Dunkeld) [1994]
Tribute (Dunkeld) [1995]
The Dougie MacLean Collection
(Putumayo) [1995]
Riof (Dunkeld) [1997]
Plant Life Years (Osmosys) [1997]

**BUDDY MACMASTER**
Fiddle. Judique, Cape Breton, Nova Scotia,
Canada.

Judique On The Floor (Sea Cape Music)
[1988]
Glencoe Hall (Independent) [1991]

**NATALIE MACMASTER**
Fiddle. Troy, Cape Breton, Nova Scotia,
Canada.

Four On The Floor (Independent) [1989]
Road To The Isle (Independent) [1991]
Fit As A Fiddle (*Rounder/Warner Music
Canada/MacMaster Music Inc.) [1993]
A Compilation (*Rounder/Warner Music
Canada) [1996]
No Boundaries (*Rounder/Warner Music
Canada) [1996]
My Roots Are Showing (Warner Music
Canada) [1998]

**RITA MACNEIL**
Singer/songwriter. Big Pond, Cape Breton,
Nova Scotia, Canada.

Born A Woman (Independent) [1975]
Part Of The Mystery (Big Pond
Productions) [1981]
I'm Not What I Seem (UCCB Press) [1983]
Flying On Your Own (Virgin/Lupins) [1987]
Reason To Believe (Virgin/Lupins) [1988]
Rita (Virigin/Lupins) [1989]
Home I'll Be (Virgin/Lupins) [1990]
Thinking Of You (Virgin/Lupins) [1992]
Once Upon A Christmas (Virgin/Lupins)
[1993]
Volume One - Songs From The Collection
(Virgin/Lupins) [1994]
Porch Songs (EMI Music Canada) [1995]

Joyful Sounds: A Seasonal Collection (EMI
Music Canada) [1996]

**MACTULLAGH VANNIN**
Isle of Man. **David Collister** (Fi); **John
Corlett** (Bod); **Peter Cubberley** (Fl, Lw,
Tw); **Sue Linglee** (g); **Mai Linglee** (Bj, m);
**David Speers** (Bz).

Mactullagh Vannin: Traditional Manx
Music (Dirt Music) [1986]

**TOMMY MAKEM**
Vocalist/multi-instrumentalist/story-teller.
Keady, County Armagh, Ireland.

Songs Of Tommy Makem. (Tradition)
[1961]
An Evening With Tommy Makem
(Shanachie)
Lonesome Waters (Shanachie)
Rolling Home (Shanachie)
Songbag (Shanachie)
Live At The Irish Pavilion (Shanachie)
From The Archives (Shanachie)
Tommy Makem's Christmas (Shanachie)
The Song Tradition (Shanachie) [1998]

**MALICORNE**
France. [1973] **Gabriel Yacoub** (g); **Marie
Yacoub**; **Hughes de Courson**; **Laurent
Vercambre**. Also: **Olivier Zdrzalik**; **Brian
Gulland**; **Jean-Pierre Arnoux**; **Dominique
Regef**; **Patrick LeMercier**; **Michel Le Cam**.

Pierre de Grenoble [1973] - Group with
Gabriel and Marie Yacoub
Malicorne (Gamma/Hexagone) [1974]

**Malicorne** (Hexagone) [1975]
**Almanach** (Gamma) [1976]
**Malicorne** (Hexagone) [1977]
**Quintessence** (Gamma/Hexagone) [c1978]
**L'extraordinaire tour de France** (Ballon
noir/WMD Acousteak) [1978]
**En public** (CBS/WMD Acousteak) [1979]
**Le Bestiaire** (Elektra/WMD Acousteak)
[1979]
**Belançoire en feu** (Elektra/WMD
Acousteak)
**Les Cathédrales de l'industrie** (Celluloid)
[1986]
**Legende: Deuxième Epoque**
(Hannibal/Rykodisc) [1989]
**Vox** (WMD Acousteak) [1996]

**TOM McCONVILLE**
Fiddle, vocalist. Newcastle-upon-Tyne,
England.

**Straight From The Shoulder** (Celtic Music)
[1988]
**Cross The River** (Old Bridge Music) [1990]

**TOM McCONVILLE WITH CHRIS
NEWMAN**
England. **Tom McConville** (Fi); **Chris
Newman** (g).

**Fiddler's Fancy** (Old Bridge Music) [1993]

**TOM McCONVILLE AND PAULINE
CATO**
England. **Tom McConville** (Fi); **Pauline
Cato** (Np).

**By Land And Sea** (Tomcat) [1996]

**JOHN McDERMOTT**
Vocalist. Scotland/Toronto, Ontario,
Canada.

**Danny Boy** (Angel/EMI) [1992]
**Old Friends** (Angel/EMI) [1994]
**Christmas Memories** (Angel/EMI) [1994]
**Love Is A Voyage** (Angel/EMI) [1995]
**When I Grow Too Old To Dream**
(Angel/EMI) [1997]

**LOREENA McKENNITT**
Harp/Vocalist/Composer. Morden, Manitoba,
Canada/Stratford, Ontario, Canada.

**Elemental** (Quinlan Road) [1985]
**To Drive The Cold Winter Away** (Quinlan
Road) [1987]
**Parallel Dreams** (Quinlan Road) [1989]
**The Visit** (Quinlan Road/Warner) [1991]
**The Mask And Mirror** (Quinlan
Road/Warner) [1994]
**A Winter Garden: Five Songs For The
Season** (Quinlan Road/Warner) [1995]
**The Book Of Secrets** (Quinlan
Road/Warner) [1997]

**RALPH MCTELL**
Singer/songwriter. Farnborough, Kent,
England.

**Eight Frames A Second**
(Capitol/Transatlantic) [1968]
**Spiral Staircase** (Transatlantic) [1969]
**My Side Of Your Window** (Transatlantic)
[1970]
**Ralph McTell Revisited** (Transatlantic)
[1970]
**You Well-Meaning Brought Me Here**
(ABC/Famous) [1971]
**Not Until Tomorrow** (Reprise) [1972]
**Easy** (Reprise) [1974]
**Streets** (Warner Bros.) [1975]
**Star Collection** (WEA) [1975]
**Right Side Up** (Warner Bros.) [1976]
**Ralph, Albert And Sydney** (Warner Bros.)
[1977]
**Maginot Waltz** (Warner Bros.) [1977]
**The Ralph McTell Collection**
(Transatlantic/Pickwick) [1978]
**Slide Away The Screen** (Road Goes On
Forever/Warner) [1979]
**Live** (Fantasy) [1979]
**Streets Of London** (BMG/20th
Century/Transatlantic) [1981]
**Love Grows** (Mays) [1982]
**Water Of Dreams** (Mays) [1982]
**Weather The Storm** (Mays) [1982]
**71/72** (Mays) [1982]
**Songs From Alphabet Zoo** (Mays) [1983]
**The Best Of Alphabet Zoo** (MFP) [1984]
**At The End Of A Perfect Day** (Telstar)
[1985]
**At His Best** (Cambra) [1985]
**Tickle On The Tum** (Mays) [1986]
**Bridge Of Sighs** (Mays) [1987]
**The Ferryman** (Mays) [1987]

Blue Skies, Black Heroes (Leola) [1988]
Stealin' Back (*Castle/Essential) [1990]
Greatest Hits (Huub) [1991]
The Boy With The Note (Leola) [1992]
Alphabet Zoo (Road Goes On Forever) [1994]
Ralph McTell (Castle) [1994]
Silver Celebration (Castle/CTE) [1994]
Sand In Your Shoes (Transatlantic) [1995]
From Clare To Here: The Songs Of Ralph McTell (Red House) [1996]
Spiral Staircase: Classic Songs (Snapper) [1997]
Definitive Transatlantic Collection (Transatlantic) [1998]
Also:
Collection Of His Love Songs (Castle)
The Best Of Ralph McTell (Castle)
Best Of Ralph McTell (Marble Arch)

## MEN OF THE DEEPS
Cape Breton, Nova Scotia, Canada. Miner's choral group.

The Men Of The Deeps (Waterloo Music) [1975]
The Men Of The Deeps III - In Concert At Glace Bay Miners' Museum (Waterloo Music) [1983]
Buried Treasures (Atlantica/EMI Music Canada) [1995]

## MILLADOIRO
Galicia, Spain. Rodrigo Romani (Celh, Mh, Oc, Bz, Ag); Moncho Garcia (d, Pc, Bod); Nando Casal (Bp, Tw, Cl, Ob, Up, m); Xosé Ferreiros (Bp, Tw, Cl, Ob, Up, m); Anton Seoane (k, Acc, Ag); Xosé Mendez (Fl,Pic); Michel Canada (Vln, Vla).

Milladoiro
A Galicia de Maeloc
O Berro Seco
Milladoiro 3
Solofria (CBS) [1982]
Galicia No Pais Das Maravillas
Castellum Honesti (Green Linnet)
Galicia No Tempo (Green Linnet)
Iacobus Magnus (Discmedi Blau)
As Fadas de Estrano Nome - Live (Green Linnet/Discmedi Blau) [1996]

## MODABO
New Brunswick, Canada. Jon Weaver (g, Fl, k, Pc, v); Mike Doyle (v); Darrell Grant (g, v).

Modabo (Modabo Promotions / Tidemark) [1995]
The Many And The One (Modabo Promotions/Tidemark) [1997]

## MATT MOLLOY
Flute. Ballaghadereen, County Roscommon, Ireland. Member of The Chieftains.

The Heathery Breeze (Polydor) [1982]
Matt Molloy with Donal Lunny (Green Linnet) [1984]
Stony Steps (*Green Linnet/Claddagh) [1987]
Heathery Breeze (Shanachie) [1988]
Music At Matt Molloy's (Real World) [1993]
Shadows On Stone (Venture) [1996]

## MATT MOLLOY/PAUL BRADY/TOMMY PEOPLES
Ireland. Matt Molloy (Fl); Paul Brady (v); Tommy Peoples (Fi).

Tommy Peoples (*Green Linnet/Mulligan) [1977/1985]

## MATT MOLLOY/SEAN KEANE/ARTY MCGLYNN
Ireland. Matt Molloy (Fl); Sean Keane (Fi); Arty McGlynn (g).

Contentment Is Wealth (Green Linnet) [1985]
The Missing Reel

## MATT MOLLOY/SEAN KEANE/LIAM O'FLYNN

The Fire Aflame (Claddagh) [1988]

## PADDY MOLONEY & SEAN POTTS W/PEADAR MERCIER

Tin Whistles (Claddagh) [1975]

## CHRISTY MOORE
Singer/songwriter. Dublin, Ireland.

Paddy On The Road with Dominic Behan [1969]
Prosperous (Tara) [1972]
Christy Moore (Polydor) [1976]
Whatever Tickles Your Fancy (Polydor) [1976]
The Iron Behind The Velvet (Tara) [1978]
Live In Dublin with Donal Lunny & Jimmy Faulkner (Tara) [1978]
Christy Moore and Friends (RTE/Tara) [1981]
The Time Has Come (*Green Linnet/WEA) [1983]
Ride On (*Green Linnet/WEA) [1984]
The Spirit Of Freedom (WEA) [1985]
Ordinary Man (*Green Linnet/WEA) [1985]
Nice 'N' Easy [1986]
Unfinished Revolution (WEA) [1987]
Christy Moore (Atlantic) [1988]
Voyage (Atlantic) [1989]
The Christy Moore Collection 1981-91 (East West) [1991]
Smoke And Strong Whisky (Newberry/Pinnacle) [1991]
King Puck (Newberry/Equator Atlas) [1993]
Christy Moore - Live At The Point (Grapevine) [1994]
Graffiti Tongue (Grapevine) [1996]
Collection Part 2 (Grapevine) [1997]

JAMES MORRISON
Fiddle. County Sligo, Ireland./New York, U.S.A.

The Professor (Viva Voce) [1989]

MOUTH MUSIC
Scotland. Martin Swan (Producer, Fi); Michaela Rowan (v); Jackie Joyce (v); Quee Macarthur (Bg); James Macintosh (d, Pc). Alumnus: Talitha MacKenzie (v).

Mouth Music (Rykodisc) [1991]
Blue Door Green Sea (Rykodisc EP) [1992]
Mo-Di (Rykodisc) [1993]
Shorelife (Rykodisc) [1995]

MOVING HEARTS
Ireland. Davy Spillane (Up); Brian Cahan; Keith Donald; Donal Lunny; Christy Moore; Eoghan O'Neill.

Moving Hearts (*Green Linnet/WEA) [1981]
The Dark End Of The Street (WEA) [1982]
Live Hearts (WEA) [1983]
The Storm (Tara) [1985]

CHRIS NEWMAN
Guitarist. England.

Chris Newman (Coast) [1981]
Chris Newman 2 (Coast) [1983]

NIAMH PARSONS & THE LOOSE CONNECTIONS
Dublin, Ireland. [1991] Niamh Parsons (v); Dee Moore (Bg); Mick Mcauley (Acc, Tw); Gavin Ralston (g); Colm Fitzpatrick (Pc).

Loosely Connected (*Green Linnet/Greentrax) [1992]
Loosen Up (Green Linnet) [1997]

MAIRE NI CHATHASAIGH
Harp. Ireland. Name pronounced Moira Née Ha-ha-sig.

The New Strung Harp (Temple) [1985]

MAIRE NI CHATHASAIGH & CHRIS NEWMAN
Ireland. Maire Ni Chathasaigh (Harp); Chris Newman (g).

The Living Wood (Green Linnet) [1988]
The Carolan Album, Vol. 1 (Old Bridge Music) [1991]
Out Of Court (Old Bridge Music) [1991]
The Carolan Album, Vol. 2 (Old Bridge Music) [1994]
The Carolan Albums (Old Bridge Music) [1994]
Live In The Highlands (Old Bridge Music) [1995]

NIGHTNOISE
Portland, Oregon, U.S.A. Johnny Cunningham (Fi); Micheal O'Domhnaill (g, k); Triona Ni Domhnaill (v, k, Syn, Acc, ); Brian Dunning (Fl); Billy Oskay (Vln).

Nightnoise (Windham Hill) [1987]
At The End Of The Evening (Windham Hill) [1988]

Something Of Time (Windham Hill) [1989]
The Parting Tide (Windham Hill) [1990]
A Windham Hill Retrospective: Nightnoise (Windham Hill) [1992]
Shadow Of Time (Windham Hill) [1993]
A Different Shore (Windham Hill) [1995]
White Horse Sessions - Live (Windham Hill) [1997]

## NOMOS

Cork, Ireland. [1990]. **Niall Vallely** (Con); **Vince Milne** (Fi); **Frank Torpey** (Bod); **Gerry McKee** (Bz); **John Spillane** (Bg, g).

I Won't Be Afraid Anymore (Green Linnet/Grapevine/Solid) [1995]
Set You Free (Green Linnet) [1997]

## CARLOS NUNEZ
Galicia, Spain. Galician Piper.

Brotherhood Of Stars (RCA Victor) [1997]

## MAURA O'CONNELL
Vocalist. Ennis, County Clare, Ireland.

The Star Spangled Molly (Ogham/Shanachie) [1981]
Maura O'Connell (Ogham) [1983]
Just In Time (Polydor/Ogham) [1986]
Western Highway (Polydor) [1988]
Always (Polydor) [1989]
Just In Time (Philo re-issue) [1989]
A Real Life Story (Warner Bros.) [1990]
Blue Is The Colour Of Hope (Warner Bros.) [1993]
Wandering Home (Hannibal/Rykodisc) [1997]

## GERRY O'CONNOR
Tenor banjo/guitar/keyboards/fiddle. Portroe, County Tipperary, Ireland.

Time To Time (Mulligan) [1990]

## LIAM O'FLYNN
Uilleann Piper. County Kildare, Ireland.

Brendan Voyage (Tara) [1980]
Liam O'Flynn (WEA) [1988]
The Fine Art Of Piping (Celtic Music) [1991]

Out To Another Side (Tara) [1993]
The Given Note (Tara) [1995]

## LIAM O'FLYNN & SHAUN DAVEY

The Brendan Voyage (Tara)

## MARY O'HARA
Celtic harp/vocalist. Ireland.

Down By The Glenside: Songs Of Ireland (Tradition) [1960]
Mary O'Hara's Ireland (Traditon/Emerald) [1973]
In Harmony (Chrysalis) [1979]
At The Royal Festival Hall (Shanachie) [1992]
Song For Ireland (Shanachie) [1992]
Live At Carnegie Hall (Valentine) [1994]
Mary O'Hara (Total Recordings) [1995]
Sings Irish Songs (Fat Boy) [1996]
Down By The Glenside: Songs Of Ireland (Tradition) [1997]
Also:
Irish Traditional Folk Songs (Columbia/Legacy)

## OLD BLIND DOGS
Aberdeen, Scotland. [1990] **Ian F. Benzie** (g, v, m); **Davy Cattanach** (Pc, v); **Jonny Hardie** (Fi, Rec, m, v); **Buzzby McMillan** (Bg, Cit, Pw, Tw, v); **Fraser Fifield** (Sx, Pi, Pw, Tw).

**New Tricks** (Lochshore/Klub)
**Close To The Bone** (Lochshore/KRL)
**Tall Tails** (Lochshore/KRL)
**Legacy** (Lochshore/KRL)
**five** (Lochshore/KRL) [1997]

## SEAN O'RIADA
Multi-instrumentalist/composer/arranger.
Cork, Ireland. Née John Reidy.

**Mise Eire** (Gael Linn) [1959]
**Mise Eire OST** (Gael Linn) [1979]
**Mise Eire - I Am Ireland** (Shanachie)
[1992]
**Le Season O Se Agus Ceoltoiri Cualann**
(Gael Linn) [1995]
**Sean O Riada** (Gael Linn) [1995]

## OSSIAN
Scotland. [1976] **Iain McInnes; Stuart
Morison; Billy Ross; Billy Jackson** (various), Alumni: **John Martin** (Fi); **Iain
MacDonald** (Hp); **George Jackson; Tony
Cuffe** (v, g).

**St. Kilda Wedding** (Iona) [1978]
**Seal Song** (Iona) [1981]
**Dove Across The Water** (Iona) [1982]
**Borders** (Iona) [1984]
**Light On A Distant Shore** (Iona) [1986]
**The Best Of Ossian** (Iona) [1995]
**The Carrying Stream** (Greentrax) [1997]

## OYSTERBAND
England. **Ian Telfer** (Fi); **Alan Prosser** (g);
**John Jones** (v, Mel); **Chopper** (Bg, Cel); **Lee**

(d); **Al Scott**. Alumni: **Ian Kearey** (Bg);
**Russell Lax** (d).

**Step Outside** (*Varrick/Cooking Vinyl)
[1986]
**Wide Blue Yonder** (Cooking Vinyl) [1987]
**Ride** (PolyGram/Cooking Vinyl) [1988]
**Little Rock To Leipzig - Live**
(Rykodisc/Cooking Vinyl) [1989]
**Freedom And Rain** with June Tabor
(Cooking Vinyl) [1990]
**Deserters** (Rykodisc/Cooking Vinyl) [1992]
**Holy Bandits** (Rykodisc/Cooking Vinyl)
[1993]
**Trawler: Best Of The Oyster Band**
(Cooking Vinyl) [1994]
**The Shouting End Of Life** (Cooking Vinyl)
[1995]
**Deep Dark Ocean** (Cooking Vinyl) [1997]

## PAPERBOYS
Vancouver, British Columbia, Canada. **Tom
Landa** (v, g, Bz, m); **Paul Lawton** (d, Bod,
Pc); **Cam Salay** (Bj, Bg); **Shona Le Mottée**
(Fi); **Shannon Saunders** (Acc, Fi, Vla, Bg,
p); **Hanz Araki** (Fl, Shk, Pw).

**Late As Usual** (Stompy Discs/Stony Plain)
[1995]
**Molinos** (Stompy Discs/Stony Plain) [1997]

## PATRICK STREET
Ireland. [1987] **Andy Irvine** (v, m, Hmc, Bz);
**Kevin Burke** (Fi); **Jackie Daly** (Acc); **Arty
McGlynn** (g). ALSO: **Gerry O'Beirne;
Donal Lunny; Declan Masterson;** and **Bill
Whelan.**

**Patrick Street** (Green Linnet) [1988]
**Number 2 Patrick Street** (Green Linnet)
[1988]
**Irish Times** (Green Linnet/Special
Delivery) [1989]
**All In Good Time** (Green Linnet) [1993]
**Made In Cork** (Green Linnet) [1997]

## PENTANGLE
England. **Bert Jansch** (g); **Jacqui MacShee** (v);
**Gerry Conway** (d); **Nigel Portman-Smith** (b);
**Peter Kirtley** (g). Alumni: **John Renbourn**
(g); **Danny Thompson** (b); **Terry Cox**
(d); **Mike Piggott; Rod Clements; Alun
Davies** (g).

**The Pentangle** (Reprise/Transatlantic) [1968]
**Sweet Child** (Reprise/Transatlantic) [1968]
**Basket Of Light** (Edsel/Transatlantic) [1969]
**Cruel Sister** (Reprise/Transatlantic) [1970]
**Reflections** (Reprise/Transatlantic) [1971]
**History Book** (Transatlantic) [1971]
**Solomon's Seal** (Reprise/Transatlantic) [1972]
**This Is Pentangle** (Transatlantic) [1973]
**Pentangling** (Transatlantic) [1973]
**The Pentangle Collection** (Transatlantic) [1975]
**Anthology** (Transatlantic) [1978]
**At Their Best** (Cambra) [1983]
**The Essential Pentangle, Vol. 1** (Transatlantic) [1987]
**The Essential Pentangle, Vol. 2** (Transatlantic) [1987]
**Open The Door** (Varrick/Making Waves) [1985]
**In The Round** (Varrick/Making Waves) [1986]
**A Maid That's Deep In Love** (Shanachie) [1987]
**So Early In The Spring** (Green Linnet/Park) [1990]
**Think Of Tomorrow** (Green Linnet/Permanent) [1991]
**The Pentangle/Sweet Child/Basket Of Light** (Demon/Transatlantic) [1991]
**Collection** (Collectors/Castle) [1992]
**Early Classics** (Shanachie) [1992]
**One More Road** (Permanent) [1993]
**People On The Highway 1968-1971** (Demon/Edsel/Pinnacle) [1993]
**Live At The BBC** (Strange Fruit) [1994]
**Live 1994** (Hypertension) [1995]
**Light Flight** (Recall) [1997]
Also:
**In Your Mind** (Ariola)

## TOMMY PEOPLES
Fiddle. St. Johnston, County Donegal, Ireland.

**Irish Fiddle & Guitar** (*Shanachie) [1992]
**The High Part Of The Road** with Paul Brady (*Shanachie) [1994]
**The Iron Man** (*Shanachie) [1995]

Also:
**Tommy Peoples**
**A Traditional Experience With Tommy Peoples**

## PLANXTY
Dublin, Ireland. **Christy Moore** (v, g); **Liam O'Flynn** (Up, Tw); **Donal Lunny**; **Andy Irvine** (v). Alumni: **Johnny Moynihan**; **Paul Brady**; **Matt Molloy** (Fl); **James Kelly** (Fi); **Noelle Casey** (Fi); **Noel Hill**; **Tony Linnane**; **Bill Whelan** (k).

**Planxty - "Black Album"** (*Shanachie/Polydor) [1972]
**The Well Below The Valley** (*Shanachie/Polydor) [1973]
**Cold Blow and The Rainy Night** (*Shanachie/Polydor) [1974]
**The Planxty Collection** (*Shanachie/Polydor) [1976]
**After The Break** (Tara) [1979]
**The Woman I Loved So Well** (Tara) [1980]
**Words & Music** (*Shanachie/WEA) [1982]

## THE POGUES
North London, England/Ireland. [1982] Peter "Spider" Stacy (v, Tw); **Jem Finer** (Bj); **Darryl Hunt** (Bg); Jamie Clarke; **Andrew Ranken** (d); James McNalley; David Coulter. Alumni: **Cait O'Riordan** (Bg); **Shane MacGowan** (v); **Terry Woods** (Cit, m); **Philip Chevron** (g); **James Fearnley** (Acc); **Joe Strummer** (v) live.

**Red Roses For Me** (*Enigma/Stiff) [1984]
**Rum, Sodomy And The Lash** (Stiff/Pogue Mahone) [1985]
**If I Should Fall From Grace With God** (Island/Stiff) [1988]
**Peace & Love** (Pogue/Island) [1989]
**Hell's Ditch** (Warner) [1990]
**The Best Of The Pogues** (WEA/Warner) [1991]
**The Rest Of The Best Of The Pogues** (Pogue) [1992]
**Waiting For Herb** (Chameleon/PM) [1993]
**Pogue Mahone** (Atlantic/Warner) [1995]
(See also Shane MacGowan and the Popes)

## MADDY PRIOR
Vocalist. England.

207

**Woman In The Wings** (Chrysalis) [1978]
**Changing Winds** (Chrysalis) [1978]
**Hooked On Winning** (Plant Life) [1982]
**Going For Glory** (Spindrift) [1983]
**Happy Families** (Progressive) [1991]
**Carols & Capers** (Park) [1991]
**Year** (Park) [1993]
**Sing Lustily And With Good Cheer** (Saydisc) [1994]
**Memento: The Best Of Maddy Prior** (Park) [1994]
**Maddy Prior And The Carnival Band-Hang Up Sorrow And Care** (Park) [1996]
**Flesh & Blood** (Park) [1998]
Also:
**Summer Solstice** (Shanachie)
**Silly Sisters** with June Tabor (Shanachie)
**Tapestry Of Carols** (Saydisc)

### THE PUNTERS
St. John's, Newfoundland, Canada. **Larry Foley** (g); **Brian Kenny** (Bg); **Patrick Moran** (Fi); **George Morgan** (d, Pc); **Jason Whelan** (g, Bz).

**The Punters** (Independent) [1995]
**Said She Couldn't Dance** (Independent) [1997]

### THE RANKINS
Mabou, Cape Breton, Nova Scotia, Canada. **Jimmy Rankin** (v, g, Pc); **Cookie Rankin** (v, Pc); **Heather Rankin** (v, p, Pc); **Raylene Rankin** (v, Pc); **John Morris Rankin** (v, Fi, p, g).

**The Rankin Family** (Independent) [1989]
**Fare Thee Well Love** (Independent) [1990]
**The Rankin Family** (EMI Music Canada) [1992]
**Fare Thee Well Love** (EMI Music Canada) [1992]
**North Country** (EMI Music Canada) [1993]
**Grey Dusk Of Eve** (EMI Music Canada EP) [1995]
**Endless Seasons** (EMI Music Canada) [1995]
**The Collection** (EMI Music Canada) [1997]
**Uprooted** (EMI Music Canada) [1998]

### HEATHER, COOKIE AND RAYLENE RANKIN
Mabou, Cape Breton, Nova Scotia, Canada.

Three sisters from The Rankins. **Heather Rankin** (v); **Cookie Rankin** (v); **Raylene Rankin** (v).

**Do You Hear . . . Christmas with Heather, Cookie and Raylene Rankin** (EMI Music Canada) [1997]

### RITA & MARY RANKIN
Mabou Coal Mines, Cape Breton, Nova Scotia, Canada. **Rita Rankin** (v); **Mary Rankin** (v).

**Lantern Burn** (CBC) [1994]
**Home** (Independent) [1997]

### RAWLINS CROSS
Atlantic Canada. **Brian Bourne** (Bg, v); **Joey Kitson** (v, Hmc); **Ian MacKinnon** (Hp, Bod, Tw, Tru, Hmc); **Dave Panting** (g, Bj, m, v); **Geoff Panting** (Bacc, Acc, p, k); **Howie Southwood** (d).

**A Turn Of The Wheel** (Ground Swell/Warner Music Canada) [1989]
**Crossing The Border** (Ground Swell/Warner Music Canada) [1992]
**Reel 'n' Roll** (Ground Swell/Warner Music Canada) [1993]
**Living River** (Ground Swell/Warner Music Canada) [1996]
**Celtic Instrumentals** (Warner Music Canada) [1997]
**Make It On Time** (Warner Music Canada) [1998]

### JEAN REDPATH
Vocalist. nr Edinburgh, Scotland.

**The Jean Redpath Scottish Ballad Book** (Elektra) [1964]
**Laddie Lie Near Me** (Elektra) [1967]
**Frae My Ain Countrie** (Folk Legacy) [1973]
**Jean Redpath** (Philo) [1975]
**Songs Of Robert Burns, V. 1** (Philo) [1976]
**Father Adam** (Philo) [1979]
**Songs Of Robert Burns, V. 2** (Philo) [1980]
**Songs Of Robert Burns, V. 3** (Philo) [1982]
**Songs Of Robert Burns, V. 4** (Philo) [1983]
**Haydn: Scottish Songs** (Philo) [1984]
**Songs Of Robert Burns, V. 5** (Philo) [1985]
**Lady Nairne** (Philo) [1986]
**A Fine Song For Singing** (Philo) [1987]

Songs Of Robert Burns, V. 6 (Philo) [1987]
First Flight (Rounder) [1989]
Songs Of Robert Burns, V. 7 (Philo) [1990]
Leaving The Land (Philo) [1990]
Song Of The Seals (Philo) [1994]
Lowlands (Philo) [1994]
The Songs Of Robert Burns (Philo) [1996]
The Songs Of Robert Burns, Volumes 1 &
2 (Philo) [1996]
The Songs Of Robert Burns, Volumes 3 &
4 (Philo) [1996]
The Songs Of Robert Burns, Volumes 5 &
6 (Philo) [1996]

## JEAN REDPATH & ABBY NEWTON

Lowlands (Philo) [1994]
Lady Nairne (Philo) [1986]

## RELATIVITY
Scotland. **Phil Cunningham; John
Cunningham; Micheal O Dhomnaill; Triona
O Dhomnaill.**

Relativity (Green Linnet) [1986]
Gathering Pace (Green Linnet) [1987]

## JOHN RENBOURN
Guitarist. Torquay, Devon, England.

John Renbourn (Reprise) [1965]
Bert And John with Bert Jansch
(Transatlantic) [1966]
Another Monday (Transatlantic) [1967]
Sir John A Lot Of Merrie Englandes Musik
Thynge And Ye Green Knyghte
(*Shanachie/Transatlantic) [1968]
The Lady And The Unicorn
(*Shanachie/Transatlantic) [1970]
The John Renbourn Sampler
(Transatlantic) [1971]
Faro Annie (Reprise/Transatlantic) [1972]
Heads And Tails (Transatlantic) [1973]
So Clear (Snapper/Transatlantic) [1973]
The Hermit (*Shanachie/Transatlantic)
[1977]
Black Balloon (*Shanachie) [1979]
Under The Volcano (Sonet) [1980]
Live In America (Flying Fish) [1981]
Live In Concert (Spindrift) [1985]
John Renbourn & Bert Jansch (Cambra)
[1985]

The Nine Maidens (Flying Fish/Spindrift)
[1986]
The Essential Collection Vol. 1: The Solo
Years (Transatlantic) [1987]
The Essential Collection Vol. 2; Moon
Shines Bright (Transatlantic) [1987]
The Folk Blues Of John Renbourn
(Demon/Transatlantic) [1988]
Ship Of Fools (Flying Fish/In-Market)
[1989]

The Mediaeval Almanack
(Demon/Transatlantic) [1989]
The Essential John Renbourn - A Best Of
(Demon/Transatlantic) [1992]
Will The Circle Be Unbroken? [1995]
Collection (Castle) [1995]
John Renbourn/Another Monday
(Essential/Castle) [1996]
Lost Sessions (Edsel) [1996]
Lady And The Unicorn/Hermit
(Essential/Castle) [1997]
Traveller's Prayer (Shanachie) [1998]
Definitive Transatlantic Collection
(Transatlantic) [1998]
Also:
Best Of John Renbour

## JOHN RENBOURN GROUP

A Maid In Bedlam
(Shanachie/Transatlantic) [1977]
Enchanted Garden
(*Shanachie/Transatlantic) [1980]

Live In America (Shanachie) [1985]
John Barleycorn (Edsel) [1996]

## JOHN RENBOURN & STEFAN GROSSMAN

John Renbourn And Stefan Grossman Live (*Shanachie/Kicking Mule) [1978]
The Three Kingdoms (Shanachie/Sonet) [1987]
Snap A Little Owl (Shanachie)

## JOHN RENBOURN & ROBIN WILLIAMSON

Wheel Of Fortune - Live (Flying Fish/Demon Fiend) [1993]

## STAN ROGERS
Singer/songwriter. Hamilton, Ontario, Canada.

Fogarty's Cove (Fogarty's Cove Music) [1977]
Turnaround (Fogarty's Cove Music) [1978]
Between The Breaks - Live! (Fogarty's Cove Music) [1979]
Northwest Passage (Fogarty's Cove Music) [1981]
For The Family (Folk Tradition) [1983]
From Fresh Water (Fogarty's Cove Music) [1984]
Home In Halifax (Fogarty's Cove Music) [1992]

## RUNRIG
Glasgow, Scotland. [1973] Bruce Guthro (v); Rory MacDonald (g); Calum MacDonald (d, Pc); Malcolm Jones (g, Acc, Bp); Ian Bayne (d); Peter Wishart (k). Alumni: Blair Douglas (Acc); Robert MacDonald (Acc) - died in 1986; Richard Cherns (k); Donnie Munro (v).

Play Gaelic (Lismor Recordings/Neptune) [1978]
The Highland Connection (Ridge) [1979]
Recovery (Ridge) [1981]
Heartland (Ridge) [1985]
The Cutter & The Clan (Ridge) [1987]
Once In A Lifetime - Live (Chrysalis) [1988]
Searchlight (Chrysalis) [1989]
Capture The Heart (Chrysalis EP) [1990]

The Big Wheel (Chrysalis) [1991]
Hearthammer (Chrysalis EP) [1991]
Flower Of The West (Chrysalis EP) [1992]
Amazing Things (Chrysalis) [1993]
Transmitting Live (Chrysalis) [1994]
Mara (*Avalanche/Chrysalis) [1995]
Long Distance - The Best Of Runrig (Chrysalis) [1996]
The Gaelic Collection 1973-1998 (Ridge) [1998]
Beat The Drum (EMI Gold) [1998]
Also:
Runrig Plays Gaelic - The First "Legendary" Recordings (Lismor)

## THE SAW DOCTORS
Galway, Ireland. [1986] Leo Moran (g); Davy Carton (v); Pearse Doherty (Bg, Tw); John Donnelly (d). Alumni: Mary O'Connor; John "Turps" Burke (m); Tony Lambert (k, Acc).

If This Is Rock And Roll, I Want My Old Job Back (Shamtown) [1991]
All The Way From Tuam (Shamtown) [1992]
Same Oul' Town (Shamtown) [1995]
Sing A Powerful Song (Paradigm) [1997]

## SCATTER THE MUD
Calgary, Alberta, Canada. Phil O'Flaherty (v, g, m); Greg Hooper (Fl, Tw, Bod, Acc); Conan Daly (Bg, v); Cam Keating (Hp, Sp, Tw, v); Dave Horrocks (d, Pc).

In The Müd (*BMG Music Canada/Independent) [1994]
Never Time To Play (Independent) [1997]

## SHANE MACGOWAN & THE POPES
North London, England. Shane MacGowan (v); Paul McGuinness (g, v,); Bernie "The Undertaker" France (Bg, v); Danny Pope (d, Pc); Tom McAnimal (Bj); Kieran Mo OHagan (g, v); Colm OMaonlai (Tw).

The Snake (ZTT/Warner Bros.) [1994]
The Crock Of Gold (ZTT/Warner Bros.) [1997]

## SHARON SHANNON
Accordion/fiddle. Nr Corofin, North Clare, Ireland.

**Sharon Shannon** (Philo/Rounder/Solid)
[1991]
**Out The Gap** (Green Linnet) [1995]
**Each Little Thing** (Green
Linnet/Grapevine) [1997]

## SHOOGLENIFTY
Edinburgh, Scotland. **Garry Finlayson**
(Banjax); **Malcolm Crosbie** (g, Tw); **James
Mackintosh** (Pc); **Angus Grant** (Fi);
**Conrad Ivitsky** (b); **Iain McLeod** (m).

**Venus In Tweeds** (Greentrax) [1995]
**Whiskey Kiss** (Greentrax) [1996]

## SILEAS
Scotland. **Patsy Seddon** (Ha, *clarsach*); Mary
**MacMaster** (Ha, *clarasch*).

**Delighted With Harps** (Lapwing) [1986]
**Beating Harps** (Green Linnet) [1988]
**Harpbreakers** (Lapwing) [1990]

## SILLY WIZARD
Scotland. Members have included **Phil
Cunningham** (Acc, k, Tw, g, v); **John
Cunningham** (Fi); **Andy M. Stewart** (v);
**Martin Hadden** (g); **Gordon Jones** (v); **Bob
Thomas** (g); **Maddy Taylor** (v); **Neil Adams**
(Bg); **Alastair Donaldson** (Bg); **Freeland
Barbour** (Acc); **Dougie MacLean** (g).

**Silly Wizard** (Xtra/Highway) [1976]
**Caledonia's Hardy Sons**
(*Shanachie/Highway) [1978]
**So Many Partings** (*Shanachie/Highway)
[1980]
**Wild And Beautiful** (*Shanachie/Highway)
[1981]
**Kiss The Tears Away**
(*Shanachie/Highway) [1983]
**The Best Of Silly Wizard** (Shanachie)
[1985]
**Silly Wizard Live In America** (Green
Linnet)
**A Glint Of Silver** (Green Linnet) [1986]
**Live Wizardry** (Green Linnet) [1988]
**Golden, Golden Live Vol. 2** (Green Linnet)
[1989]

## SIN E
Ireland. **Steafan Hannigan** (Up, Pi, Bz, Tw,
Pc); **Taz** (v, g, Tw, Fi, Bod); **James O'Grady**
(Up, Tw, Fi); **Teresa Heanue** (Fi, Tw, v);

**Mike Cosgrave** (k, g, Bz); **Ansuman Biswas**
(Pc, Tab, Cg).

**Sine E** (Rhiannon) [1996]
**It's About Time** (Rhiannon) [1997]

## SKYEDANCE
U.S.A. **Alasdair Fraser** (Fi); **Eric Rigler**
(Pi); **Chris Norman** (Fl); **Peter Maund** (Pc);
**Mick Linden** (Bg); **Paul Machlis** (p, k).

**Way Out To Hope Street** (Culburnie)
[1997]

## SLÀINTE MHATH
Sydney Mines, Cape Breton, Nova Scotia,
Canada. Pronounced "Slawn-cha Va." **Lisa
Gallant** (Fi, Sd); **Boyd MacNeil** (Fi, Pc);
**Ryan MacNeil** (k); **Bruce MacPhee** (Hp,
Pi); **Stephanie Hardy** (v, g). Alumnus:
**Bhreagh MacDonald**.

**Prophecy** (Independent) [1996]
**Music For The Kilted Generation**
(Independent) [1998]

## LAURA SMITH
Singer/songwriter. London, Ontario,
Canada/Cape Breton, Nova Scotia, Canada.

**Laura Smith** (CBC Maritimes) [1989]
**B'tween The Earth and My Soul**
(Cornermuse Recordings/Atlantica/EMI)
[1994]
**It's A Personal Thing** (Universal) [1997]

## SOLAS
New York, U.S.A. **Seamus Egan** (Fl, Tw, Bj,
m, Bod); **John Doyle** (g, Mc, v); **John
Williams** (Bacc, Con); **Winifred Horan** (Fi);
**Karan Casey** (v).

**Solas** (Shanachie) [1996]
**Sunny Spells and Scattered Showers**
(Shanachie) [1997]

## DAVY SPILLANE
Uilleann pipes. Ireland.

**Davy Spillane Band: Out Of The Air**
(Tara)
**Atlantic Bridge** (Tara) [1986]
**Shadow Hunter** (Tara)
**Pipedreams** (Tara) [1991]
**East Wind** with Andy Irvine (Tara) [1992]

A Place Among The Stones
(Columbia/Sony) [1994]

## SPIRIT OF THE WEST
Vancouver, British Columbia, Canada.
[1983] **John Mann** (v); **Geoffrey Kelly** (Fl,
Bod, g); **J. Knutson** (m, Bg); Alumni: **Hugh
McMillan**; **Linda McRae** (Acc, Bg, v); **Vince
Ditrich** (d).

**Tripping Up The Stairs** (Stony Plain)
[1978]
**Spirit Of The West** {Stony Plain] [1983]
**Tripping Up The Stairs** (Philo) [1987]
**Old Material** 1984-1986 (Stony Plain)
[1987]
**Labour Day** (Flying Fish) [1988]
**Save This House** [1990]
**Go Figure** (Warner Bros.) [1991]
**Faithlift** (Warner Bros.) [1993]
**Two-Headed** (Discovery) [1995]
**Open Heart Symphony** (Warner Music
Canada) [1996]
**Weights & Measures** [1997]

## STEELEYE SPAN
England. [1969] **Maddy Prior** (v); **Gay
Woods** (v, Con); **Peter Knight** (Fi, Bj, m, v);
**Nigel Pegrum** (d, Pc, Fl); **Bob Johnson** (v,
g); **Tim Harries** (v, Bg); **Liam Genokey** (d,
Pc). Alumni: **Ashley "Tyger" Hutchings**
(Bg); **Terry Woods** (v, g, m); **Gerry Conway**
(d); **Dave Mattacks** (d); **Martin Carthy** (v,
g); **Tim Hart** (v, Dul, g); **Rick Kemp** (Bg, v);
**Mark Williamson** (Bg); **Chris Stains** (Bg);
**John Kirkpatrick** (v, g, Bacc, Con);

**Hark The Village Wait** (*Shanachie/RCA)
[1970]
**Please To See The King** (*Shanachie/Big
Tree/B&C) [1971]
**Ten Man Mop Or Mr. Reservoir Butler
Rides Again** (*Shanachie/Pegasus) [1971]
**Below The Salt** (*Shanachie/Chrysalis)
[1972]
**Individually And Collectively** [1972]
**Parcel Of Rogues** (*Shanachie/Chrysalis)
[1973]
**Almanack** [1973]
**Now We Are Six** (*Shanachie/Chrysalis)
[1974]
**Commoner's Crown** (*B.G.O./Chrysalis)
[1975]

**All Around My Hat**
(*Shanachie/Chrysalis/Mobile Fidelity)
[1975]
**Rocket Cottage** (*B.G.O./Chrysalis) [1976]
**Original Masters** (*B.G.O./Chrysalis) [1976]
**Storm Force Ten (Beat Goes On)**
(*B.G.O./Chrysalis) [1977]
**Live At Last!** (*B.G.O./Chrysalis) [1978]
**Adam Catched Eve** (Chrysalis) [1979]
**Time Span** [1979]
**Sails Of Silver** (Chrysalis) [1980]
**Steeleye Span** [1980]
**Recollections** [1981]
**That's Steeleye Span** [1982]
**On Tour** [1983]
**Dogs And Ferrets** [1983]
**The Best Of Steeleye Span** (Chrysalis)
[1984]
**Back In Line** (*Shanachie/Park/Flutterby)
[1986]
**Portfolio** (*Shanachie/Chrysalis) [1988]
**Tempted And Tried** (*Shanachie/Dover)
[1989]
**The Early Years** (Connoisseur) [1989]
**The Best Of & The Rest Of Steeleye Span**
(Action) [1991]
**Tonight's The Night - Live** (Shanachie)
[1991]
**The Collection** (Castle) [1991]
**The Collection-In Concert** (Park) [1994]
**Spanning The Years** (Chrysalis) [1995]
**Time** (*Shanachie/Park) [1996]
**A Snack Of Steeleye Span** [1996]
**Sails Of Silver** with three extra live tracks
(Park) [1997]

## ANDY M. STEWART
Vocalist/bouzouki/guitar. Scotland.

**By The Hush** (*Green Linnet/Highway)
[1982]
**Fire In The Glen** with Phil Cunningham
and Manus Lunny (Shanachie) [1986]
**Dublin Lady** with Manus Lunny (Green
Linnet) [1987]
**Songs Of Robert Burns** (Green Linnet)
[1990]
**At It Again** (Green Linnet) [1990]
**Man In The Moon** (Green Linnet) [1994]
**Donegal Rain** (Green Linnet) [1997]

## ANDY M. STEWART & MANUS LUNNY

**Dublin Lady** (Green Linnet) [1987]

## ALAN STIVELL
Celtic (Breton) Harp/Multi-instrumentalist. Britanny, France. Née Alan Cochevelou.

*Telenn Geltiek* (Mouez Breiz) [c1964]
**Reflets/Reflections** (Fontana) [1970]
**Renaissance de l'harpe Celtique/Renaissance Of The Celtic Harp** (Fontana) [1971]
**A l'Olympia - Live** (Fontana) [1972]
**Chemins de terre/From Celtic Roots** (Fontana) [1974]
*E. Langonned*/A Homecoming (Fontana) [1974]
**Grand Succes d'Alan Stivell** (Fontana) [c1975]
**E Dulenn/Live In Dublin** (Keltia III) [1975]
**Celtic Rock** (Vertigo) [1976]
*Trema'n inis*/Vers l'ile (Keltia III) [1976]
*Raok Dilestra*/Avant d'accoster/Before Landing (Keltia III) [1977]
*Un Dewezh barzh ger*/Journee a la maison (Keltia III) [1978]
**Suzy Macguire** (Impact) [1978]
**International Tour** (Keltia III) [1979]
**Symphonie Celtique/Celtic Symphony** (Keltia III) [1980]
**Journee à la maison** (Rounder) [1981]
**Alan Stivell** (Impact) [1982]
**Renaissance de l'harpe Celtique/Renaissance Of The Celtic Harp** (Rounder) [1982]
**Legende** (Keltia III) [1983]
**Terre des vivantes** (Disc AZ)
**Celtic Symphony** (Rounder) [1984]
**Harpes du nouvel age** (Rounder/Keltia III) [1986]
**Symphonie Celtique/Celtic Symphony** (Rounder) [1986]
*Raok Dilestra*/Avant d'accoster/Before Landing (Rounder) [1987]
**Live In Dublin** (Dreyfus) [1988]
**The Mist Of Avalon** (Keltia III) [1991]
**Alan Stivell** (Master Series/PolyGram France) [1991]
**Again** (Keltia III/Dreyfus) [1994]
**The Mist Of Avalon** (Dreyfus) [1994]

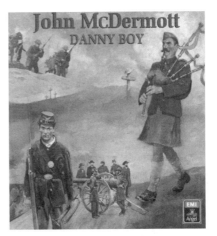

**Legende** (Dreyfus) [1995]
**Brian Boru** (Dreyfus) [1996]
**70/95 Zoom** (Dreyfus) [1997]
**1 Dour/1 Earth** with Youssou N'Dour, Khaled and others (Dreyfus) [1998]

## STOCKTON'S WING
Ireland. **Maurice Lennon** (Fi, Vla, v); **Paul Roche** (Fl, Tw, v); **Mike Hanrahan** (v, g); **Peter Keenan** (k, v); **Dave McNevin** (Bj, m, g).

**Stockton's Wing** (Tara) [1978]
**Take A Chance** (Tara) [1980]
**Light In The Western Sky** (Tara) [1982]
**American Special** (Tara) [1984]
**Take One - Live** [1985]
**Full Flight** [1986]
**Celtic Roots Revival** [1988]
**The Stockton's Wing** (Tara) [1991]
**The Crooked Rose** (Shanachie/Tara) [1992]
**Letting Go** (Tara) [1996]
**Celtic Collections** (K-Tel) [1997]

## BRENDA STUBBERT
Fiddle/piano/step-dancing/composer. Point Aconi, Cape Breton, Nova Scotia, Canada.

**Tameraker Down** (Independent) [1987]
**House Sessions** (Independent) [1992]
**In Jig Time** (Celestial Entertainment) [1995]

## MAIRÉID SULLIVAN
Vocalist. Lisheen, Kealkill, West Cork, Ireland/U.S.A.

**Dancer** (Lyrebird Music) [1996]
**For Love's Caress — A Celtic Journey**
(Lyrebird Music) [1997]

**SWEENEY'S MEN**
Dublin, Ireland. [1966] **Johnny Moynihan**
(Bz, Tw); **Terry Woods** (Bj, v); **Henry
McCullogh**. Alumni: **Joe Dolan; Andy
Irvine** (v, g, m, Hmc).

**Sweeney's Men** (Transatlantic) [1968]
**The Tracks Of Sweeney** (Transatlantic)
[1969]
**The Legend Of Sweeney's Men** (Demon)
[1988]
**Time Was Never Here 1968-69**
(Transatlantic/Demon) [1994]

**TANNAHILL WEAVERS**
Scotland. **Roy Gullane** (g,v); **Phil Smillie**
(Fl, Bod, Tw, Pw); **Leslie Wilson** (g, Bz, k);
**John Martin** (Fi, Cel, Vla, v); **Duncan J.
Nicholson** (Hp, Pi, Tw, Pw, k). Alumni:
**Hudson Swan; Dougie MacLean; Mike
Ward; Alan MacLeod; Bill Bourne; Iain
MacInnes; Ross Kennedy; Stuart Morrison;
Kenny Forsyth**.

**Are Ye Sleeping Maggie?** (Hedera) [1976]
**The Old Woman's Dance** (Hedera) [1978]
**The Tannahill Weavers** (Hedera) [1979]
**Tannahill Weavers IV** (Hedera) [1981]
**Passage** (Green Linnet) [1983]
**Land Of Light** (Green Linnet) [1986]
**Dancing Feet** (Green Linnet) [1987]
**The Best Of The Tannahill Weavers:
1979-1989** (Green Linnet) [1989]
**Cullen Bay** (Green Linnet) [1990]
**The Mermaid's Song** (Green Linnet) [1992]
**Capernaum** (Green Linnet) [1994]
**Leaving St. Kilda** (Green Linnet) [1995]
**The Tannahill Weavers Collection: Choice
Cuts 1987-1996** (Green Linnet) [1997]

**TARTAN AMOEBAS**
Scotland. **Fraser McNaughton** (Fi, Pi, k); **J.
Simon van der Walt** (Pc, Horns) et al.

**Tartan Amoebas** (Kaya) [1993]
**Imaginary Tartan Menagerie** (Iona) [1995]
**Evolution** (Iona) [1997]

**RICHARD THOMPSON**
Guitarist/songwriter. England.

**Henry The Human Fly** (Hannibal) [1972]
**Richard Thompson Live! (More Or Less)**
(Island) [1976]
**Strict Tempo!** (Hannibal) [1981]
**Hand Of Kindness** (Hannibal) [1983]
**Small Town Romance** (Hannibal) [1984]
**Across A Crowded Room** (Polydor) [1985]
**Daring Adventures** (Polydor) [1986]
**Amnesia** (Capitol) [1988]
**Invisible Means** (Windham Hill) [1991]
**Rumor And Sigh** (Capitol) [1991]
**Sweet Talker: Original Music From The
Movie** (Capitol) [1992]
**Watching The Dark** (Hannibal/Rykodsic)
[1993]
**Mirror Blue** (Capitol) [1994]
**World Is A Wonderful Place** (Green
Linnet) [1994]
**Live At Crawley 1993** (Flypaper) [1995]
**You? Me? Us?** (Capitol) [1996]
**Industry** (Hannibal) [1997]

**RICHARD AND LINDA THOMPSON**
England. **Richard Thompson** (g, v); **Linda
Thompson** (v).

**I Want To See Those Bright Lights Tonight**
(Carthage) [1974]
**Hokey Pokey** (Carthage) [1975]
**Pour Down Like Silver** (Carthage) [1975]
**First Light** (Hannibal) [1978]
**Sunnyvista** (Hannibal) [1979]
**Shoot Out The Lights** (Hannibal) [1982]

**KATHRYN TICKELL**
Northumbrian smallpipes/fiddle. Wark,
Northumberland, England.

**On Kielder Side** (Saydisc) [1984]
**Borderlands** (Black Crow) [1987]
**Common Ground** (Black Crow) [1988]
**The Kathryn Tickell Band** (Black Crow)
[1991]
**Signs** (Black Crow) [1993]
**The Gathering** (Park) [1997]
**The Northumberland Connection** (Park)
[1998] as Kathryn Tickell & Friends

**TRI YANN**
Britanny, France. [1971] **Jean-Paul
Corbineau** (g, v); **Jean Chocun** (v, m, g, Mc,
Dul); **Gérard Goron** (v, d, Pc, Mc); **Louis-
Marie Seveno** (v, Bg, Vln, Fl); **Jean-Luc
Chevalier** (g); **Christophe Le Helley** (v, k,

Fl, Ch). Alumni: **Jerome Gasmi** (d); **Bruno Sabathé** (v, k)

***Tri Yann an Naoned:* Les Prisons de Nantes** (Kellen) [1972]
**Dix Ans, Dix Filles** (Kellen) [1973]
**Suite Gallaise** (Marzelle) [1974]
**La Decouverte ou L'Ignorance** (Marzelle) [1976]
**Urba** (Marzelle) [1978]
***An Heol A Zo Glaz:* Le Soleil Est Vert** (Marzelle) [1981]
**Cafe Du Bon Coin** (Marzelle) [1983]
**Anniverscene - Live** (Marzelle) [1985]
**Le Vaisseau De Pierre** (Marzelle) [1988]
**Belle Et Rebelle** (Marzelle) [1991]
**Inventaire 1970-1993** (Marzelle) [1993]
**Portraits** [1995]
**Tri Yann En Concert** [1997]

## WATERBOYS
Scotland/Ireland/U.S.A. **Mike Scott** (v, g, p). Alumni: **Anthony Thistlethwaite** (Sx, m); **Karl Wallinger** (k); **Steve Wickham** (Fi, Ho, v); **Sharon Shannon** (Acc, Fi); **Trevor Hutchinson** (b, Bz).

**The Waterboys** (Chrysalis) [1983]
**A Pagan Place** (Chrysalis/Alliance) [1984]
**This Is The Sea** (Chrysalis/Alliance) [1985]
**Fisherman's Blues** (Ensign/Alliance) [1988]
**Room To Roam** (Ensign/Alliance) [1990]
**The Best Of The Waterboys 1981-1991** (Chrysalis/Ensign)
**Dream Harder** (Geffen/Ensign) [1993]
**The Secret Life Of The Waterboys 1981-1985** (EMD/Chrysalis)
**Still Burning** - Mike Scott solo (Chrysalis) [1998]

## WATERSON: CARTHY
England. **Martin Carthy** (g); **Norma Waterson** (f); **Eliza Carthy** (v).

**Waterson: Carthy** (Topic) [1995]
**Common Tongue** (Topic) [1997]

## BILL WHELAN
Composer. Ireland.

**The Seville Suite** (Tara) [1992]
**Riverdance** (Celtic Heartbeat/Atlantic) [1995]
**Some Mother's Son** (Atlantic) [1996]

**Roots Of Riverdance** (Celtic Heartbeat/Atlantic) [1997]
**Seville Suite: Kinsale To La Coruna** (Uptown/Universal) [1997]

## ROBIN WILLIAMSON
Multi-instrumentalist/vocalist/story-teller. Edinburgh, Scotland. ROBIN WILLIAMSON AND HIS MERRY BAND: **Sylvia Woods** (Ha); **Chris Caswell** (various); **Jerry McMillan** (Fi)

**Myrrh** (Edsel) [1972]
**Journey's Edge** [1977] as Robin Williamson And His Merry Band
**Words And Music** [1977] as Robin Williamson And His Merry Band
**American Stonehenge** (Edsel) [1978] as Robin Williamson And His Merry Band
**A Glint At The Kindling** (Tmc) [1979] as Robin Williamson And His Merry Band
**Songs Of Love & Parting** (Flying Fish)
**Music For The Mabinogi** (Cerddoriaeth Ar Gyfer y Mabinogi) (Flying Fish) [1984]
**Legacy Of The Scottish Harpers** (Flying Fish/Claddagh) [1984]
**Legacy Of The Scottish Harpers, V. 2** (Flying Fish) [1986]
**Winter's Turning** (Flying Fish) [1986]
**Songs For Children Of All Age** (Flying Fish/Claddagh) [1987]
**Ten Of Songs** (Flying Fish) [1988]
**Music For The Newly Born** [1990]
**Wheel Of Fortune** with John Renbourn [1993]
**Mirrorman Sequences 1961-1966** (Pig's Whisker) [1997]
**Dream Journals 1966-1976** (Pig's Whisker) [1997]
**Celtic Harp Airs & Dance Tunes** (Greentrax) [1997]
Also:
**Songs Of Love And Parting + Five** (Tmc)
**Island Of The Strong Door** (Tmc)

## WOLFE TONES
Ireland. **Noel Nagle** (Fl, Tw, Up); **Tommy Byrne** (g, v); **Derek Warfield** (v, various).

**Let The People Sing** [1963] (Shanachie)
**25 Years Of Greatness** [1963] (Shanachie)
**Spirit Of The Nation** [1964] (Shanachie)

215

Live Alive-Oh [1986] (Shanachie)
A Sense Of Freedom [1987] (Shanachie)
Profile [1991] (Shanachie)
Sing Out For Ireland [1993] (Shanachie)
Rifles Of The IRA (Shanachie)
Across The Broad Atlantic (Shanachie)
Belt Of The Celt (Shanachie)
Irish To The Core (Shanachie)
Celtic Collection (KCDE)

## WOLFSTONE
Scotland. Ivan Drever (g, v, Cit, Tw, Ma, Pi); Duncan Chisholm (Fi); David Foster (b, d, Syn); Roger Niven (g); Stuart Eaglesham (g, v); Struan Eaglesham (k); Iain MacDonald (pi, Tw, Fl).

Unleashed (*Green Linnet/Iona/Lismore) [1991]
The Chase (*Green Linnet/Iona) [1992]
Burning Horizons (Iona EP) [1993]
Wolfstone (Celtic Music) [1994]
Year Of The Dog (Green Linnet) [1994]
Wolfstone, Vol. 1 (Celtic Music) [1995]
The Half Tail (Green Linnet) [1996]
Wolfstone, Vol. 2 (Celtic Music) [1996]
Pick Of The Litter [1997]
The Strange Place (Green Linnet) [1998]

## BRENDA WOOTTON
Vocalist. Cornwall, England.

My Land (RCA) [1984]
'B' Comme Brenda (Musidisc) [1985]

## THE WRIGLEY SISTERS
Orkney Island, Scotland. Jennifer Wrigley (Fi); Hazel Wrigley (g, p).

Dancing Fingers (Attic) [1991]
The Watch Stone (Attic) [1994]
Huldreland (Greentrax) [1997]

## COMPILATIONS/VARIOUS ARTISTS/SOUNDTRACKS

A Celebration Of Scottish Music (Temple) features Battlefield Band, Cilla Fisher, Hamish Moore and others.

A Celtic Collection (Putumayo) [1996] features Capercaillie, Dougie MacLean, Andy M. Stewart, Sharon Shannon, Old Blind Dogs, Figgy Duff, and Mary Jane Lamond, among others.

A Celtic Tapestry (Shanachie) features Dolores Keane

A Celtic Tapestry - Volume 2 (Shanachie) features Clannad, Solas, Talitha MacKenzie, Silly Wizard, Planxty, Arcady, Karan Casey and others.

A Controversy of Pipers (Temple) [1983]

A Treasury Of Irish Songs (Shanachie) features Mary Black, Delores Keane, Clannad (featuring Maire Ni Bhraonian), Mairead Ni Mhaonaigh (of Altan) and others.

A Woman's Heart (Dara) [1992] features Mary Black, Frances Black, Eleanor McEvoy, Delores Keane, Maura O'Connell and Sharon Shannon.

A Woman's Heart 2 (Dara) [1994] features Frances Black and others.

Bakerswell (Claddagh) features Sean Potts, Sean Og Potts, Kevin Glackin, John Kelly Jr., John McEvoy, Mick Hand, Noirin O'Donoghue.

Ballinasloe Fair: Early Recordings Of Irish Music In America, 1920-1930 (Traditional Crossroads) [1998] features Packie Dolan, John Sheridan, Dan Sullivan, Frank Murphy, Murty Rabbett & others.

The Best Of British Folk Rock (Park) [1996] features Capercaillie, Steeleye Span, Oyster Band, The Strawbs, Fairport Convention, Runrig, Pentangle, Lindisfarne and more.

Best Of The Celtic Tradition, Vol. 1 (Tradition) features The Clancy Brothers & Tommy Makem; Clancy, Makem, Family & Friends; and Seamus Ennis.

Best Of Irish Folk (Transatlantic) features The Dubliners, Finbar & Eddie Furey, Sweeney's Men and The Johnston's and others.

Blasta! The Irish Traditional Music Special (Shanachie) features De Dannan, Clannad,

Tony MacMahon & Noel Hill, Maighread Ni Dhomnaill, Mary Bergin, Delores Keane, Paddy Glackin, Triona Ni Dhomhnaill, Paddy Keenan and others.

**Brave Hearts - New Scots Music** (Narada) [1998] features Capercaillie, Blair Douglas, Mary Jane Lamond, Ashley MacIsaac, Dougie MacLean, Karen Matheson, Old Blind Dogs, Skyedance and others.

**The Bridges of Cape Breton County** (Celestial) [1998] features Brenda Stubbert, Carl MacKenzie, Winnie Chafe, Dave MacIsaac and others.

**Bringing It All Back Home** (BBC) music from the BBC TV series featuring a wide variety of Irish traditional artists as well as musicians and singers from other genres who have been influenced by the ancient music.

**Cape Breton Fiddlers On Early LPs** (Breton Books and Music)

**Cape Breton Island** (Nimbus) features Buddy MacMaster, among others.

**Cape Breton Night At The Cohn** (CBC) [1982] features Rita MacNeil, Cape Breton Symphony and others.

**Cape Breton Scottish Fiddle, Vol. 2** (Topic) [1978]

**Celtic** (Putumayo)

**Celtic Brittany** (ARC Music) features Bleizi Ruz, La Bagad du Moulin Vert, Tonnerre de Brest, Y. Etienne Gwendal and Dan Ar Bras, among others.

**Celtic Colours Of The World** (Allegro) [1998] features Johnny Cunningham with Seamus Egan, Puirt A Baroque, Dervish, Fernhill, Brendan Begley and others.

**Celtic Fiddle Festival** (Green Linnet) [1993] features Johnny Cunningham, Kevin Burke and Christian Lemaitre.

**Celtic Fiddle Festival: Encore** [1998]

**Celtic Heartbeat Collection 2** (Celtic Heartbeat) [1998] features Christy Moore, members of U2, Bill Whelan, Sinead O'Connor, among others.

**Celtic Love Songs** (Shanachie) [1998] features Boys of the Lough, Clannad, Planxty, Solas, Steeleye Span, Arcady, Cathie Ryan, John Renbourn Group and others.

**Celtic Music Live From Mountain Stage** (Blue Plate Music) [1997] features The Tannahill Weavers, Dougie MacLean, Altan, The Battlefield Band, and others.

**Celtic Odyssey** (Narada) [1993] features Altan, Capercaillie, Alasdair Fraser, Relativity and others.

**Celtic Tides** (Putumayo) [1998]

**Celtic Treasure: The Legacy Of Turlough O'Carolan** (Narada)

**Celtic Twilight** (Hearts O'Space) features Mychael Danna, John Doan, Joanie Madden and Bill Douglas, among others.

**Celtic Twilight II** (Hearts O' Space) features Loreena McKennitt, Nightnoise, Jeff Johnson & Brian Dunning, Mychael Danna, Talitha Mackenzie and John Doan, among others.

**Celtic Twilight III: Lullabies** (Hearts O'Space) features Mairéid Sullivan, Talitha MacKenzie and Noirin Ni Riain, among others.

**Celtic Twilight IV: Celtic Planet** (Hearts O'Space) features Davy Spillane, John Doan, Anuna, Sheila Chandra, Aoife Ni Fhearraigh and Carreg Lafar, among others.

**Celtic Voices** (Narada) [1995] features Emma Christian and others.

**Columbia World Library: England** (Rounder) [1998]

**Columbia World Library: Ireland** (Rounder) [1998]

**Columbia World Library: Scotland** (Rounder) [1988]

**Common Ground** (EMI Premiere) [1996] features Maire Brennan, Sharon Shannon, Paul Brady, Bono, Sinead O'Connor, Brian Kennedy, Elvis Costello, Kate Bush, Andy Irvine, Davy Spillane and Donal Lunny, Christy Moore, among others.

217

**Dance Of The Celts** (Narada) [1997] features Celtic jigs, reels and hornpipes performed by Altan, Old Blind Dogs, Pat Kirtley, Dervish, Mary Bergin, John Whelan, Pat Kilbride, John McGann and others.

**Datgan** (Fflach Tradd) features traditional music of Brittany, Ireland, Scotland and Wales sung unaccompanied by Annie Ebrel, Lillis O Laoire, Mairi Smith and Julie Murphy.

**Dog Big & Dog Little** (Claddagh) features Ben Lennon, Gabriel McArdle, Seamus Quinn & Ciaran Curran.

**The Drones And The Chanters** (Claddagh) [1994] features Willie Clancy, Seamus Ennis, Paddy Moloney, Leo Rawsome & others.

**The Drones and The Chanters, V. 2** (Claddagh) [1995] features Ronan Browne, Robbie Hannan, Liam O'Flynn, Sean Potts & others.

**Etoiles Celtiques** (Keltia Musique) features Loreena McKennitt, Barzaz, Altan, Milladoiro, Dan Ar Braz, among others.

**Faces Of The Harp, Celtic and Contemporary** (Narada) [1997] features Sylvia Woods, Alison Kinnaird, Derek Bell, Sileas and others.

**Ffidil** (Fflach Tradd) [1997] features 12 traditional Welsh fiddlers including Bob Evans, Gareth Whelan, Huw Roberts, Stepehn Rees, Mike Lease, Jane Ridout, Marc Weinzwig, Dan Morris, Bernard Kilbride, Gerard Kilbride, Julie Higginson and Sian Phillips.

**Fiddlers Of Eastern Prince Edward Island** (Rounder) [1997]

**Fiddlers Of Western Prince Edward Island** (Rounder) [1997]

**Fire In The Kitchen** (Unisphere/BMG) [1998] features Ashley MacIsaac, Leahy, The Rankins, Natalie MacMaster, Mary Jane Lamond, Laura Smith, Great Big Sea, The Barra MacNeils, Rita MacNeil, The Ennis Sisters and La Bottine Souriante.

**Folk Heroes** (RTE) features The Bothy Band, Altan, Sweeney's Men, The Clancy Brothers & Tommy Makem, Stockton's Wing, The Johnstons and The Ludlows, among others.

**French Fiddling In America** (Rounder) [1998]

**From Galway To Dublin; Early Recordings Of Irish Traditional Music** (Rounder) [1993] features Michael Coleman, James Morrison, Leo Rowsome, Delia Murphy, Paddy Killoran, Neil O'Boyle and Liam Walsh.

**Gaelic Roots - Boston College Irish Studies Program Celebrates...** (Kells) [1997] features Seamus Egan, Joe Derrane, Eileen Ivers, Natalie MacMaster and others.

**Gathering** (Greenhays) [1981] features Paul Brady, Peter Browne, Andy Irvine, Donal Lunny, Matt Molloy, Tommy Potts.

**Happy To Meet, Sorry To Part** (Globestyle) [1996] features John Doherty, Josie McDermott, Willie Clancy, Micho Russell, Tommy McMahon, Bernard Russell and others.

**Harpestry: A Contemporary Collection** (Imaginary Road) [1997] features Derek Bell, Andrea Piazza, Michele Sell and Deborah Henson-Conant and others.

**Heart Of Ireland: A Collection Of Traditional And Modern Celtic Songs** (Music Club) [1998] features Clannad, Delores Keane & John Faulkner, Triona Ni Dhomhnaill, Paddy Keenan and others.

**Heart Of Scotland: A Collection Of Traditional And Modern Gaelic Songs** (Music Club) [1998] features Catherine-Ann MacPhee, Jennifer & Hazel Wrigley, Boys Of the Lough (with Aly Bain), Deaf Shepherd, Ceolbeg, The McCalmans and others.

**Heart Of The Celts - Love Songs** (Narada) [1997] features Capercaillie, Connie Dover, Aoife Ni Fhearraigh and others.

**Holding Up Half The Sky: Voices Of Celtic Women** (Shanachie) [1997] features Maire Brenna (Clannad), Delores Keane, Mary Black, Karan Casey, Maura O'Connell (with De Dannan, Cathy Jordan (with Dervish) and others.

**Indigenous Tribes** (Iona) [1997] features Rock, Salt & Nails, Wolfestone, Tartan Amoebas, Hamish Imlach and others.

**Irish Dance Music** (Topic) [1995] features Michael Coleman, John McKenna, Tom Morrison, and Frank Lee.

**Legends Of Ireland** (Rhino) [1998] features The Pogues, Clannad, The Dubliners and others.

**L'Imaginaire Irlandais** (Keltia Musique) features The Pogues, The Chieftains, Clannad, among others.

**Live From The Mountain Stage** (Shanachie) features The Tannahill Weavers, Dougie MacLean, Altan, the Battlefield Band, and others.

**Long Journey Home** OST (Unisphere) [1998] features The Chieftains, Mary Black, The Irish Film Orchestra, Van Morrison, Elvis Costello, Vince Gill, Sinead O'Connor, Liam O Maonlai; Mick Moloney; Sissel; Eileen Ivers.

**Mactullagh Vannin'** (Dirt Music) [1986] features the best of traditional and original music from the Isle of Man.

**Magic and Mystery — Majestic Music From Scotland and Ireland** (Temple) [1997]

**Mighty Session!** (Kells) [1997] features Delores Keane, Sharon Shannon, Begley & Cooney, Vinnie Kilduff & Gerry O'Connor and others.

**Milestone At The Garden: Irish Fiddle Masters From The 78 RPM Era** (Rounder) [1996] features Michael Coleman, James Morrison and Hugh Gillespie.

**The Music and Songs Of Greentrax: The Best Of Scottish Music** (Greentrax) [1996]

**Music From The Western Isles** (Scottish Tradition Series/Greentrax) features Gaelic songs with examples of mouth music and pibroch songs.

**The Music Of Cape Breton, Vol. 1, Gaelic Tradition in Cape Breton** (Topic) [197

**Out Of Ireland** OST (Shanachie) features

Eileen Ivers, Mick Moloney, Seamus Egan and others.

**The Piping Concert - Live At Celtic Connections '97** (Lochshore) [1997] features Dr. Angus MacDonald, Paddy Keenan, Pauline Cato & Tom McConville and others.

**Playing With Fire: The Celtic Fiddle Collection** (Green Linnet) features Kevin Burke, Eileen Ivers, Sean Keane, John Cunningham and others.

**Remembering Stan Rogers: An East Coast Tribute I** features The Irish Descendants, Laura Smith, Terry Kelly, Rita and Mary Rankin, Evans & Doherty, Modabo and Lennie Gallant and others.

**Riverdance: Music From The Show** (Celtic Heartbeat) [1995] features Bill Whelan's original score performed by Davy Spillane, Anuna, Maire Breatnach, and Katie MacMahon, among others.

**The Road Home/An Rathad Dhachaigh** (Stephen MacDonald Productions) [1997] features Mary Jane Lamond, Natalie MacMaster, Sharon Shannon, Capercaillie, Ashley MacIsaac, The Barra MacNeils, Buddy MacMaster, among others. Released to coincide with the first annual Celtic Colours International Festival on Cape Breton Island, Nova Scotia, Canada in Oct. 1997.

**The Secret Of Roan Irish OST** (Daring) [1995] features Maire Breatnach & Cormac,

Ronan Browne, Mason Daring, Billy Novick and others.

**Shetland Fiddle Music** (Scottish Tradition Series/Greentrax) features Tom Anderson, George Sutherland and others.

**The Shetland Sessions, Vol. 1** (Lismor Folk)

**The Shetland Sessions, Vol. 2** (Lismor Folk)

**The Silver Bow** (Topic) features Tom Anderson and Aly Bain.

**Songs Of The Cape** (Atlantica) [1992] features suite of the same name composed by Scott Macmillan and performed by Jerry Holland, John Morris Rankin, Dave MacIsaac and Kinnon Beaton, among others.

**Songs Of The Wooden Boat** (Duckworth/Atlantica/EMI Music Canada) [1996]

**STUC Centenary Album - If It Wisnae For The Union** (Greentrax) [1996] features Luke Kelly and the Dubliners, Capercaillie, Dick Gaughan, Runrig, Christy Moore, Eric Bogle, Battlefield Band, Ewan MacColl, The McCalmans and others.

**Traditional Music Of Scotland** (Green Linnet) [1997] features Andy Stewart and Manus Lunny, The Tannahill Weavers, Capercaillie and others.

**Voices - English Traditional Songs** (Musica Pangaea/Amicus International) [1997] features Maddy Prior, The Watersons, Martin Carth and others.

**Waulking Songs From Barra** (Scottish Tradition Series/Greentrax)

**The Wheels Of The World: Early Irish American Music, Vol. 1** (Shanachie). Two volume set features flutist John McKenna, piper Patrick J. Touhey, fiddlers James Morrison and Michael Coleman among others.

**The Wheels Of The World: Early Irish American Music, Vol. 2** (Shanachie)

**Women Of The World: Celtic** (Putumayo) [1995] features Mary Black, Maire Brennan, Maura O'Connell, Capercaillie, Altan, and Maire Breatnach, among others.

**Women Of The World: Celtic II** (Putumayo) [1997] features Karen Matheson, Eileen Ivers, Natalie MacMaster with Cookie Rankin, Susan McKeown, Mary Jane Lamond and Pamela Morgan, and others.

**Woody Lives - A Tribute To Woody Guthrie** (Black Crow) [1987] with Dick Gaughan, Bert Jansch and others.

# Celtic Music Festivals

The festivals listed below feature Celtic music, or a particularly high percentage of it, as part of their programming. Though the information provided is correct to the best of our knowledge and research, we strongly suggest that you contact any festival you are interested in attending prior to making your travel arrangements.

## JANUARY

**Celtic Connections**
Glasgow, Scotland. 0141-287-5511; fax 0141-353-4134. Press & Media: 0141-332-6633.

## FEBRUARY

**Celtic Flame**
(Feb-Mar) Cork, Limerick, Galway and Dublin, Ireland. 01-602-4000; fax 01-602-4100; e-mail: online@munster-express.ie

**Gothenburg Irish Festival**
Gothenburg, Sweden. fax 031-774-0488; e-mail: irish@reab.se

**Savannah Irish Festival**
Savannah, Georgia, U.S.A. (912)234-8444; 1-800-436-3746; e-mail: SavIrish@BellSouth.net

## MARCH

**Celtic Spring Festival**
Derry, Ireland. 01504-365151; fax 01504-264858.

**Gatehouse of Fleet Spring Festival of Music, Arts and Crafts**
Dumfries and Galloway, Scotland. 01557-814030.

**National St. Patrick's Day Festival**
Dublin, Ireland. 01-671-3788; fax 01-677-4633; e-mail: info@paddyfest.ie

**San Francisco Celtic Music & Arts Festival**
San Francisco, California, U.S.A. (415)252-9992; fax (415)252-9995; e-mail: iaf@iaf.org

**St. Patrick's Week**
Downpatrick, Co. Down, Ireland. 01396-610800; fax 01396-610801.

**Traditional Music Festival**
Kinsale Town, Kinsale, Co. Cork, Ireland. 021-772382; fax 021-774085

*APRIL*

**Alaska Folk Festival**
Juneau, Alaska, U.S.A. (907)780-4213.

**Chatham Folk Days**
Chatham, Kent, England. 01634-403868.

**The Craic Irish/Celtic Festival**
Atotod, De Meern, Netherlands. (31)10 4163367.

**Edinburgh Harp Festival**
Edinburgh, Scotland. 0131-332-8692; e-mail: harpfest@scotweb.co.uk

**Glenfarg Village Folk Feast**
Glenfarg, Perthshire, Scotland. 01383-823471; e-mail: duncan.mcnab@virgin.net

**Inverness Folk Festival**
Inverness, Scotland. 01463-238586.

**Kapunda Celtic Music Festival**
Kapunda, SA, Australia. 08-8566-3236.

**Morpeth Northumbrian Gathering**
Morpeth, Northumberland. 01670-519466; fax 01670-510191.

**Normandy Celtic Festival**
Normandy, Tennessee, U.S.A. e-mail: andy-gay@edge.net

**Oporto Interceltic Festival**
Oporto, Portugal. (351)2 5193100; fax (351)2 5193109. e-mail: discantus@mail.telepac.pt

**Pan-Celtic Festival**
Ennis, Co. Clare, Ireland. 065-23382; fax 065-23382.

**Rootin' About**
Aberdeen, Scotland. 01224-642230; fax 01224-6308888.

**Shetland Folk Festival**
Lerwick, Shetland, Scotland. 01595-695381; fax 01595-695381. e-mail: sffs@zetnet.co.uk

**Shoots & Roots** (formerly Edinburgh Folk Festival) (April & Nov.)
Edinburgh, Scotland. 0131-554-3092; web site: http//www.netreal.co.uk/edfolkfest/

**Southern Illinois Festival of Irish Music and Dance**
Carbondale, Illinois, U.S.A. (618)453-3478.

*MAY*

**Athboy Blue Jeans Festival**
Athboy, Co. Meath, Ireland. 049-47971.

**Banchory Festival of Scottish Music**
Banchory, Kincardshire, Scotland. 01330-822705.

**Boolavogue Weekend**
Boolavogue, Co. Wexford, Ireland. 054-89205.

**Chippenham Folk Festival**
Chippenham, Wiltshire, England. 01249-657190; e-mail: chippfolk@aol.com

**Doune & Dunblane Fling**
Doune Castle, Doune, Scotland. 01786-824092.

**Dundalk International Maytime Festival**
Dundalk, Co. Louth, Ireland. 042-35253; fax 042-26317.

**Fleadh By the Feale/May Traditional Weekend**
Abbeyfeale, Co. Limerick, Ireland. 068-31701.

**Fleadh Cheoil Luimnigh/Limerick Music Festival**
Kilmallock, Co. Limerick, Ireland. 061-397684.

**Fleadh Nua**
Ennis, Co. Clare, Ireland. 065-40884; fax 065-42525; e-mail: ceoltrad@iol.ie; web site: http://www.execpc.com/~jimvint/fleadh.html

**The Galway Early Music Festival**
Galway City, Ireland. 091-524411.

**Girvan Traditional Folk Festival**
Girvan, Scotland. 01465-712128.
http://www.girvan.traditional.folk.festival@ai
lsa.almac.co.uk

**Heineken Green Energy International Music Festival**
Temple Bar, Dublin, Ireland. 01-670-8085;
fax 01-670-8084.

**Highland Festival** (May/June)
Various locations, the Highlands, Scotland.
01463-719000; fax 01463-716777; e-mail:
info@highlandfestival.demon.co.uk

**Josie McDermott Memorial Festival**
Ballyfarnon, Boyle, Co. Roscommon,
Ireland. 078-47096 or 078-47024.

**Mayfest**
Glasgow, Scotland. 0141-552-8000; fax
0141-552-6612.

**Mick Carr Memorial Traditional Music Weekend**
Meenaneary, Carrick, Co. Donegal, Ireland.
073-39009.

**Mid-Wales May Festival**
Newtown, Wales. 01686-621975; fax
01686-622425; e-mail:
ffidil@lrc.ruralwales.org

**Northern Lights Festal**
Ballycastle, Ireland. 012657-62225; fax
012657-62515.

**Orkney Traditional Folk Festival**
Stromness, Orkney Islands, Scotland.
01856-851331; fax 01856-851636.

**Paddy Music Expo Limerick**
Limerick City, Ireland. 061-410777; fax
061-315634.

**Sligo Arts Festival**
Sligo Town, Ireland. 071-69802; fax
071-69845.

**St. Magnus Festival**
Kirkwall, Orkney Island, Scotland.
01856-872669.

**Thoresby Fest Noz**
Thoresby Park, nr Newark, Notts., England.
0115-977-4435; fax 0115-977-2428; e-mail:
arts@ls.nottscc.gov.uk

*JUNE*

**Clitheroe Great Days of Folk**
Clitheroe, Lancashire, England. 01254-
397623; fax 01254-397623; e-mail: rodgers-
clan@ndirect.co.uk

**Connaught Fleadh**
Ballinasloe, Co. Galway, Ireland.
0905-42600.

**Feis na nGleann**
Cushendall, Co. Antrim, Ireland.
012667-71349.

**Festival "Na Fir Bolg"** (Irish Folk Festival)
Vorselaar, Belgium. 0032-0-14-500363;
fax 0032-0-14-500363; e-mail:
festival@mail.dma.be

**Fleadh Amhran agus Rince**
Ballycastle, Co. Antrim, Ireland.
012657-63703.

**Gaelic Roots Music, Song & Dance Summer School and Festival**
Boston College, Boston Massachusetts,
U.S.A. (617)552-0490.

**Gaelic Roots: A Music, Song and Dance Summer School and Festival**
Chicago, Illinois, U.S.A. (708)687-9323.

**Galowan**
Penzance, Cornwall, England. 01736-
331733; fax 01736-332211; e-mail:
10661/71@compuserve.com

**Glasgow International Folk Festival**
Glasgow, Scotland. 0141-552-8605.

**Gower Folk Festival**
Parkmill, Gower Peninsula, Wales.
01792-850803; fax 01792-233476.

**Guinness Fleadh New York**
New York, New York, U.S.A. Ticketmaster
NY: (212)307-7171.

**Guinness Fleadh Chicago**
Arlington International Race Course,
Chicago, Illinois, U.S.A. Ticketmaster
Chicago: (312) 559-1212.

**Guinness Fleadh San Jose**
Spartan Stadium Fields, San Jose, California,
U.S.A. Bass SJ: (408) 998-2277.

**Guinness Fleadh**
Finsbury Park, London, England.
0181-963-0940 (Info only).

**Highland Traditional Music Festival**
Dingwall, Ross-shire, Scotland.
01349-830388; fax 01349-830599. e-mail:
robgibson@sol.co.uk

**Isle of Arran Folk Festival**
Kildonan, Isle of Arran, Scotland.
01770-820231; fax 01770-820231
http://www.netreal.co.uk/arranfolkfest

**Killin Traditional Music & Dance Festival**
Killin, Perthshire, Scotland 01567-820224;
fax 01567-820342; e-mail: fstewart@com-
puserve.com

**Kilmore Celtic Festival**
Assumption College, Kilmore, Australia.
03-5781-1711; fax 03-5781-1832; e-mail: ser-
vice@theruralstore.com.au

**Potomac Celtic Festival** (formerly Oatlands
Celtic Festival)
Leesburg, Virginia, U.S.A. (703)451-4492;
fax (703)451-4492; e-mail:
argent@access.digex.net; web-site:
http://www.shirenet.com

**Skagen Festival**
Skagen, Denmark. 45-98446677; fax
45-98446377.

**Sligo County Fleadh Cheoil**
Tubbercurry, Co. Sligo, Ireland. 071-85596.
West Waterford Festival of Early Music -
Lismore, Co. Waterford, Ireland. 058-54975.

JULY

**Bally Shannon Folk and Traditional
Music Festival**
Bally Shannon, Co. Donegal, Ireland.
072-51088; fax 072-52832.

**Boyle Arts Festival**
Boyle, Co. Roscommon, Ireland. 079-62066;
fax 079-62894; e-mail: taxinfo@iol.ie

**The Cambridge Folk Festival**
Cambridge, England. 01223-457245; e-mail:
marketing@cambridge.gov.uk

**Catskills Irish Arts Week Program**
East Durham, New York, U.S.A. e-mail:
irish@francomm.com

**Cleveland Irish Cultural Festival**
Cleveland, Ohio, U.S.A. e-mail: info@cleve-
landirish.org

**Collingwood Celtic Continuum**
Collingwood, Ontario, Canada.
(705)444-7750.

**Conception Bay Folk Festival**
Carbonear, Newfoundland, Canada.
(709)596-3324; e-mail:
gstrong@terra.nlnet.nf.ca

**The Continental Ceilidh**
Lanark, South Lanarkshire, Scotland.
0141-631-3390; fax 0141-887-9991; e-mail:
team.slceuro@cableol.co.uk

**Fiddler's Green Folk Festival**
Rostrevor, Co. Down, Ireland.
016937-38052; fax 016937-38052; e-mail:
phil.tom@dnet.co.uk

**Fleadh Cheoil na Mumhan/Munster Fleadh**
Cheoil - Cashel, Co. Tiperary. 062-61800;
fax 062-62513.

**Galway Arts Festival**
Galway City, Ireland. 091-587169; fax
091-587169; e-mail: gaf@iol.ie

**Harpe des Celtes**
Plounéour-Menez, France. 02-98789325.

**Hebridean Celtic Festival**
Stornoway, Isle of Lewis, Scotland.
07071-878787; fax 01851-860759; e-mail:
celtfest@sol.co.uk

**Irish Festival on the Miramichi**
Miramichi, New Brunswick, Canada.
(506)778-8810; fax (506)778-8686; e-mail:
barque@nbnet.nb.ca

**Isle of Bute International Folk Festival**
Isle of Bute, Scotland. 01700-504964; e-mail:
peter.morrison@virgin.net

**The James Morrison Traditional Music Festival**
Riverstown, Co. Sligo, Ireland. 071-65283.

**Mariposa in Muskoka**
Bracebridge, Ontario, Canada.
(416)588-3655; fax (416)536-4021; e-mail:
ufojoe@interlog.com

**Newcastleton Traditional Music Festival**
Newcastleton, Scotland. 01450-377165.

**Rothbury Traditional Music Festival**
Rothbury, Morpeth, Northumberland,
England. 01669-620178.

**Sesiwn Fawr Dolgellau**
Dolgellau, Gwynedd, Wales. 01341-423355;
fax 01341-423355; e-mail: myfyr@sesiwn-
fawr.demon.co.uk

**Sidmouth International Festival of Folk Arts**
Sidmouth, East Devon, England.
01296-433669; fax 01296-392300; e-mail:
sid@mrscasey.nildram.co.uk

**Skye and Lochalsh Festival/Feis an Eilein**
Isle of Skye, Scotland. 01471-844207; fax
01471-844441.

**Skye Folk Festival**
Portree, Isle of Skye. 01470-582224; fax
01470-582346.

**South Sligo Traditional Music Festival**
Tubbercurry, Ireland. 071-61201.

**Stan Rogers Folk Music Festival**
Canso, Nova Scotia, Canada.
1-888-554-7826; e-mail: info@stanfest.com

**Stonehaven Folk Festival Stonehaven,**
Kincardshire, Scotland. 01569-763519; fax
01569-766356; e-mail: pat.cruse@virgin.net

**Summer Festival of Traditional Music**
Inverness, Scotland. 01463-715757; fax
01463-713611.

**The Welsh Fiddle Convention**
Builth Wells, Powys, Wales. 01982-552555;
e-mail: box@wyeside.co.uk

**West Cornwall Maritime Festival**
Penzance, Cornwall, England.
01736-362341.

**Westport Street Festival**
Westport, Co. Mayo, Ireland. 098-35178.

**Winnipeg Folk Festival**
Winnipeg, Manitoba, Canada.
(204)231-0096; 1-888-655-5354;
fax (204)231-0076.

**Yn Chruinnaght**
Ramsey, Isle of Man. 01624-814559.

AUGUST

**All-Ireland Fleadh/Fleadh Cheoil na hEireann**
Ballina, Co. Mayo, Ireland. 096-73395 or
096-70905; fax 096-70711; e-mail:
MVRird@iol.ie

**Auchtermuchty Festival Traditional Music Weekend**
Auchtermuchty, Scotland. 01337-828732.

**Ballyshannon Folk/Traditional Music And International Festival**
Ballyshannon, Co. Donegal, Ireland.
072-51088; fax 072-52832.

**Ben Eoin Fiddle and Folk Festival**
Ben Eoin, Nova Scotia, Canada.
(902)567-6302; e-mail:
bvmckinnon@ns.sympatico.ca

**Bray International Festival of Music and Dance**
Bray, Co. Wicklow, Ireland. 01-286-0080.

**Brimstone Head Folk Festival**
Fogo Island, Newfoundland, Canada. e-mail:
gwinsor@calvin.stemnet.nf.ca

**Cahersiveen Celtic Music Weekend**
Cahersiveen, Co. Kerry, Ireland. 066-72777;
fax 066-72993.

**Croppy Boy Festival**
Boolavogue, Co. Wexford, Ireland.
054-66282; fax 054-66898.

**Cropredy Festival Cropredy, nr Banbury,**
Oxon., England. 01869-337142.

**The Durham Gathering**
Durham, England. 0191-222-1717; fax
0191-230-2484; e-mail: folkworks@folk-
works.demon.co.uk

**Earth, Air, Fire and Water: Celtic Roots
Festival**
Goderich, Ontario, Canada. (519)524-8221;
fax (519)524-8221; e-mail:
celtic.festival@odyssey.on.ca

**Edinburgh Festival Fringe**
(Aug-Sept)
Edinburgh, Scotland. 0131-226-5257; fax
0131-220-4205; http://www.edfringe.com/

**Edinburgh International Festival**
(Aug-Sept) Edinburgh, Scotland.
0131-473-2001; fax 0131-473-2002;
http://www.ed.ac.uk/~eif/eif98/

**Edmonton Folk Music Festival**
Edmonton, Alberta, Canada. (403)429-1999;
1-888-878-3378; e-mail: artfests@compus-
mart.ab.ca

**Feakle Traditional Music Week**
Feakle, Co. Clare, Ireland. 061-925125 or
061-925027.

**Fergus Scottish Festival**
Fergus, Ontario, Canada. (519)787-0099; fax
(519)787-1274; e-mail: scottish@sentex.net

**Festival by the Sea**
Saint John, New Brunswick, Canada.
(506)632-0086; fax (506)632-0994.

**Granard Harp Festival**
Co. Longford, Ireland. 043-86556; e-mail:
Granard.Harp@mayo-ireland.ie
Heineken Roots Rave

**Irish Week by the Sea**
Beach Meadows, Nova Scotia, Canada.
(902)354-2980 or (410)235-7490; fax
(410)662-5664; e-mail:
shipwhistle@msn.com

**Lorient Interceltic Festival/Festival
Interceltique De Lorient**
Lorient, Brittany, France. (33)2 97212429;
fax (33)2 97643413; e-mail:
jppichard@wanadoo.fr

**Lunenburg Folk Harbour Festival**
Lunenburg, Nova Scotia, Canada.
(902)634-3180; fax (902)634-9568; e-mail:
folkharb@auracom.com

**Marymass Folk Festival**
Irvine, Ayrshire, Scotland. 01294-551047.

**Michael Shanley Traditional Weekend**
Kiltyclogher, Co. Leitrim, Ireland.
072-54222; fax 072-54044.

**Milwaukee Irish Fest**
Milwaukee, Wisconsin, U.S.A.
(414)476-3378; e-mail: ifest@execpc.com;
web site: http://www.irishfest.com/

**Miramichi Folk Song Festival**
Miramichi, New Brunswick, Canada.
(506)623-2150 or (506)622-1780; fax
(506)623-2261; e-mail: icinfo@mibc.nb.ca

**Mitchelstown International Music Festival**
Mitchelstown, Co. Cork, Ireland.
025-24500; fax 025-84325

**Mull of Kintyre Music Festival**
Mull of Kintyre, Scotland. 01586-551053;
fax 01586-554972.

**Newfoundland and Labrador Folk Festival**
St. John's, Newfoundland, Canada.
(709)576-8508; fax (709)576-2323; e-mail:
lindar@morgan.ucs.mun.ca

**Newport Irish Music Festival**
Fort Adams State Park, Newport, Rhode
Island. (401)849-2028; e-mail:
IrishFest@aol.com

**O'Carolan Harp and Traditional Music**
Festival Keadue, Co. Roscommon, Ireland.
078-47204; fax 078-20229.

**Oul' Lammas Fair**
Ballycastle, Co. Antrim, Ireland.
012657-62024.

**Puck Fair**
Killorglin, Co. Kerry, Ireland. 066-62366;
fax 066-62059; e-mail: puckfair@iol.ie; web
site: http://www.iol.ie/puckfair.

**Rose of Tralee International Festival**
Tralee, Co. Kerry, Ireland. 066-21322; fax
066-22654.

**Scoil Eigse**
Ballina, Co. Mayo, Ireland. (see All-Ireland Fleadh)

**Speyfest**
Fochabers, Scotland. 01343-820611.

**Tonder Festival**
Tonder, Denmark. 45-74725400; fax 45-74720123; web site: http://www.tf.dk

SEPTEMBER

**Appalachian & Bluegrass Music Festival**
Omagh, Co. Tyrone, Ireland 01662-243292.

**Braemar Night**
Blairgowrie, Scotland. 01250-872960.

**Cincinnati Celtic Music and Cultural Festival**
Cincinnati, Ohio, U.S.A. (513)533-4822; e-mail: cfl@fuse.net.

**Celtic Classic Highland Games & Festival**
Bethlehem, Pennsylvania, U.S.A. e-mail: info@celticfest.org; web site: http://www.celticfest.org/home.htm

**Celtic Fest Chicago**
Chicago, Illinois, U.S.A. (312)744-0532.

**Chicago Uilleann Pipers' Tionol**
(associated with Celtic Fest)
Chicago, Illinois, U.S.A. (815) 943-0611 e-mail: jgaffney@mc.net

**Culross Folk Festival**
Culross, Scotland. 0138-880225.

**Culzean Castle & Country Park Festival of Scottish Music & Dance**
Maybole, Ayrshire, Scotland. 01655-760274.

**Dunbar Traditional Music Festival**
Dunbar, East Lothian, Scotland. 01368-863301.

**Galway International Oyster Festival**
Galway, Ireland. 091-527282; fax 091-527282.

**The Heart of Scotland Music Festival**
Aberfeldy, Perthshire, Scotland. 01887-829651; e-mail: tayview@msn.com

**Heineken Celtic Ceilidh**
Harbourfront Centre, Toronto, Canada. (416)973-3000; e-mail: info@harbourfront.on.ca

**Irish 2000 Music And Arts Festival**
Altamont, New York, U.S.A. 1-888-41-IFEST; e-mail: i2000@hibernians.com; web site: http://www.hibernians.com/i2000.htm

**Kirriemuir Festival**
Angus, Scotland. 01575-574986.

**KVMR Celtic Festival and Marketplace**
Nevada County Fairgrounds, Grass Valley, California, U.S.A. (530)265-9073; fax (530)265-9077; e-mail: kvmr@kvmr.org

**Pittsburgh Irish Festival**
Station Square, Pittsburgh, Pennsylvania, U.S.A. (412)422-5642; fax (412)441-1814; e-mail: pghirishfest@juno.com

**Sebastopol Celtic Festival**
Sebastopol, California, U.S.A. (707)829-7067; e-mail: cloud@monitor.net; web site: http://www.monitor.net/celtic/

**Washington Irish Folk Festival**
Gaithersburg, Maryland, U.S.A. (301)565-0654; e-mail: ncta@aol.com

OCTOBER

**Austin Celtic Festival**
Austin, Texas, U.S.A. e-mail: auscelt@io.com

**Ballintogher Annual Feis**
Ballintogher, Co. Sligo, Ireland 071-64250.

**Celtic Colours International Festival**
Cape Breton Island, Nova Scotia, Canada. (902)539-8800 or (902)562-6700; fax (902)539-9388; e-mail: colours@chatsubo.com; web site: http://www.chatsubo.com/colours/

**Celtic Festival Japan**
Tokyo, Japan. 81-3-3701-5656; fax 81-3-3701-5656; e-mail: celtic@gol.com

**Celtic Nations Heritage Festival**
New Orleans, Louisiana, U.S.A. e-mail: laurie@celticnationsworld.com; web site: http://www.celticnationsworld.com/festival.htm

**O'Carolan Harp and Cultural Festival**
Nobber, Co. Meath, Ireland. 046-52115; e-mail: nobber@harp.net

**Penicuik Folk Festival**
Penicuik, Scotland. 01968-678153.

**Lowender Peran Celtic Festival**
Perranporth, Cornwall, England. 01872-554034; fax 01872-553413.

**Santa Barbara Celtic Arts & Music Festival**
Warren Showgrounds, Santa Barbara, California, U.S.A. (805)966-9894.

*NOVEMBER*

**Belfast Festival At Queen's**
Belfast, Northern Ireland. 01232-667687; fax 01232-665577.

**Castlemilk Folk Festival**
Castlemilk, Glasgow, Scotland. 0141-631-1166.

**Celts in Kent**
Kent, England. 01622-696489; fax 01622-696419.

**Ennis November Trad Music Festival**
Ennis, Co. Clare, Ireland. novtradfest@clarenet.ie

**The Entrance Celtic Festival**
The Entrance, Central Coast, Australia. 02-4332-7768.

**Highland Fiddle Festival**
Inverness, Scotland. 01463-715757; fax 01463-713611.

*DECEMBER*

**Edinburgh's Hogmanay** (Late Dec/Early Jan)
Edinburgh, Scotland. 0131-473-1998; fax 0131-473-2003; web site: http://www.go-edinburgh.co.uk/hogmanay/

**Woodford Mummer's Feile**
Woodford, Co. Galway, Ireland. 0509-49248 or 0509-49063.

# Celtic Sites, Pubs, Museums & More

One way of getting the feel for the *sean nos* is to visit the various pubs, records stores, archives, and museums in Ireland, Scotland, and Cape Breton featuring traditional Celtic music. Here is a layman's guide.

## IRELAND

*Selected Traditional Music Pubs in Dublin*

Baggot Inn
143 Baggot St., Dublin 2. 01-676-1430.

Blue Light
Barnacullie, Sandyford. 01-295-4682.

Brazen Head
20 Lower Bridge St., Dublin 8.
01-677-9549.

Clifton Court Hotel
11 Eden Quay, O'Connell Bridge, Dublin
1. 01-874-9869.

Comhaltas Ceoltoiri Eireann, Belgrave
Square, Monkstown, County Dublin, Ireland
353-01-280-0295; Fax 353-01-280-3759

Fiddler's Green
Newmarket, Dublin 8. 01-473-2567.

Fitzsimons
21/22 Wellington Quay, Temple Bar, Dublin
2. 01-677-9315.
Ha'penny Bridge Inn: 42 Wellington Quay,
Dublin 2. 01-677-0616.

Harcourt Hotel
60 Harcourt St., Dublin 2. 01-478-3677.

Hughes Pub
19 Chancery St., Dublin 7. 01-872-6540

Johnnie Fox's Pub
The Dublin Mountains, Glencullen, County
Dublin. 01-295-5647.

Kitty O'Shea's
23-25 Grand Canal St., Dublin
4. 01-660-9965.

Meeting Pint
100 Upper Dorset St., Dublin
7. 01-830-5735.

Merchant
Bridge St., Dublin 8. 01-679-3797.

Molloy's
4 Lower George St., Dun Laoghaire,
01-280-1238.

Molly Malone's
Central Hotel, Exchequer St., Dublin
2. 01-679-7302.

Mother Redcap's Tavern
Back Lane, Christchurch, Dublin
8. 01-453-3960.

O'Donaghue's
15 Merrion Row, Dublin
2. 01-661-4303/01-660-7194.

O'Shea's Hotel
19 Talbot St., Dublin 1. 01-836-5670.

Paddy Hannan's
James St., Dublin 8. 01-679-0526.

Searson's
42 Upper Baggot St., Dublin
2. 01-660-0330.

Sinnotts
South King St., Dublin 2. 01-478-4698.

Slattery's
29 Capel St., Dublin 1. 01-872-7971.

Slattery's of Rathmines
217/219 Rathmines Rd. Lower, Dublin
6. 01-497-2052.

Whelan's
25 Wexford St., Dublin 2. 01-478-0766.

White Horse Inn
1 Georges Quay, Dublin 2. 01-478-3677.

Wood Quay Bar & Restaurant
Fishamble St., Temple Bar, Dublin
2. 01-679-8428.

Wynn's Hotel
Abbey St., Dublin 1. 01-874-5131.

## Selected Traditional Music Pubs in Ireland/Northern Ireland

The Errigle Inn
Ormeau Rd., Belfast 01232-641410.

Kelly's Cellars
30 Bank St., Belfast 01232-744524.

Maddens
Smithfield, Belfast 01232-244114.

Durty Nelly's
Bunratty. 061-364072.

An Bodhran
42 Oliver Plunkett St., Cork 021-274544

An Spailpan F Mac
29 South Main St., Cork 021-277949.

Dan O'Connell's
Knocknagree, NW Cork, County Kerry 064-56238.

The Cotton Tree
Slaney Place, Enniscorthy. 054-33179.

Leo's Tavern
Menalek, Crolly. 075-48143.

The Clarendon Bar
44 Strand Rd., Derry 01504-263705.

Dungloe Bar
Waterloo St., Derry 01504-267716.

Gweedore Bar
Waterloo St., Derry 01504-263513.

Gus O'Connor's
Doolin. 065-74168.

MacDermott's
Doolin. 065-74328.

McGanus
Doolin. 065-74133.

Stanford's Inn
Main St., Dromahair. 0716-4140.

The Archway Bar
Main St., Ennistimon. 065-71080.

The Quays
11 Quay St., Galway. 091-68347.

The Slate House
Cross St. Upper, Galway. 091-68820.

Taaffe's Bar
19 Shop St., Galway. 091-64066.

Ti Neachtain
Quay St., Galway. 091-68820.

Maggie Holland's
St. Kieran's St., Kilkenny. 056-62273.

Buckley's Bar
College St., Killarney. 064-31037.

The Laurels
Main St., Killarney. 064-31149.

Kieran's Folk House Inn
Guardwell, Kinsale. 021-772382.

The 1601
Pearse St., Kinsale. 021-772529.

The Spaniard Inn
Scilly, Kinsale. 021-772436.

The Locke
3 George's Quay, Limerick. 061-413733.

Nancy Blake's
Upper Denmark St., Limerick. 061-416443.

Culturlann na h'Eireann
Belgrave Square, Monkstown, County Dublin
01-1280-0295.

Smuggler's Creek Inn
Russnowlagh. 072-52366.

Bailey's Corner
Tralee, County Kerry 066-26230.

T and H Doolin
George's St., Waterford. 051-72764.

Matt Molloy's
Bridge St., Westport. 098-26655.

Westgate Tavern
Westgate, Wexford. 053-22086.

### Record Stores, Museums, Archives, Tours, etc.

Claddagh Records
2 Cecilia St., Temple Bar, Dublin 2. 01-677-8943; e-mail: claddagh@crl.ie. Bills itself "Dublin's only specialist traditional Irish record shop." Mail order available.

Irish Traditional Music Archive
63 Merrion Square, Dublin 2 (1)661-9699; FAX (1)662-4585; web site: http:www.itma.ie Mulligan - 5 Middle St. Court, Middle St., Galway 091-564-961; FAX 091-564-961. Large selection of Irish and Scottish Traditional Music & Folk Music from all over the world. Catalogue available on request.

Rock 'n' Stroll Trail
16 plaques erected in Dublin at sites that were significant in the development of the musical careers of such local luminaries as The Chieftains, Sinead O'Connor, U2, Bob Geldof and Thin Lizzy. For the guidebook, Rock 'n' Stroll contact Dublin Tourism, 14 Upper O'Connell St. 01-747733.

Scoil Eigse
Comhaltas Ceoltoiri Eireann, Belgrave Square, Monkstown, County Dublin 01-280-0295; FAX 01-280-3795. Summer school of traditional music in Dublin.

Traditional Irish Musical Pub Crawl
Dublin. 01-478-0193; FAX 01-475-1324; e-mail: musical.pub.crawl@officelink.eunet.ie

Two professional musicians, who perform a number of songs along the way, guide this tour of a variety of Dublin pubs while telling the story of Irish Music and its influences on contemporary world music.

Traditional Music Shop
Doolin 065-74407. Comprehensive stock of music and print materials on the local music culture. Proprietors Noirin and Harry Hamilton.

## SCOTLAND

Balnain House: Home of Highland Music
40 Huntly Street, Inverness, Scotland IV3 5HR 01463-715757; fax 01463-713611. A Georgian mansion on the banks of the River Ness that houses a permanent interactive exhibit on the history of Highland music, a gift shop and café and hosts live music events and an estimated 60,000 visitors each year. A pilgrimage site for anyone interested in Celtic music.

Comunn na Gàidhlig
5 Mitchell's Lane, Inverness, Scotland IV2 3HQ 01463-234138; FAX 01463-237470; e-mail: fios@cnag.org.uk Society dedicated to the preservation and promotion of the Gaelic language.

The Piping Centre
30-34 McPhater Street, Cowcaddens, Glasgow, Scotland G4 0HW 0141-353-0220; FAX 0141-353-1570. Centre dedicated to the promotion and enjoyment of the bagpipes.

Scottish Music Information Centre - 1 Bowmont Gardens, Glasgow, Scotland G12 9LR 0141-334-6393; FAX 0141-337-1161; e-mail: smic@glasgow.almac.co.uk Documents and promotes all forms of Scottish music.

Traditional Music & Song Association of Scotland (TMSA) 95-97 St. Leonard's Street, Edinburgh, Scotland EH8 9QY 0131-667-5587; Fax 0131-662-9153; e-mail: e.cowle@tmsa.demon.co.uk. TMSA promotes Scottish traditional music at festivals, ceilidhs, concerts and competitions, and, through its good works, helps to create an environment in which it can flourish. As the TMSA is actively involved in many of the traditional music festivals in Scotland, they are a great resource for updates on upcoming events.

## CAPE BRETON

The Ceilidh Trail School of Celtic Music, P.O. Box 455, Greenbutsh, MA 02040, U.S.A. (actual location — Inverness, Cape Breton, Nova Scotia, Canada) e-mail: j9rand@aol.com

Gaelic College of Celtic Arts & Crafts, P.O. Box 9, Baddeck, Cape Breton, Nova Scotia B0E 1B0 (902) 295-3411; Fax (902) 295-2912; e-mail: gaelcoll@atcon.com

# Bibliography

Beaton, Virginia and Stephen Pedersen. *Maritime Music Greats: Fifty Years Of Hits And Heartbreak*. Nimbus Publishing Ltd, 1992.

Bianchi, Anne and Adrienne Gusoff. *Music Lovers Guide To Great Britain & Ireland*. Passport Books, 1996.

Burns, John. "Money Changes Everything." Style & Travel, *Sunday Times*, June 12, 1994.

Carson, Ciaran. *Irish Traditional Music*. Appletree Press, 1986.

Carson, Ciaran. *Last Night's Fun*. Pimlico, 1996.

*CD International: CD World Reference Guide — Popular Music Edition, "Major Markets" 1998*. CDI Publishing Corporation, 1998.

*Celtic Wales*. Pitkin, 1997.

Cheyney, Tom. "Paddy Goes Native." *Pulse! Magazine*, February 1997.

Clark, Douglas. *The Dubliners Discography*. http://www2.bath.ac.uk/~exxdgdc/music/dublin12.html with contributions from Eddie Kelly, Willy Veurheulpen, Jens Kilian, Oskar Itzinger, Suzanne Uniacke, Claudia Weissman-Stahl, Peter Dwyer, Per Solli & Olli Serin.

Corbin, Carol and Judith A. Rolls. *The Centre of the World at the Edge of a Continent: Cultural Studies of Cape Breton Island*. University College Of Cape Breton Press, 1996.
Cole, Robert. *A Traveller's History of France*. Interlink Books, 1995.

*Cornwall: The Cultural Construction of Place*. Edited by Ella Westland. The Patten Press/University of Exeter, 1997.

Cotterell, Arthur. *Celtic Mythology*. Anness Publishing Ltd, 1997.

Creighton, Helen. *The Best of Helen Creighton*. Lancelot Press, 1988.

d'Arcy, Susan. "As Others See Us: The Pub Tour Guide." *Irish Sunday Times*, October 1997.

Deary, Terry. *The Cut-Throat Celts*. Scholastic Books, 1997.

Delaney, Frank. *The Celts*. Harper Collins Publishers, 1993.

*The Dublin Sessions*. Discover Dublin Ltd., 1997.

Donnington, Robert. *The Instruments of Music*. University Paperbacks/Methuen, 1969.

Duigan-Cabrera, Anthony. "Celtic Inc." *Entertainment Weekly*, March 20, 1998.

Ellis, P. Berresford. *The Story of the Cornish Language*. Tor Mark Press, Date.

Filbee, Marjorie. *Celtic Cornwall*. Constable & Co., 1996.

Fisher, Andrew. *A Traveller's History of Scotland*. Interlink Books, 1997.

Frost, David. *Talking with David Frost: Michael Flatley*. David Paradine Television, Inc. & WETA-TV, 1998.

Gillis, Rannie. *Travels in the Celtic World*. Nimbus Publishing, 1994.
"Garth Brooks Sells Out Third Dublin Date." *Communique*, January 1997.

Glatt, John. *The Chieftains: The Authorized Biography*. St. Martin's Press, 1997.

233

*Ireland: Insight Pocket Guide.* APA Publications, 1995.

*Ireland: Eyewitness Travel Guide.* Dorling Kindersley, 1995.

Jenner, Henry. *King Arthur in Cornwall.* Oakmagic Publications, 1996.

King, John. *The Celtic Druids' Year: Seasonal Cycles of the Ancient Celts.* Blandford, 1995.

Larkin, Colin. *The Virgin Encyclopedia of Popular Music.* Virgin Books/Muze UK Ltd., 1997.

*Loreena McKennitt: No Journey's End* (video). Quinlan Road Limited, 1996.

Lotz, Pat and Jim. *Cape Breton Island.* David & Charles/Stackpole Books, 1974.

Macinnes, Sheldon. *A Journey in Celtic Music — Cape Breton Style.* University College of Cape Breton Press, 1997.

MacLeod, John. *Highlanders: A History of the Gaels.* Sceptre, 1996.

Makem, Tommy. *Tommy Makem's Secret Ireland.* St. Martin's Press, 1997.

Matthews, Caitlin. *The Elements of the Celtic Tradition.* Element Books, 1997.

McGrail, Steve. "Tunes of Glory." *Scottish Life,* Winter 1997.

McNamara, Christy and Peter Woods. *The Heartbeat of Irish Music.* Roberts Rinehart Publishers, 1997.

Millar, Will. *Children of the Unicorn.* McClelland and Stewart, 1974.

Munro, Ailie. *The Democratic Muse: Folk Music Revival in Scotland.* Scottish Cultural Press, 1984.

Murley, Colin, Ray Pascoe and Rod Nute. *Cornwall: One of the Four Nations of Britain.* Cornish Stannary Publications, 1996.

Murphy, Peter. *Buddy McMaster: The Master of Cape Breton Fiddle.* Seabright Murphy Video Productions.

"Nashville Writers Travel to Ireland." *Communique.* December 1997.

Nettl, Bruno. *Folk and Traditional Music of the Western Continents.* Prentice-Hall, Inc., 1965.

Neville, Peter. *A Traveller's History of Ireland.* Interlink Books, 1995.

O'Casey, Sean. *Sunset and Evening Star.* Macmillan, 1954.

O'Connor, Nuala. *Bringing It All Back Home: The Influence of Irish Music.* BBC Books, 1991.

O'Neil, Pat. *A Traveller's Guide to Cape Breton.* Solus Publishing, 1996.

Osborne, Brian D. & Ronald Armstrong. *Scottish Dates.* Birlinn, 1996.

Pearlman, Edward Scott. "Scotland in Music." *Scottish Life,* Winter 1997.

*The Rough Guide to World Music.* Rough Guides, 1994.

*Rock, Rhythm and Reels.* Edited by Lee Fleming. Ragweed: The Island Publisher, 1997.

Powell, T.G.E. *The Celts.* Frederick A. Praeger Publishers, 1960.

Ross, James. *Coronach's Instruments: An Illustrated Concert Guide.*

Rowley, Eddie. *A Woman's Voice.* O'Brien Press, 1993.

Rublowsky, John. *Music in America.* Crowell-Collier Press, 1967.

Rutherford, Ward. *Celtic Mythology.* Thorsons/Harper/Collins, 1987.

Self, Geoffrey. *Music in West Cornwall: A Twentieth Century Mirror.* Geoffrey Self, 1997.

Spencer, Peter. *World Beat.* A Cappella Books, 1992.

Sullivan, Mairéid. *Celtic Music For A "New World Paradigm."* 1997.

Sweeney, Philip. *Virgin Directory of World Music.* Virgin Books, 1991.

Taylor, Timothy. *Global Pop: World Music, World Markets.* Routledge, 1997.

The Ultimate Encyclopedia of Musical Instruments. General Editor: Robert Dearling. Carlton, 1996.

UhBriain, Kathleen (team leader). The Timeline of Celtic History. Clannada na Gadelica, 1998.

The West Country Book. Edited by J.C. Trewin. Webb & Bower, 1981.

Williamson, Robin. English, Welsh, Scottish & Irish Fiddle Tunes. Oak Publications, 1976.

Woodhouse, Harry. Cornish Bagpipes: Fact Or Fiction. Dyllansow Truran, 1994.

Writing the Wind: A Celtic Resurgence. Edited by Thomas Rain Crowe with Gwendal Denez & Tom Hubbard. New Native Press, 1997.

Zinck, John R. The East Coast Ceilidh: A Look at Atlantic Canada's Music Scene. VanMarkin Publications, 1998.

# Acknowledgements

⊕ On behalf of Hallway Entertainment, I would like to express our gratitude and thanks to everyone involved in the making of *Celtic Tides*, the television show, including George Anthony and Fred Nicolaidis at the CBC Television Network in Canada; Doug Hall; Paul Cadieux; Dave Goard; Richard Saint-Pierre; Jerome Corbeil; Nathalie Vallerand; Chantal Rousseau; Diane Bryson; Joyce Butterworth; Christine Curchaud; Isabelle Marin; Pete Tessier; Keith Lynch; Brigette Lauzon; Vince Amari; Serge Harve; Donald Milaure; Josee Trottier; Ted Samuels; and Chantale-Marie Dallaire. Facilitators included Mickey Quase, Karen Maxwell, Jenny MacLean, Ian Blackaby, Bill Bruce, Jayne Boyce, Tom Sherlock, Dan MacDonald, Kathy Parkington, Donald Shaw, Jane Skinner, Steve Macklam, Darrell Gilmour, Cindy Byram, Sheri Jones, Phyllistine Landry, Andre Bourgeois, Ian Middleton, Philip King, John Masterson, Mark Littlewood, Joe O'Reilly, Chris Roslin, Diane Ernst, Jeff Laramie, Peter Murphy, Roy Harris, John Dalton, David Kines, National Capital Commission of Canada, and Sandusky State Theatre.

In the writing of this book, there are a number of people who deserve thanks for their interest, help, and encouragement. The list includes Mark and Greg Hall at Hallway Entertainment, whose interviews accompany mine through the text of the book; Kristen Topping for her early, ground-breaking work on the project; Bob Hilderley and Susan Hannah at Quarry Press for their valuable input and perspective; my cousin Steve Thorndike in Wakefield, England; David Farrell of *The Record* for the unexpected notoriety in Rothesay; Kathy Hahn; Mairead Sullivan; Frank Ferrel; Philip King, Hummingbird Productions, Dublin for his kind permission to use selected quotes from his television production with Maire Brennan of Clannad; Peter Murphy, Seabright Murphy Video Productions, Nova Scotia, Canada for his kind permission to use selected quotes from his documentary *Buddy MacMaster: Master of the Cape Breton Fiddle*; Paul White and Beth Gibbs, KOCH International, Toronto; Cindy Byram, Shanachie Entertainment, New York; Georgina Porter, Balnain House, Inverness, Scotland; Graham Roberts, Union Hotel, Penzance, England; Katherine Wallace, Penzance Bookshop, Penzance, England; Janice

& Charles Soane, The Ardyne-St. Ebba Hotel, Rothesay, Isle of Bute, Scotland; Joella Foulds, Max MacDonald, Pat O'Neil and Iain MacLean, Rave Entertainment, Sydney, Nova Scotia, Canada; Phil Debinsky; Richard Dermer, Celtic Aire Records; Eric Sanzen, World Park Productions; Char Power, S.L. Feldman & Associates; Tom Landa, Stomp Productions, Vancouver; Jerry Liebowitz, Label Director, Rykodisc Canada; EMI Canada; Mercury Records; Bob Chacra, President, Musique Alternative Chacra Inc.; Alan Leith, The Compact Disc Depot, Sydney, Nova Scotia, Canada; Jane Boyce, Quinlan Road; Jeff Remedios, Virgin Music Canada; Murdock Smith (GEM Photo), Sydney, Nova Scotia, Canada; and The Chieftains' publicist, Charlie Comer, a character of the first order, who introduced me to Paddy Moloney and the magic in the music during the group's association with Island Records in the mid-1970s.

Photographs of the artists were provided courtesy of the artists or their recording companies. Thank you all for your cooperation. Other photographs and ephemera are from the author's collection, except the photograph of Mary Jane Lamond on page 160 which was provided courtesy of Murdoch Smith.

A tip of the hat also goes to Edinburgh, Scotland-based Fiona Ritchie, producer of the internationally syndicated radio show *The Thistle & Shamrock*; Gerard Manning (ceolas@celtic.stanford.edu), Steve Winick, Colin Irwin and others who continue to document the living tradition that is Celtic music and culture as it moves into the 21st century.

Finally, a big hug of love and gratitude to my sister Christine Broster, a Celtic music fan who has become somewhat of an expert on the genre after undertaking an odyssey of discovery as the researcher on this book. Pete, Heather, and Nicholas, the computer's now free. We're off to Cynthia's for lunch!

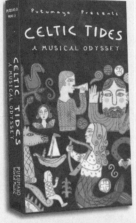
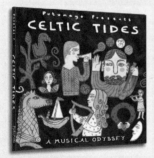

# QUARRY MUSIC BOOKS

❑ *Neil Young: Don't Be Denied*
by JOHN EINARSON

$21.95 CDN / $15.95 US

❑ *Magic Carpet Ride: John Kay & Steppenwolf*
by JOHN KAY and JOHN EINARSON

$21.95 CDN / $15.95 USA

❑ *American Woman: The Guess Who*
by JOHN EINARSON

$21.95 CDN / $15.95 USA

❑ *Building a Mystery: Sarah McLachlan*
by JOHN EINARSON

$21.95 CDN / $15.95 USA

❑ *Encyclopedia of Canadian Rock, Pop & Folk Music*
by RICK JACKSON

$26.95 CDN / $19.95 USA

❑ *Encyclopedia of Canadian Country Music*
by RICK JACKSON

$26.95 CDN / $19.95 USA

❑ *The Real Patsy Cline*
by DOUG HALL

$21.95 CDN / $15.95 USA

❑ *Snowbird: Anne Murray*
by BARRY GRILLS

$21.95 CDN / $15.95 USA

❑ *The Hawk: Ronnie Hawkins and The Hawks*
by IAN WALLIS

$21.95 CDN / $15.95 USA

❑ *Ironic: Alanis Morissette*
by BARRY GRILLS

$21.95 CDN / $15.95 USA

❑ *For What It's Worth: Buffalo Springfield*
by JOHN EINARSON

$21.95 CDN / $15.95 USA

❑ *Falling Into You: Céline Dion*
by BARRY GRILLS

$21.95 CDN / $15.95 USA

❑ *The Mamas and The Papas*
by DOUG HALL

$21.95 CDN / $15.95 USA

---

Available at your favorite bookstore or directly from the publisher:
Quarry Press, P.O. Box 1061, Kingston, ON K7L 4Y5, Canada.
Te. (613) 548-8429, Fax. (613) 548-1556, E-mail: order@quarrypress.com.

Name _____

Address _____

_____ Postal Code _____ Telephone _____

Visa/Mastercard# _____ Expiry _____

Signature _____

Your books will be shipped with an invoice
enclosed, including shipping costs, payable
within 30 days in Canadian or American currency
(credit card, check, or money order).